PRAISE FOR
CENTRAL AMERICA'S FORGOTTEN HISTORY

"This is a text that is sorely needed, and there is nothing like it available, a brilliant, deeply researched, and concise 'forgotten' history, not only of Central America but also of US military occupations and interventions that have created the refugees at the US-Mexico border."

—ROXANNE DUNBAR-ORTIZ,
author of *An Indigenous Peoples' History of the United States*

"Aviva Chomsky's *Central America's Forgotten History* is essential reading, an antidote to mainstream coverage that ignores the larger context of the crisis. Its roots, as Chomsky concisely and convincingly reveals, are deep, and many of them snake back to Washington, to a century of catastrophic security and economic policies."

—GREG GRANDIN,
author of *The End of the Myth: From the Frontier to the Border Wall in the Mind of America*

"In this breathtaking book, Aviva Chomsky reminds us of the intertwined histories of Central America and the United States. With compelling arguments and rigorous evidence, Chomsky demonstrates how US policies allowed corporations to build astronomical wealth by impoverishing and exploiting the lives and labor of the people of Central America. Equally important, *Central America's Forgotten History* chronicles Indigenous organizing and international solidarity movements that should guide contemporary efforts to reform US foreign policies vis-à-vis the Global South."

—PAUL ORTIZ,
author of *An African American and Latinx History of the United States*

"For decades, policy makers and the public have grappled with the problem of undocumented immigrants and have at the same time ignored the reasons why so many Central Americans, in particular, are fleeing in caravans of thousands to the US. These reasons lie in the history of that region—a history in which the US government is implicated in forcefully establishing the conditions so intolerable as to impel people to flee. Until we understand the US' role and continued complicity in perpetuating these conditions, a true solution to the immigration 'problem' will remain out of reach. Professor Chomsky's book illuminates this willfully forgotten history."

—PATRICIA MONTES,
executive director, Centro Presente

"*Central America's Forgotten History* is more than a compelling account of how colonialism made and remade Central America and the United States from the distant past to Trump's border wars. With rich detail and accessible analysis, Aviva Chomsky demonstrates how the colonial crucible itself is ultimately a fight over how history is remembered—and why such history is so important for advancing popular struggle."

—STEVE STRIFFLER,
author of *Solidarity: Latin America
and the US Left in the Era of Human Rights*

"I have been waiting for *Central America's Forgotten History* for the past decade. This thorough and thought-provoking book revives the history that has long been severed from the Central American experience in US discourse, especially around immigration. Chomsky demonstrates that you can't divorce centuries of colonialism and settler colonialism, US-supported dictators and death squads, and decades of neoliberal economic deprivation and dispossession from the people who arrive every day to the militarized US frontier. And just as important, in the long history of cross-border organizing she chronicles, there might be a solution in the solidarity to this crisis of displacement: not in more misguided border enforcement but—and this will be quite clear when you set the book down—in justice-based reparations."

—TODD MILLER,
author of *Storming the Wall: Climate Change,
Migration, and Homeland Security*

CENTRAL AMERICA'S FORGOTTEN HISTORY

CENTRAL AMERICA'S FORGOTTEN HISTORY

REVOLUTION, VIOLENCE, AND THE ROOTS OF MIGRATION

AVIVA CHOMSKY

BEACON PRESS
BOSTON

Beacon Press
Boston, Massachusetts
www.beacon.org

Beacon Press books
are published under the auspices of
the Unitarian Universalist Association of Congregations.

24 23 22 21   8 7 6 5 4 3 2 1

This book is printed on acid-free paper that meets the uncoated paper
ANSI/NISO specifications for permanence as revised in 1992.

Text design and composition by Kim Arney

Central America map created by Daniel Feher, https://www.freeworldmaps
.net/centralamerica/centralamerica-printable-map.jpg.

Library of Congress Cataloging-in-Publication Data
Names: Chomsky, Aviva, author.
Title: Central America's forgotten history : revolution, violence, and the
    roots of migration / Aviva Chomsky.
Description: Boston : Beacon Press, [2021] | Includes bibliographical
    references and index.
Identifiers: LCCN 2020032641 (print) | LCCN 2020032642 (ebook) |
    ISBN 9780807056486 (hardcover) | ISBN 9780807056547 (ebook)
Subjects: LCSH: Central America—History. | Central America—Politics and
    government. | Central America—Emigration and immigration. | United
    States—Emigration and immigration. | Central America—Relations—
    United States. | United States—Relations—Central America.
Classification: LCC F1436 .C48 2021 (print) | LCC F1436 (ebook) |
    DDC 972.8—dc23
LC record available at https://lccn.loc.gov/2020032641
LC ebook record available at https://lccn.loc.gov/2020032642

CONTENTS

PART I

A CRISIS
WITH
DEEP ROOTS

CHAPTER 1

INVISIBILITY AND FORGETTING

Central American migrants carry the inheritance of centuries of history, much of it forgotten or obliterated. Indigenous identities were suppressed in Nicaragua and El Salvador in projects of nation building and the aftermath of repression. Activist and revolutionary projects have also been crushed, and evidence of massacres and violence buried. The United States has labored to erase its role in creating the crises in Central America. While historical memory projects struggle to recover histories, many Central Americans simply hope to survive or to escape. In the United States, Central Americans remake identities to adjust to their new context. Most US Americans, even those who decry the abusive treatment of immigrants, remain blissfully oblivious to the histories migrants carry.

What is memory? Different disciplines give different answers. For psychologists, memory may be individual, part of an individual's construction of self and identity. But memory is also collective. Societies and cultures preserve and create memory through oral traditions and religions, and through written records and shared commemorations and narratives. The way a society or group of people understands its past infuses its culture and the way people understand and act in the present.

All memory is, in a sense, constructed. As individuals or as members of groups, we privilege some memories over others, and we create coherent and meaningful stories and understandings of our past and present out of fragments of memory.

Forgetting is an inevitable part of memory. By highlighting—remembering—certain details, events, or interpretations, we erase or forget others. We forget because our individual and collective histories overflow with detail that would form a chaotic blur if we did not form them into coherent narratives. But when we rely on one narrative, we may be suppressing others.

Historians think a lot about memory. We create memory by writing histories. We read primary sources from the periods we study, understanding that even though they are original documents or firsthand accounts, they still tell us only part of the story—often the perspective of educated elites who are literate and control the resources to preserve and document their version of the past. We try to read them again, "against the grain," to find clues as to what some of the invisible, unheard voices hidden within them might have to say.

When we listen to individuals talk about the past, too, we know that their memories are selective and often shaped by things that may have happened after the incidents they are describing. Even two people who witnessed or participated in the same event may have very different recollections of it.

Struggles over historical memory can be very political. History, we often hear, is told by the victors. The victors have every interest in justifying their own victory, celebrating their greatness, and decrying the misdeeds of the vanquished. They may suppress the language and the culture of those they vanquish in their attempts to suppress their memories.

Many Americans are aware of clashes over historical memory with respect to World War II. Sometimes it's too simple to claim a clear distinction between victor and vanquished, and battles over who controls the historical narrative continue. Germany and Japan were defeated in World War II. But both of them are thriving, wealthy countries. Some of the leaders of their wartime regimes were punished, but others escaped or continued to hold political and economic power. The Jewish population of eastern Europe was decimated, even if they were not officially on the losing side of the war. Who, then, were the winners and the losers? Who gets to tell the story?

In Germany and elsewhere in Europe, the Holocaust is officially denounced, and apologies and reparations to Jewish survivors continue. In parts of Europe, Holocaust denial—forgetting—is a punishable crime. In contrast, survivors of Japanese atrocities are still struggling to have their stories acknowledged. Koreans and Chinese have protested the efforts of Japanese nationalists to deny wartime aggression or eliminate its mention from textbooks.

Or another example. In Vietnam, the Americans lost the war, but it was the Vietnamese who suffered millions of deaths and whose country was destroyed. And the experiences of a population within a country are never uniform. Some Vietnamese fought with, and others fought against, the Americans. Whether among the winners or the losers, official narratives may diverge sharply from open or suppressed memories of different people and groups.

In Central America, forgetting is layered upon forgetting. Spanish conquerors slaughtered and enslaved Indigenous people, prohibited Indigenous religions, and denigrated Indigenous cultures and languages. After independence in the early 1800s, European-oriented elites labored to construct national narratives that rationalized their own privilege and a version of progress that compounded it. Some called the century after independence the "second conquest," as a new export economy based on coffee and bananas pushed peasants off their land and forced them into plantation labor.

By the late nineteenth century, Central America's economies became tightly interwoven with US investment, and US political and military intervention followed. Resistance and rebellion were frequent, but brutally suppressed. By the 1920s, protests coalesced around politicized goals. In Nicaragua, Augusto C. Sandino led a peasant movement to drive US occupiers out of his country. In El Salvador, communist leader Farabundo Martí organized urban workers, while Indigenous peasants in the coffee region took up arms to regain control of their lands and villages. In Guatemala, a revolutionary government tried to reform the country's land and labor systems from 1944 to 1954. All of these uprisings were followed by fierce repression, and by rewriting and forgetting.

Forgetting can be a form of oppression and silencing, but silence can also be a form of protection and resistance. Guatemalan Indigenous activist Rigoberta Menchu began her acclaimed 1983 *testimonio* by pondering the meanings of memory and of silence. She began by explaining the meaning of testimonio: "This is my testimony. I didn't learn it from a book and I didn't learn it alone . . . My story is the story of all poor Guatemalans. My personal experience is the reality of a whole people."[1]

But at the same time that she insists on the importance of recounting her story—testimony—Menchu places a lot of emphasis on what she will not tell. Under fire and oppression, she suggests, some memories can best be preserved by hiding them. Menchu quotes the ancient Mayan text Popol Vuh: "Learn to protect yourselves, by keeping our secret." "Indians have been very careful not to disclose the details of their communities," she elaborates. "And the community does not allow [children] to talk about Indian things." Parents must teach their children "to keep the secrets of our people, so that our culture and customs will be preserved." Parents recount tales of Indigenous heroes who fought the Spanish, insisting "let no landowner extinguish all this, nor any rich man wipe out our customs. Let our children, be they workers or servants, respect and keep our secrets." "We Indians have always hidden our identity and kept our secrets to ourselves . . . we know we must hide so much in order to preserve our Indian culture and prevent it being taken away from us."[2]

The secrets became inherent to what it means to be Indigenous. They formed part of the centuries-long tradition of Indian resistance against Spanish control and nourished the communities' clandestine organizing against the Ladinos and landlords who were dispossessing Indigenous communities in the 1970s and '80s. As communities organized self-defense measures, Menchu wrote that "[n]o-one must discover our community's secret now, compañeros. It's secret what we are doing here. The enemy must not know, nor must our other neighbours." "When we began to organize ourselves, we started using all the things we'd kept hidden. Our traps—nobody knew about them because they'd been kept secret. Our opinions—whenever a priest came to our village we'd all keep our mouths shut." "This is why Indians are thought to be stupid. They can't think, they don't know anything, they say. But we have hidden our identity because we needed to resist."[3]

REMEMBERING MATTERS

One of the arguments of this book is that history matters, and how we tell and remember history matters. Not because, as the famous quote by George Santayana suggests, "Those who cannot remember the past are condemned to repeat it." A more important question is *how* we remember the past: what stories we tell ourselves about the past. Those stories inform what we believe about the present and how we act in the present. If we erase important parts of our own and Central American countries' histories, we can believe that they are simply, inherently, "shit-hole countries" (as President Trump suggested in early 2018), filled with "criminals" with "blatant disregard for our border & sovereignty."[4] "This is an invasion of our Country," he tweeted.[5]

US Americans, in that case, are the victims of people who are invading us. The roots of this narrative are as deep as the roots of migration. To understand what's happening today, we will challenge that narrative and emphasize our intertwined common histories.

TWO KINDS OF COLONIALISM, NORTH AND SOUTH

Both the United States and Central America trace their contemporary histories back to European colonialism. An ascendant and Catholic Spain controlled vast and lucrative Indigenous empires with dense populations a century before small British contingents established beachheads on the eastern coast of North America. The English-speaking world developed a historical narrative known as the "Black Legend," which portrayed the Spanish as cruel and backward *conquistadores* who murdered and plundered their way through the Caribbean and Latin America. The British, in contrast (according to their own account), were hard-working, forward-looking colonists (rather than colonizers) who industriously set up self-sufficient farming villages on empty lands.

This narrative conveniently explains contemporary inequalities between the United States and Latin America by implying a "historical" narrative in which English speakers in particular, and northern Europeans in general, through their moral and developmental superiority, deserve their exalted place in the world.

Of course, the legend is just that—a legend. It serves to cover up some more inconvenient similarities, contrasts, and connections between the British and the Spanish colonial worlds, later to become the United States and Latin America. Contrary to popular mythology in the United States, British colonizers were just as interested as the Spanish in converting Native peoples and extracting wealth from their colonies. By the time the British got involved, the Spanish had already taken control of the most immediately profitable areas, but the British also quickly developed plantation production in their Caribbean colonies.

Rather than the quasi-racial distinction between northern and southern Europeans that characterizes the Black Legend, differences among the American contexts shaped the ideologies and tactics of the colonizers. The Spanish encountered empires with dense populations and well-developed systems for extracting resources and labor. They focused their colonial project on dominating these preexisting systems. The British in North America, in contrast, found much smaller populations, already decimated by European diseases that frequently preceded their arrival. With little potential in the way of precious metals or plantation agriculture, the colonizers had no choice but to find ways to sustain themselves. Once they realized the potential for plantation agriculture in the US South and the Caribbean, they enthusiastically orchestrated forced-labor systems every bit as cruel and exploitative as those their Spanish counterparts utilized in their territories.

Where populations were small and virtually impossible to control, as in North America, the British developed a kind of colonial enterprise called *settler colonialism*. Rather than *ruling over* the people they colonized—like the Spanish in Mexico and Peru, or the British themselves in India—settler colonial projects were based on *eliminating* the people who were there and *replacing* them with a white, European population. (Where there was sufficient economic potential, settler colonial rulers imported racially defined subject populations to engage in forced labor.) In this respect, British settler colonialism in the Americas resembles the way it ruled Australia, New Zealand, and Canada, but is different from British colonialism in India.

Traditional colonialism and settler colonialism shared an ideology of European superiority that continues to infuse the world today, now commonly termed *racism*. What we today call *people of color* are formerly colonized peoples. Simply acknowledging the colonial roots of race and racism helps us to understand how profoundly the past has shaped the present.

It's also worth noting that most of the wealth and power in today's world is concentrated in the former colonial powers (the United States and Europe), while most of the poverty is concentrated in their former colonies (Africa, Latin America, the Caribbean, South and Southeast Asia). This division too has its roots in a long history of colonialism.

But colonialism ended a long time ago, right? And the United States was a colony—and it's the richest and most powerful of all. So those old white people who founded the United States must have done something right, while their counterparts to the south must have done something wrong.

Well, yes and no. Latin America and the United States both achieved independence from their colonizers, the story goes, around two hundred years ago. But let's think about who were the colonizers, and who were the colonized, and who exactly achieved independence from whom. In

British North America, it was the British colonizers themselves who demanded independence—in order to continue to advance their settler colonial project. The "founding fathers" and new leaders of the country were slaveholders, land surveyors, and expansionists. The colonized people of British North America—that is, the Native American and African and Afro-descended populations, were still colonized after independence. The only difference was that now their colonial ruler was the United States instead of the British.

The strongest contrast to the US experience of independence occurred just a few years later, in Haiti. There, it was not the French colonizers who rose up and called for independence—it was the colonized, enslaved Africans. They threw out their French masters and abolished slavery and the plantation system. Nothing of the sort happened in the United States.

Latin America—including Central America—fell somewhere in between. Spanish-descended elites led the independence struggles and ended up in control of the new countries' economies and political institutions. But they were outnumbered almost everywhere by African, Indigenous, and mixed-race populations that also saw independence as a chance to claim their rights.

Bringing in the concepts of colonialism and settler colonialism offers a new perspective for understanding the history of the United States and of Central America, and of their long and tortured relationship. It's a concept that's deliberately obscured and forgotten by versions of the present that try to erase the past. But using it completely changes the way we think about colonialism in the United States. Rather than quaint stories about Pilgrims, Thanksgivings, old-fashioned clothes, and a revolution for freedom that relegated colonialism to the past, we could tell stories about a settler colonial project that did not end in 1776. Instead, it mushroomed after the colonizers became independent of Britain and, freed from British restraints, set out to conquer and colonize a continent.

In Central America, too, independence did not mean the end of colonialism. A neocolonial relationship of economic and ideological dependence on Europe and, by the end of the nineteenth century, on the United States was one way that colonialism continued to cast a shadow. Internally, European-descended elites and new European immigrants continued to dominate the countries' Indigenous populations politically and economically. The latter was true in the United States, too, of course.

But the two intersected as the United States extended its political, military, and economic reach into Central America in what many called *neocolonialism*. These relationships and ideologies also shaped how the countries' histories were written.

So let's begin by looking at the nature of conquest and colonial rule in Central America. In the next chapter we'll carry the story forward into the first hundred years of independence and look more deeply at how the settler colonial nature of the United States in the long nineteenth century shaped its relations with its newly independent neighbors.

ERASING INDIANS FROM THE CONQUEST OF CENTRAL AMERICA

As Rigoberta Menchu suggested, memories of Indigenous culture, language, identity, and resistance have been subject to repeated challenge over the centuries in Central America. Spanish colonizers included people with religious, political, and economic aims. The Catholic Church sent priests and missionaries, while the Spanish Crown sent bureaucrats, and contracted or allowed individuals to pursue their own economic goals. Each of these groups had different motivations for attacking, or preserving, Indian identities. The church wanted souls; the government wanted subjects and taxes; the conquistadors wanted gold. In each case, they needed people, and they needed people identified as Indian. But they each sought to remake Indigenous peoples to fit their own desires. The church claimed rights to evangelize Indigenous peoples, the Crown to tax them, and the conquistadors to enslave them. As they jostled for control, they subjected Indigenous forms of religion, governance, and labor to their sometimes-competing objectives.

Thus, at the same time as they denigrated and destroyed Indigenous lifeways, they relied on them both materially and ideologically. They needed Indian allies in warfare to overthrow Indigenous empires, they needed Indian elites to collaborate in enforcing their new labor and taxation systems, they needed Indian workers and peasants to supply them with labor and tribute, and they needed Indian flocks to be converted. Paradoxically, they needed Indians to be Indians at the same time they needed to define all that was Indian as inferior and in need of Spanish domination.

While traditional accounts of the Spanish conquest of Central America generally attribute it to the military leader Pedro de Alvarado, just as the conquest of Mexico is attributed to Hernán Cortés or the discovery of America to Christopher Columbus, that tale is only one kind of memory making. More recent historiography of the conquest challenges the conquistador myth in several ways. In fact, Mexico and Central America had been home to rival and sometimes warring empires for hundreds of years before the Spanish arrived. The celebrated Spanish military conquests were actually carried out primarily by rival Indigenous groups, rather than by the small Spanish force that accompanied them. The Spanish may have thought they were using Native allies, but Indigenous groups were using the Spanish newcomers for their own purposes. In the long term, the Spanish indeed came to dominate, but that long-term process has come to distort our memories of what we term the "conquest."

One lingering testimony to the role of Mexican Indigenous groups in the so-called Spanish conquest of Central America is the prevalence of place names in the Mexican Nahuatl language. Even today many places in Guatemala are known by the names given them by the Indians who accompanied (or led) the Spanish. Mexican place names like Quetzaltenango are sprinkled among Spanish names like San Marcos, and some towns—like Santiago Atitlán—combine Spanish (Santiago) and Nahuatl (Atitlán).[6] Many smaller towns retain new or old names in local Mayan languages.

Most accounts emphasize that the role of European disease made the Spanish "conquest" dramatically different from the long history of imperial jockeying and conquest that preceded their arrival. Europeans were heir to centuries of infection and plague that gave survivors a huge biological advantage. Over time, and through the early deaths of many of their population, European populations had developed resistance or immunity to many of the microbes they inadvertently carried with them to the Americas. What Alfred Crosby called "ecological imperialism," rather than superior weapons or tactics, was what devastated the Indigenous populations, bringing a demographic collapse in which up to 90 percent died in the century after contact, leaving the Spanish to impose their rule.[7]

Historians estimate the preconquest population of Central America at between 5 and 6 million. This dropped drastically during the first 150 to 200 years after the Spanish arrived, then stabilized and began a slow recovery. By the time of independence in the early nineteenth century, the Native population was a little under 600,000. They were joined by some 20,000 Africans (most of them enslaved), 45,000 Spaniards, and 375,000 "castas" or mixed-race people.[8]

In some ways, Spain's supposed domination remained fragile. Despite the demographic collapse, Spaniards were greatly outnumbered by non-Spaniards. Indigenous survivors of the holocaust found many ways to evade and contest Spanish control. They incorporated Catholic religious symbols into their own worldviews and practices; some historians wondered if the missionaries actually converted Indians or were converted themselves as they adopted Indian language and customs to gain acceptance in the communities. Indians continued to speak their languages and engage in traditional economies and village life, while complying minimally with Spanish tax and labor demands as they had under preconquest imperial rulers. They used Spanish law and bureaucracy to protect their rights and autonomy. They fled into unconquered areas. And they rose up in arms against Spanish officials who intruded too deeply into their livelihoods and cultures.

Indian resistance and survival were especially strong in areas like Central America that were more rural and held less economic draw for the Spanish. The Spanish set up their rule in the ashes and infrastructure of the Aztec empire in Mexico and the Inca empire in Peru. Far from the bureaucratic center in Mexico's old—and new—capital, in the diocese of Guatemala, which included today's Guatemala and El Salvador, there was no single, dramatic military conquest. The Spanish engaged in "Catholic colonialism" by sending Franciscan and Dominican missionaries to "reduce" the Indian populations to controlled settlements. In the Indigenous highlands of Guatemala, throughout the 1500s "recalcitrant Indians were repeatedly rounded up from the hills and reintroduced into the settlements, as others were continually exhorted not to abandon them in the first place." "Indian neophytes, ushered into the early churches by their leaders" who had bribed them with gifts, "either ignored or interpreted in their own way the garbled sermons they received from their priests" who neither spoke nor understood the languages of those they had supposedly converted. The missionaries relied heavily on local authorities, plying them with gifts and offering them roles in the new church, reinforcing rather than undermining or challenging Native hierarchies. "By organizing the cult through the traditional social hierarchies in Indian villages, the monastic orders reinforced ancient social patterns instead of eroding them."[9]

Even when the missions were secularized and parish priests replaced the missionary orders in the late 1700s, the syncretic system that had grown under the missionaries, based in the *cofradías* (village-level brotherhoods) and saints' cults, persisted. Few priests were willing to serve in remote rural areas, and even those who could did not speak local languages. Until the late nineteenth century, one study concluded, "despite the introduction of new tools and plants and animals and beneath a gloss of religious and political change, [Guatemala's] rural population largely continued to create and inhabit its own socioeconomic and political spaces and to suffer only limited outside interference on a day-to-day basis."[10]

Even in these remote areas, though, "starting deep in the colonial period, Indian [elites] had grown to rely on Spaniards and then Ladinos to pursue their interests and maintain their authority."[11] Local leaders trod an uneasy path as they sought to maintain legitimacy in their communities and also with Spanish authorities. Their power and position depended on both.

Nicaragua, to the south of Guatemala, served as a source of slaves to feed the rapacious labor demands of silver mining in Peru and transportation in Panama, where Spain's trade with South America passed. Some two hundred thousand, or more than one-third of Nicaragua's Indigenous population, were enslaved and transported out of the country in the first decades after conquest before the trade was ended in 1550. The enslavement and transport of such large numbers of Central American Indians, wrote historian Murdo MacLeod, constituted "one of the most tragic and forgotten aspects of Spanish Pacific history."[12]

Another population that has been virtually invisibilized in Central American history is the Caribbean coast peoples, descendants primarily of Caribbean-facing Indigenous peoples and Afro-Caribbean escapees from slavery or post-emancipation migrants. The Atlantic or Caribbean coastline of Belize, Guatemala, Honduras, Nicaragua, and Costa Rica has been isolated from interior, highland, and Pacific Central America since pre-Columbian times. (El Salvador, ensconced on the Pacific coast, does not share this Caribbean history with the rest of Central America.) While some Mayan populations live in the northern sector, especially in Mexico and Belize, most of the Indigenous and their languages, like the Miskitu, Mayangna (Sumo), or Rama in Nicaragua, or Talamanca in Costa Rica, belong to Caribbean and northern South American Arawak- and Chibcha-related groups. Many of these have mixed over the centuries with Afro-descended peoples, some forming new ethnicities like the Black Carib or Garifuna and Creole.[13] Their colonial interactions were with the British Caribbean and Protestant missionaries rather than the Spanish- and Catholic-dominated mainland. The divide continued in the late nineteenth century when much of the Caribbean area was taken over by US-based banana companies, which brought new waves of Black Caribbean migrant workers. Even today, the Atlantic (or Caribbean) coast regions of Central America are physically and culturally distant from the capital cities and the mainstream of national life.

THE SPANISH COLONIAL ORDER

Spanish colonial rule was based on tightly controlled trade, close relations between church and state with a strong role of the church in governance, and strict hierarchical division of the population. At the top were *peninsulares*—Spaniards born in Spain, who controlled government and economy. Below them were Creoles, the American-born offspring of Spaniards. And at the bottom were the Indians or Indigenous people. In the heartland of Spain's empire, the Indigenous were subject to brutal labor and tribute demands. But in the backwaters like Central America, which lacked gold, silver, or the potential for plantation agriculture, the Spanish system of "two republics"—the Republic of Indians and the Republic of Spaniards—provided a significant degree of protection and autonomy for Indigenous communities. Meanwhile the presence of a growing population of mixed-race people, Indigenous people increasingly immersed in the Spanish world, and free and enslaved Black people complicated the Spanish claim about the two republics.

Murdo MacLeod described the first thirty years after conquest as the phase of "looting": "the invading Spaniards simply took the resources most readily and obviously available and sent them out of the country. Thus human beings and surface gold (also extracted by enslaved Indians) were exported in large quantities for the first thirty years after the conquest."[14] The Spanish then developed other export products, principally cacao, which became a popular drink in Europe and North America; cochineal, a red dye produced by insects that live on the nopal cactus in the 1600s; and especially after the 1700s, indigo, a plant producing a deep blue dye. The dyes were used in Europe's growing textile industries.

Cacao and cochineal prompted new forms of labor coercion after Indian slavery was officially (though not always really) abolished after the

1550s. Both were lowland crops. To force workers to migrate to the plantations, the Spanish imposed tribute, a special tax in cash and goods, on Indian highland communities. To pay the tax, Indians had no choice but to comply with Spanish labor demands. Indigo grew mostly wild or semi-wild in eastern Guatemala and in parts of El Salvador and was often combined with cattle grazing. Cattle required little labor, and indigo only during the short harvest season, so these had less impact on highland Indigenous communities.

WHY PEOPLE FORGET

Conquerors, triumphant elites, and perpetrators of atrocities might have obvious self-interested reasons for wanting to forget the crimes, suffering, and injustice involved in their rise to dominance. Since they control institutions, education, government, and the press, they have the means to promote their version of history.

Sometimes, popular memories that counter these official histories are maintained and passed down through oral traditions, families, cultural activities, and communities. Rigoberta Menchu wrote about such subversive histories as a form of resistance. But sometimes popular memories are buried or suppressed. People repress memories out of shame, disillusionment, fear, and self-preservation. Remembering the past may be too painful, or may bring a real threat of torture, murder, or disappearance, especially if the oppressors remain in power as they do in much of Central America.

The revolutionary movements that swept Nicaragua, Guatemala, and El Salvador in the 1970s drew on buried memories of resistance, as Rigoberta Menchu's testimony argues. In the repression that swept Guatemala and El Salvador, especially after the 1979 revolutionary victory in Nicaragua, government forces savagely attacked suspected activists, their suspected supporters, and the memories, hopes, and dreams of a new social order that motivated the revolutions. The isthmus was left riddled with broken communities, broken bodies, and broken memories.

In the documentary *Guatemala: Journey to the End of Memories*, narrator Nancy Peckenham travels with photos of a Guatemalan family from a refugee camp in Mexico back to their highland village, hoping to find family members who had remained there when those in Mexico fled the violence. When she arrives at the village, she is followed by soldiers, and the villagers she encounters react with fear and unanimously deny recognizing any of the refugees in the photos. Yet when she returns to Mexico with video footage of villagers, the refugees quickly recognize and even claim family relationships with several of them. "In Guatemala," Peckenham concludes, "to remember is dangerous."

In another haunting scene, she visits a "model village," a concentration camp where hundreds of displaced villagers deemed to be "subversive" are brought for reeducation. We are shown scenes of stony-faced residents lining up and reciting progovernment propaganda. It's a stark vision of what the "end of memories" means for the victims of violence.

For intellectuals and elites, invisibilizing and forgetting are a way of creating blissful ignorance that allows them to enjoy their privilege without acknowledging its basis in exploitation. Forgetting allows them to avoid the shame that would come from seeing. When one Guatemalan plantation owner remarked innocently that she had nothing to hide, a local activist retorted angrily that "[s]he's got plenty to hide, even if she doesn't know it."[15]

Author Daniel Wilkinson offered an anecdote to reflect on how the beneficiaries of the plantation economy soothe their consciences by evading and forgetting. A plantation owner drives hurtling down a rural dirt road, going far too fast as they pass through a village. Suddenly a rooster darts into the road in front of them. The driver shrugs as he runs it down. "What could I do?" he demands defensively.[16]

Indeed. By ignoring his actions—driving too fast—that led up to the accident, it's easy to cast himself as blameless. And, as Wilkinson rudely and repeatedly reminds his American readers, they are just as implicated in the system as the Guatemalan elites that Wilkinson invites readers to scorn for their arrogance.

Two poems from the 1980s, one by Guatemalan guerrilla fighter Otto René Castillo and the other by American poet and activist Carolyn Forché, explore the violence of wealth and poverty, and how Central American elites construct particular kinds of invisibility and forgetting. But the poems also speak to US audiences, reminding us quietly that we too are part of the systems they describe, and if we don't know it, it's because we are engaged in our own rituals of forgetting.

Castillo directs his attention at the "apolitical intellectuals" who from their ivory towers distance themselves from the misery of the poor and work hard to ignore their complicity in the system that sustains their privilege. Every day they avert their eyes from those who labor to maintain the intellectuals' comfort, while they enjoy "their dress, their long siestas after lunch" and their self-important ruminations on Greek mythology or "the idea of the nothing." But one day, Castillo imagines, "they will be interrogated by the simplest of our people. . . . Those who had no place in the books and poems of the apolitical intellectuals, but daily delivered their bread and milk, their tortillas and eggs, those who drove their cars, who cared for their dogs and gardens." Those invisibilized workers will finally ask their own question: "What did you do when the poor suffered, when tenderness and life burned out of them?" The apolitical intellectuals will be unable to answer: "A vulture of silence will eat your gut. . . . You will be mute in your shame."[17]

American poet Carolyn Forché, who spent many of the war years in El Salvador, also addressed the question of willful ignorance, shame, and forgetting in her best-known poem "The Colonel," written in 1978. But while she described the Salvadoran colonel's brutality and forgetting, she addressed her poem in English to an American, not a Salvadoran, audience.

The poem describes in spare terms the complacency of El Salvador's bourgeoisie and the normalization of violence. But it implicitly accuses Americans who are funding the war of the same kind of willful ignorance and self-righteousness that she describes in the colonel's family. "What you have heard is true," she begins ominously, implying that her US readers have surely heard whispers about the atrocities in El Salvador, but have perhaps dismissed them as too outrageous—or too potentially discomfiting—to be true.

The scene in the colonel's house is familiar, almost banal. His wife brings a tray of coffee, his daughter files her nails, his son goes out for the evening, the television displays a "cop show" in English. "There were daily papers, pet dogs . . ." But in the same sentence, "a pistol on the cushion beside him." The pistol is so casual that it could perhaps be overlooked, but just as the reader is lulled into the familiarity of the scene, their attention is drawn to the violence simmering just below the surface, the "broken bottles . . . embedded in the walls around the house to scoop the kneecaps from a man's legs or cut his hands to lace."

The scene gets more tense as "there was some talk then of how difficult [the country] had become to govern," and the colonel tells the parrot to "shut up" when it says hello. He leaves the room and returns "with a sack used to bring groceries home." But when he dumps the sack on the table out spill human ears. "What you have heard is true," the reader remembers. "I am tired of fooling around," the colonel then informs Forché. "As for the rights of anyone, tell your people they can go fuck themselves." With these words, the colonel derides US Americans for *their* privilege of forgetting, which allows them to blame Salvadorans for human rights violations while erasing their own culpability in El Salvador's situation.[18]

MIGRATION AND FORGETTING

The politics of forgetting took on a new significance in the United States as more and more Central Americans fled their homes to make new lives in *el norte* (the North). Large-scale Central American migration to the United States dates to the civil wars of the 1980s and came primarily from El Salvador and Guatemala. Most came fleeing political violence, and their presence became politically very inconvenient for the Reagan administration, which was seeking to justify its support for these countries' governments. Others were economic refugees. Either way, the refugees gave the lie to Reagan's claims of the governments' legitimacy and right to US support.

Central Americans had been migrating for centuries, of course. Their populations were shaped and reshaped by waves of migration even before the arrival of the Spanish, forming patchworks of languages and evolving cultures and ethnicities. Spanish migrants moved themselves and moved Indigenous peoples to take advantage of land and labor, and for political and religious control. The coffee and banana economies of the nineteenth century likewise shifted land and labor patterns. Population growth, land exhaustion, export agriculture, and state-sponsored colonization schemes after World War II pushed peasants from land-scarce El Salvador—the most densely populated country of Central America—to Honduras, and from the Guatemalan highlands north to the rain forests of the Ixcán and the plains of the Petén. When they came to the United States, Central Americans followed the routes established by Mexicans, to California and Texas, but also to Washington, DC, and other urban centers, and to new destinations in the US South.

In 1986, the Reagan administration signed a landmark piece of immigration legislation, the Immigration Reform and Control Act. IRCA attempted to address the problems created in part by the 1965 Immigration and Nationality Act that for the first time set quotas limiting

Mexican and other Latin American immigration. The INA turned millions of mostly Mexican seasonal migrants into undocumented or "illegal" immigrants. IRCA sought to regularize the status of many of these migrants while sanctioning employers who hired undocumented workers and setting the stage for the anti-immigrant and wall-building hysteria that began in the 1990s and continues today.

IRCA was aimed primarily at legalizing Mexican migrant workers. It excluded those who had arrived after 1982—thus, many of the Central American refugees. But some, like the Mayans from Totonicapán in highland Guatemala who settled in Houston, had arrived early enough to take advantage of the law. Migrants have always followed family members, and legal status gave some the ability to formally sponsor relatives, creating another path for growing communities.

After Central America's peace treaties of the 1990s, the region's political, economic, and military relations with the United States only tightened. Peace, neoliberal reforms, and structural adjustment loans set the stage for a flood of US investment. Closer economic ties served as an additional spur to migration, as they did elsewhere. Yet Central America became ever more invisible to the US public, even as its migrants periodically hit the front pages.

FORGETTING CENTRAL AMERICA IN THE UNITED STATES

Many historians and other investigators in Central America have encountered the challenges of closed doors, destroyed and missing records, and silences there. The same kinds of silences face investigators into the US role in Central America.

A group of researchers visited the US Embassy in El Salvador in 1985 to ask about human rights abuses there, in particular, a massacre of seventy-four Indian peasants on a cooperative. "They gently scold us for visiting," the visitors reported, "for journeying into what they consider El Salvador's past. 'It's terrible what happened—but that was two years ago!' they say. 'Americans have to stop dwelling on the sins of this country's past. This is Day One in El Salvador, a new beginning.'"[19]

Even now, US government records are classified or heavily redacted. One of the few CIA cables to be released from the height of the repression in Guatemala included a page in which every line except one was covered with heavy black marker. US censors are literally obliterating the past.[20]

When then vice president Nixon visited Latin America in 1958, he was shocked to be greeted by anti-American protests. When President Reagan toured in 1982, he reported in wonder that "you'd be surprised . . . they are all individual countries!"[21] Very few US Americans can name a single political leader in Central America. We have the privilege of "forgetting" about these countries.

Yet US political leaders, parties, and policies are the stuff of everyday conversation in Central America. People there don't have the luxury of ignoring or forgetting what is going on in the United States, because they know that US presidential elections, policy decisions, and economic developments are likely to deeply affect them.

CHAPTER 2

MAKING THE UNITED STATES, MAKING CENTRAL AMERICA

Bananas, Coffee, Savages, and Bandits

The nineteenth century was a period of economic development and state and nation building in both the United States and the Central American countries, and these processes were interrelated. Political independence meant the establishment of new institutions and ideologies and trying to implement governance over people and territories. The United States and the Central American countries spent the nineteenth century at war: wars fought in part over the nature of the new nations. All grappled with questions of citizenship and race. By late in the century, their paths were deeply intertwined.

One of the conceits of forgetting in the United States is the idea that colonialism ended in 1776 when the new country declared independence. Central American countries, too, celebrate their independence heroes and wars as historical milestones. But in both regions, the colonial roots ran deep and profoundly shaped the new countries. In the United States, independence meant a surge of settler colonial expansion that incorporated Central America into its sights. In Central America, colonial racial hierarchies shaped the new nations even as the United States imposed new forms of neocolonial rule.

HOW COLONIALISM SHAPED THE UNITED STATES

Settler colonialism characterized US history from its earliest days to the present. The country was established as a white nation, in a land inhabited by many nonwhite people. It was established by colonizers motivated by an unquestioning belief in their own right, or even duty, to expand. Entrenched in settler colonialism were ideas about race and freedom. For a country founded on the basis of slavery, expansion, and expulsion, it's remarkable how central the concept of freedom has been to its self-image and ideology. But freedom for white people required the land, labor, and resources of nonwhite people. Thus, the concept of freedom itself—so central still to US American identity—has always been deeply racialized.

One result of this outlook is that throughout US history, domestic policy and foreign policy have been entangled. If only the white residents of the original thirteen colonies became citizens of the new country, then what exactly were the nonwhite—primarily Native American and African American—residents? Even when free, Blacks could not be citizens of the United States. They were permanent outsiders within.

Most Native Americans, of course, lived outside the borders of the new country and were simply foreigners, to be dealt with through diplomacy, war, trade, and treaty. But others lived inside the borders of the thirteen colonies that declared independence, and those borders constantly expanded. The century after independence was one of nonstop warfare and conquest. The incorporation of new territories meant the incorporation of new peoples. "For Americans, the Revolution was a war for independence, and it was also a war for Indian land," wrote Colin Galloway. "Establishing the sovereignty of the United States required wrestling with the sovereignty of Indian nations and their place in American society."[1] As the new country extended its reach into Indian country, newly conquered Indians became redefined as "domestic dependent nations."[2]

Historian John Grenier called this the United States' "first way of war," laying out a pattern of total war against civilian populations and destruction of their subsistence economies that shaped the US military. It was also a first way of thinking that rested on convictions about racial superiority and a racialized concept of freedom. This arrogance and self-righteousness formed a deadly mix justifying US domination of non–Anglo-Saxons and has shaped US relations with Central America ever since.[3]

CENTRAL AMERICA

Today's Central American countries formed part of Spain's colonial Audiencia of Guatemala, a district of its Viceroyalty of New Spain, based in the heartland of the old Aztec empire in the Central Valley of Mexico. In 1786, as part of a campaign to streamline governance of its empire, Spain further divided the Audiencia into intendancies, thus creating administrative divisions and power brokers that laid the foundation for the countries that emerged after independence.

Central American independence came in stages in the nineteenth century, first as part of Mexico in 1821, then breaking away two years later as the United Provinces and then the Federal Republic of Central America; then in 1838, primarily through elite squabbles over power and territory, into the countries as we know them today (though not without continuing border disputes). As elsewhere in Latin America, independence brought new autonomy, ideologies, and economic projects for Creole (that is, American-born, Spanish-ancestry) elites, and new relationships with British, German, and soon US burgeoning industrial economies.

Consolidation of a new post-independence order took several decades. Elite factions split into Liberals and Conservatives, whose essential goals overlapped despite differences that contributed to ongoing civil wars. Conservatives hoped to maintain much of the colonial social order, including legal status for Indian communities and a role for the church in governance. Liberals sought to overturn the colonial caste system and its legal intermediaries in order to exert direct state control over the population. Liberals were also committed to the idea of progress based on foreign investment and the development of an export economy. Liberals and Conservatives shared deeply elitist and racist views, shaped by colonialism, that placed Euro-descendants at the top of the social hierarchy and saw Indians, in particular, and the rural poor majority, in general, as an obstacle to progress, fit only for service to their social and racial betters.

When the Liberals triumphed toward the end of the century, two of the main victims were Indian communities and the church. While Indians had been marginalized and treated as inferior under the colonial system, the Spanish had also recognized a fair degree of autonomy and especially communal land rights. The church, too, held large tracts of land. Liberals wanted a strong state that would eliminate or control these alternate sources of power. Abolishing collective land holdings and putting land for sale on the free market, they believed, would be the key to stimulating export production and economic progress.

As elites consolidated power under new Liberal regimes, they turned to new militaries and proliferating police agencies (agricultural police, rural police, civil guards, etc.) to back up the expropriation of Indigenous lands and peasants' forced incorporation into the new export economies. As in the United States, the road to progress was paved with racism and violence.

BETWEEN INDEPENDENCE AND CONSOLIDATION

Guatemalan Liberals took power in 1829 and began a concerted attack on colonial institutions. Indian communities lost their legal status and land rights, and Indians were subject to a new head tax. The government expropriated religious orders and expelled the archbishop and missionaries from the country. The state began to auction off church property, declared freedom of religion, and took control of church-run cemeteries and schools. The military was a main beneficiary of confiscated church property, and also moved in to fill the spaces left by the church in rural areas, becoming the first and main government presence there.[4]

The reforms, and a cholera epidemic that many rural poor saw as yet another government ploy to take their lands, provoked multiple rebellions, often in concert with religious authorities. In the late 1830s, these culminated in the triumph of Conservative Rafael Carrera. Many authors concur that Carrera's reign was "something of a golden age in the Guatemalan highlands for community autonomy and freedom from outside intervention . . . The communities, abandoned by the church and the central government . . . were left for a generation largely to themselves."[5]

This did not mean that rural life was conflict-free. The retreat of outside authorities allowed Indian elites to consolidate wealth and power in their communities.[6] Communities also battled each other over land. "Whereas the Spanish colonial regime had been able to enforce a minimum of order, if not justice, in the countryside, with the near collapse of the central state the villages laid into each other with enthusiasm and ferocity."[7] Later in the century, as the population increased and the plantation economy started to demand more land, these struggles only increased.

The fact that Indian communities battled internally and with each other reminds us that we can't essentialize either ethnic or class identities. Indian communities were stratified, hierarchical, and divided. Loyalties and identities are contingent and change over time.

Historian Erik Ching described El Salvador's nineteenth century this way: "Between 1824 and 1842 El Salvador participated in forty interstate battles . . . State institutions were born defunct, and no single political group could generate sufficient strength to consolidate authority. Instead of one great pyramid, the political system of El Salvador consisted of numerous little pyramids, distinct patronage networks that battled one another for control over the central state—however decrepit and insolvent it may have been."[8] His words could apply to all of Central America prior to the 1870s.

THE NEW LIBERAL ORDER AFTER 1870

The Liberal governments that consolidated power by the end of the century were eager to shake off colonial restrictions and modernize their countries with the help of European loans and investment. Progress, they believed, would come from building an export economy. In both Guatemala and El Salvador, a new Liberal hegemony based on promoting coffee production united the oligarchy by the late nineteenth century. For Central America's poor majorities, the elite vision of progress entailed new forms of repression and coercion.

In the mid-nineteenth century, most of the region's land and labor was still in the hands of its Indigenous villages. The coffee boom brought land grabs, plantation agriculture, railroads, and forced labor to Indigenous populations in the cool Pacific volcanic highlands. Some historians termed it a "second conquest," as local oligarchs and foreign investors implemented new systems to gain control of Indigenous lands and labor.[9] They also reformulated ideologies that defined Indians as backward, primitive, relics of a past that must be transcended in the interests of modernization, productivity, and integration in world markets.

In Guatemala, German immigrants played a key role in developing the industry. In El Salvador, the infamous "fourteen families" (rather than nuclear families, these were more like tightly interlocked clans) are sprinkled with the names of European immigrants (some via the Caribbean) like Hill, de Sola, Parker, Dalton, and D'Aubuisson. These oligarchies controlled politics, the economy, and the military.

In Nicaragua and Honduras, the United States held greater sway. In both countries, a strong British presence on their extensive Atlantic coasts dated back to the 1600s and drew sustained US attention, especially after the British declared the area a protectorate in 1844. In Nicaragua, the struggle between Liberals and Conservatives remained more acute in part because of the outsized US influence and presence there. In Honduras, too, a weak state and dependence on foreign investors in the banana and mining industries slowed the emergence of a coffee oligarchy.

Even in Guatemala and El Salvador, where elites were more powerful and autonomous, to look at them in isolation constitutes its own kind of forgetting. There were larger global forces behind Central America's nineteenth-century coffee boom. Central American coffee was not the only tropical stimulant that Europeans invested in, produced, imported, sold, and consumed during their second industrial revolution. As English and French peasants left their farms for the factories, their diets shifted from grains and vegetables that they produced themselves to sugar, coffee, and tea produced in the colonies, in a counterpart to the mass production for profit in the home countries. US coffee came first from France's slave plantations in the Caribbean, then from Brazil and Colombia, and increasingly from Cuba and Puerto Rico—two colonies that the United States took from Spain in 1898—and, in the twentieth century, from the nominally independent countries of Central America that soon were swept into the US sphere of influence. The new coffee oligarchies rose to power at home but remained subordinate in the global order.

REMAKING GUATEMALA FOR COFFEE

Guatemala offers a prime example of how Liberal dictators and coffee oligarchs built a strong state that relied on military repression of the population. Coffee revenues subsidized the state's repressive apparatus, and repression was necessary to force peasants to give up their land and to provide cheap labor for the new coffee plantations. A series of "liberal dictators" used an iron hand to impose liberal priorities of "order and progress." Especially long-lived and notorious were Justo Rufino Barrios (1871–1885), Manuel Estrada Cabrera (1898–1920), and Jorge Ubico (1931–1944). Estrada Cabrera served as the model for Guatemalan Nobel Prize–winning author Miguel Ángel Asturias's harrowing 1946 novel *El Señor Presidente*, which became a classic illustrating the ways the dictator used physical and psychological terror to control the population.

The Conservative Carrera era ended, and the Liberal state came back with a vengeance with the 1871 revolution that brought coffee planter Justo Rufino Barrios to power. Barrios invested massively in physical and banking infrastructure to support the new coffee economy and passed reforms privatizing communal and church lands, thus facilitating the transfer of land from communities to the new plantation owners. Loss of land forced many peasants into selling their labor to the plantations, but Barrios left nothing to chance: he also established new systems of forced labor to ensure that plantations had enough workers.

First came the *mandamiento*—a colonial-style forced-labor draft imposed on Indigenous communities between 1877 and 1894. Mandamiento was complemented by debt peonage. If a planter could indenture a worker through debt, the worker was released from the state-organized mandamiento and became subject to their creditor. Debt peonage created a privatized alternative to the state system of forced labor, but it only worked because state security forces backed it up.

Jorge Ubico recentralized the system in 1931 by replacing debt peonage with a new Vagrancy Law that required all men who did not own property to labor in public works or private plantations for 100 to 150 days a year. Both debt peonage and vagrancy laws mirrored those implemented in the US South after the abolition of slavery, except in Central America both applied almost exclusively to Indians.

Thus "the creation of Guatemala's agrarian proletariat took place along clearly defined ethnic lines. Coffee production parasitically attached itself to indigenous communities, slowly draining pueblos of their subsistence autonomy. Indian towns were obvious sources of labor, and at times whole communities, either through the mandamiento or peonage, became the captive workforce of specific planters." Because coffee was a seasonal crop that required large numbers of workers only for the harvest, planters could also benefit by allowing villages to maintain minimal subsistence lands to sustain themselves when their labor was not needed.[10]

Incorporation in the coffee economy also transformed relations within many Indigenous communities. When communal holdings were abolished, Indigenous as well as Ladino elites were able to purchase land. Within Indigenous communities, "macehuales [commoners] became mozos [peons] and principales [community leaders] became patrones [bosses]."[11] As the state reinforced Indigenous landlords' power, what were formerly relations of reciprocity within communities became more coercive.

Historian Greg Grandin investigated how the system worked in one heavily Indian city, Quetzaltenango. Landed Indigenous elites "still actively participated in the city's cofradía system and continued to bind individuals to them in relations of dependent paternalism. Large K'iche' landholders provided land to poorer Indians to live on and cultivate, in exchange for labor or crops." The cofradías evolved to take a larger role in community governance and elites' roles strengthened. The export economy and its beneficiaries thus found ways to take advantage of existing community identities and institutions.[12]

As Indigenous power holders increased their sway over poorer community members, they also relied more on Ladino brokers and the state to uphold their authority. "The liberal state did not arrive unexpectedly in communities in 1871," Grandin writes. "[I]t was invited in." Over the course of the liberal/coffee period, "relations of deference and obligation gradually weakened as expectations of subsistence rights withered away. The power of principales became much more directly tied to the punitive function of the state."[13]

The coffee revolution also brought Ladinos into the heart of Indian communities. As labor contractors, merchants, moneylenders, and politicians, they provided the glue that tied Indian workers to migrant labor on the coffee plantations.

Indigenous elites shared with their Ladino counterparts "many of the liberal assumptions regarding progress, civilization, education, and economic prosperity" and the essentially backward nature of Indian society. However, they "categorically refused to accept the Ladino equation of race and class, which grew increasingly powerful as Guatemala became transformed into a coffee-producing nation." As Indians were defined as coffee pickers, Indian elites sought to create a cultural and political space in which they could be both Indian and wealthy.[14] These debates about the nature and meaning of Indian identity would persist and evolve over Guatemala's later history.

EL SALVADOR

El Salvador's coffee lands were concentrated in the heavily populated and heavily Indigenous western portion of the country. The legislative revolution began in 1881 when the government abolished the legal status of Indigenous communities and privatized communal landholdings. As in Guatemala, new laws forced the recently dispossessed to work on the growing coffee plantations. To enforce the new order and repress peasant uprisings in the 1880s and '90s, the government established a military training school in 1900 and a new rural police force, the Guardia

Nacional, in 1912. As Indian communities lost their lands and legal rights, their people were forced into underpaid, grueling, wage labor on the new coffee plantations.

Still, the first decades of the coffee revolution were less draconian in El Salvador than they were in Guatemala. In El Salvador, some peasants, including Indigenous peasants, managed to acquire small plots of land and participate in the coffee export boom. True "proletarianization and dispossession" in the western coffee region accelerated in the coffee boom of the 1920s as "the peasantry suffered an agonizing decomposition" that becaome catastrophic after the Depression hit.[15]

Despite the loss of land, Indian communities "remained a vibrant part of the socio-political fabric of western El Salvador" in the first decades of the twentieth century, held together through their cofradías and community identity and institutions.[16] Some spoke the Indigenous Nahua language and wore traditional dress, though many did not. Indian peasants shared a similar structural position to Ladino peasants: most were poor, illiterate, and lacked access to land. It was their less visible shared history and collective identity and, in particular, their Indigenous cofradías that distinguished El Salvador's Indian peasants.[17]

El Salvador's high population density and levels of urbanization fostered a strong organizational culture. By the 1930s, San Salvador was home to a small Salvadoran Communist Party, the communist mutual support organization International Red Aid, and the Regional Federation of Salvadoran Workers, which founded a People's University and to which some 10 percent of the country's workers belonged.

Student activist Farabundo Martí left El Salvador for Nicaragua in 1927 to fight against the US occupation there. He returned in 1929 to join his country's burgeoning organizational life and founded the Salvadoran Communist Party. In addition to organizing among workers in the capital, the party sought contacts among rural coffee workers. The collapse of coffee prices during the Great Depression meant that jobs disappeared and wages contracted. Indebted smallholders lost their lands, yet there were no jobs. "In the summer of 1931, thousands of desperate, hungry workers were on the roads."[18]

The US attaché to Central America described the situation in early 1932, after a military general, Maximiliano Hernández Martínez, toppled the reformist-elected government in a coup: "There is practically no middle class between the very rich and the very poor . . . I imagine the situation in El Salvador today is very much like France was before its revolution, Russia before its revolution and Mexico before its revolution. The situation is ripe for communism . . . A socialistic or communistic revolution in El Salvador may be delayed for several years, ten or even twenty, but when it comes it will be a bloody one."[19]

The revolution was not long in coming. In the January 1932 local elections, communist and leftist candidates won in numerous municipalities, but the coup government refused to recognize the results. In some Indian communities, the conflicts were between Indian and Ladino candidates. Popular anger coalesced into a plan to coordinate peasant takeovers of local town halls with a workers' strike in the capital on January 22. The plans leaked and the government mobilized, arresting Martí a few days before the planned protest.

In the coffee region, the rebellion went on as planned. Armed peasants took over municipal buildings, sacked archives, and attacked Ladino power holders. Across the region, some fifty to one hundred were killed. The rebellion was "heavily shaped by racial tension, and indigenous perceptions of the 'Spanish' and ladinos as invaders and occupiers," wrote Virginia Tilley. The revolt should "be granted a long-denied place in history as one of the last great Indian uprisings of the twentieth century." Indigenous rebels sought "freedom for an indigenous community (which had its own elite and class divisions) from ladino racial domination . . . Its anticolonial and antiladino flavor . . . was rooted in collective memory of the conquest."[20]

What followed was "a racial reign of terror" carried out mostly not by the army but by armed Ladino vigilante groups. Estimates of those killed range from ten thousand to over thirty thousand. Tilley described the vicious brutality as "a brief flare of racial extremism that swept the hearts and minds of ladinos in the area, drawing normally quiet people, prone to ethnic cohabitation within a familiar caste system, into deadly participation."[21] At the national level, the threat of US intervention also goaded the Martínez government to react with ruthless violence to prove its capacity to maintain order.[22]

The mass killings, or *matanza*, enabled Ladinos to assert power in village after village, especially control over land and water. The killing itself was only one form of silencing and erasure. After the slaughter, "[c]andid public discussion of the events was suppressed, archives were off-limits, documents were destroyed, lost, or stolen, and many people who witnessed the events were exiled or killed, or remained silent."[23] If histories recalled the uprising, it was through the lens of communism and anti-communism, even though the Communist Party played only a small role in the events.

After the matanza, Salvadoran intellectuals and government officials joined an international trend to erase the country's Indians altogether. The government eliminated racial categories from the census and all municipal records. "By 1958 the Salvadoran legislature would claim simply that 'in our country indigenous populations do not exist.'"[24] Instead, the country celebrated a myth of racial unity and race mixture or *mestizaje.* Intellectuals followed those in Mexico and elsewhere who proposed a "cosmic" or "Latin" race as a source of national pride and of resistance to European and especially US imperialism.

But national unity rested on forgetting. Tilley explains that "in El Salvador, no sense of moral responsibility about that trauma, or even glancing concern, lingers in the national conscience. No one thinks of compensation for the massacre's survivors, or truth commissions, or any of the measures that today, in other countries, surround the aftermath of ethnic cleansing . . . The Matanza is admitted to have targeted and terrified an entire ethnic population. But the ethnic group targeted in that massacre is presumed to have disappeared." "Tucked conceptually into an unreachable past, they absolve the nation of any collective guilt or further action following the Matanza."[25]

The campaign of silence and the rewriting of history shaped the memories of the victims as well, but in different ways. Decades later, researchers found that while survivors could vividly recount the slaughter, they erased their own histories of activism. The trauma and the ongoing repression encouraged survivors to emphasize their victimhood over their mobilization. "The common phrase 'mataron justos por pecadores' (they killed the just instead of the sinners) synthesizes this perspective. In other words, Indians did not participate in the rebellion but became the scapegoats in the bloody repression."[26] Although they buried their memories, Indian villages did not obediently abandon their identity and institutions. The meaning and uses of Indigenous identity continued to evolve.

NICARAGUA AND HONDURAS UNDER US SWAY

The United States had more than a passing affinity for Central America's nation- and state-building elites. US policy makers shared the view that

Indians belonged to the past, and that progress required that their land and autonomy be eliminated in the interests of capitalist development. They believed that US loans and US investment in Central America could build an export economy that would help them enrich themselves individually and as a group. As for the poor at home in the United States, their revolutionary potential would be dampened by the blessings of consumer society. For this, the United States needed Indigenous lands in the West and beyond, including in Central America, to feed its factories and its workers. At the bottom of the hierarchy were Central American workers, who would be put down by force if they challenged the system.

In Guatemala and El Salvador, US influence remained mostly indirect, cultural, and economic. The United States offered ideologies, loans, markets, and, by late in the century in Guatemala, a new export industry in the remote Atlantic coast—bananas. (See below.) In Nicaragua and, to a lesser extent, Honduras, the intervention was more direct.

The Monroe Doctrine

In 1823 President James Monroe articulated the first official statement of US policy in the Americas, upon which so many future interventions would be based. "The American continents," he proclaimed, "are henceforth not to be considered as subjects for future colonization by any European powers . . . We should consider any attempt on their part to extend their system to any portion of this hemisphere as dangerous to our peace and safety." The statement was aimed at Europeans. But in fact, despite some European claims, in 1823 most of the Americas still belonged to sovereign Native American tribes or was claimed by newly independent Latin American countries. Many of the latter, like the United States, also claimed sovereignty over land that was still under Native control. Monroe took Native and Latin American claims so lightly as to not even merit mention: his concern was competition with European colonizers.

At the time Monroe announced the doctrine, the United States occupied only the eastern portion of North America. His statement made it clear that the new country claimed sole rights to colonize the rest of the continent. And the new country immediately set about doing so.[27]

In 1829, Latin American independence leader Simón Bolívar articulated his interpretation of the US stance. The United States, he wrote, "seems destined by Providence to plague America with miseries in the name of Freedom."[28] (He uses "America" in the conventional Latin American way, to refer to the continent that includes North, Central, and South America, rather than to the country of the United States. Just one other thing that the United States tends to forget: that America is a continent, and people in the United States are not the only "Americans.")

The century after US independence was the heyday of the settler colonial project there. "Manifest Destiny" and "westward expansion" are common euphemistic terms to describe the colonial conquest of Native lands. But much of the land to the west of the United States was also part of Latin America—Mexico, to be precise. Central America, too, played a key role in westward expansion. Because most of the territory between the East Coast and California was still under Native control, gold rushers heading for California looked for a southern route. Railroad and shipping tycoon Cornelius Vanderbilt descended on Nicaragua to build roads and shipping infrastructure to carry thousands of easterners every month on the fastest and cheapest route to California. Just as relations with Indian tribes and nations blurred the line between domestic and foreign policy, so did relations with Central America.

Manifest Destiny was a public-private collaboration, as when Anglo settlers moved to Mexican Texas (or Comanchería, since most of the land claimed was under Comanche control) and then demanded annexation to the United States.[29] Thousands of privateers or filibusterers organized private military expeditions into Latin America after 1848.[30] The most successful and notorious, William Walker, allied with Nicaragua's Liberals against the Conservative government and succeeded in taking control of the country from 1855 to 1857, bringing in his wake some twelve thousand US settlers. US president Franklin Pierce quickly recognized his regime there. One historian termed his mission "nascent U.S. liberal imperialism in the form of overseas settler colonialism," that likewise transcended the line between domestic and foreign policy.[31] Walker's invasion and occupation, and the Central American armies that joined forces to oust him and restore Nicaragua's independence, have been mostly airbrushed out of US history. But Central Americans remember these events as formative.

The Civil War temporarily distracted the United States from western, southern, and overseas expansion, but by the end of the nineteenth century, Central America again was feeling its weight. The war created new markets and government largesse for railroads and steel manufacturers, setting the stage for massive development of the country's industrial and financial sectors. For Central America, this meant a flood of investment in the new banana industry as well as the coffee industry, and in a transportation infrastructure to export these goods to the United States. Investment also flowed into gold and silver mining, and into private utilities, to serve the growing urban populations.[32]

The Roosevelt Corollary

President Theodore Roosevelt proclaimed his famous "corollary" to the Monroe Doctrine in 1904. "The most civilized powers," he announced, clearly including the United States in this category, had an obligation to arm themselves and "police" their racial and economic inferiors. "If a nation shows that it knows how to act with reasonable efficiency and decency in social and political matters, if it keeps order and pays its obligations, it need fear no interference from the United States," he went on. However, "chronic wrongdoing, or an impotence which results in a general loosening of the ties of civilized society, may . . . ultimately require intervention by some civilized nation, and . . . may force the United States, however reluctantly, in flagrant cases of such wrongdoing or impotence, to the exercise of an international police power."[33]

The Monroe Doctrine declared that the United States would keep Latin America off-limits to Europeans. The Roosevelt Corollary now claimed a US right to intervene if it simply disapproved of the way a Latin American country was handling its internal affairs. If Central American governments failed to protect the US investors and bankers who were playing growing roles there, the US military would intervene to protect them.

Dollar Diplomacy

In 1912, President William Howard Taft announced that US economic expansion meant "substituting dollars for bullets" in US foreign policy, formalizing what became known as "dollar diplomacy." But in Central America, the flood of dollars after the Civil War and the Roosevelt Corollary brought about the opposite result. To protect US investments from both European and local challenges, military interventions and the use of Roosevelt's "international police power" became increasingly common. Woodrow Wilson (US president, 1913–1921) declared that European investment in or extension of credit to Central America constituted a threat to US interests there. US warships patrolled the Caribbean, and the United States did not hesitate to intervene repeatedly to protect "the persons and property of [US] citizens" in Central America, in the words of Calvin Coolidge (US president, 1923–1929).[34]

US Marine major general Smedley Butler caustically described his role in carrying out this policy in a 1933 speech. Serving in the Marines, he said, "I spent most of my time being a high class muscle-man for Big Business, for Wall Street and for the Bankers. In short, I was a racketeer, a gangster for capitalism. I helped in the raping of half a dozen Central American republics for the benefits of Wall Street."[35] While the Central American countries were nominally independent, it was clear to all who the kingmakers were.[36]

NICARAGUA

The longest US occupation was in Nicaragua, where the United States orchestrated the defeat of the Liberal Party government of José Santos Zelaya in 1909, directly occupied in 1912, and remained in control until 1933. Since taking power in 1893, Zelaya had challenged US hegemony in the region. He refused to grant the United States rights to build a canal across Nicaragua (leading to US machinations to create a new puppet state in Panama and build its canal there), and asserted his right to negotiate with British and Japanese investors independently of the United States. In 1909, US forces occupied Bluefields on Nicaragua's Atlantic coast and supported a rebellion there, succeeding in installing a more compliant government in Managua.

A few years later, when a group of Zelaya supporters led by Benjamín Zeledón took up arms against the US-supported Conservative government, the US Marines quickly landed to quash the rebellion. Zeledón was captured and killed by Nicaraguan government troops, and his body dragged through the small town of Niquinohomo before being buried. Teenager Augusto C. Sandino witnessed the events, which he later said made his "blood boil with rage." Within a few years, he would be leading another rebellion, this time against the full-fledged US occupation that followed the rebels' defeat in 1912.[37]

The Marines remained in Nicaragua until 1933. They allowed the presidency to remain nominally in the hands of consecutive Conservative leaders, though US officials took control of the country's central bank and customs collection. They also succeeded, finally, in obtaining a treaty (the Bryan-Chamorro Treaty of 1914) granting the United States the right to build an inter-oceanic canal through the country, along with a ninety-nine-year lease to the Corn Islands in the Caribbean and the right to build a naval base in the Gulf of Fonseca.

Nicaragua under occupation received *less* foreign investment than almost any other Latin American country during the same years. US priorities in Nicaragua were less economic than geopolitical: to ensure that no other European power built a canal there to rival its own in Panama. The United States quickly withdrew most of its army and "essentially governed Nicaragua through representatives of Wall Street banks." Rather than the loans they showered elsewhere in Latin America during the 1920s, the banks imposed fiscal discipline on Nicaragua.[38] Nicaragua's landed elites suffered as they lost access to government-funded infrastructure and sources of credit. Thus, for better or worse, Nicaragua did not experience the extremes of dispossession and land concentration that characterized Guatemala. Most of the country's coffee lands remained in the hands of smallholders before the 1930s.

For Nicaragua's Indigenous population, debt peonage reigned under US occupation as it did in Guatemala. A Nicaraguan legislator wrote that "[t]here are at least 70,000 indígenas who live, together with their wives and children, in true slavery . . . The police chiefs receive payments from the hacendados, especially the foreigners so that they are always willing to order the captures and searches of Indians' homes whom they then carry off, tied up, to the hacienda, where they have to work for an indefinite period of time."[39]

As in Guatemala, Indian elites often found a way to prosper as middlemen in the exploitative system, contributing to deepening divides in Indian communities. "The epoch's defining image of indigenous life," historian Jeffrey Gould writes of the early twentieth century, was "the *amarrados* (the bound ones), a long file of Indians with their hands tied behind their backs, led by their ethnic brethren on horseback toward an army encampment or to the peons' quarters of the plantation." Many fled their communities for the mountains.[40]

In Nicaragua, as in El Salvador, Ladinos elaborated histories and ideologies lauding Nicaragua's mestizaje as progressive and even anti-imperialist, and dismissing Indians as primitive relics. Also, as in El Salvador, Indians themselves contributed to the erasure of memories of ethnic repression and resistance.

In one Indian town, Gould describes decades of attacks on land and institutions, the spectacular murder of a Ladino land-grabber, and the subsequent vicious repression against the community. Years later, the community still struggled with grinding poverty, landlessness, and isolation. Elders mourned not only the material losses, but the fact that "the youth do not want to know our history; they do not care about our history." "Fear, shame, and flight have disintegrated the bonds of the Indian community," Gould concludes. Today "no one under forty easily accepts an Indigenous identity." Shame that their struggles failed, shame that community bonds fragmented, and shame because resistance gave way to "complicity with [their] own oppressors."[41]

By the mid-1920s, the United States was ready to divest itself of Nicaragua, leaving power in the hands of its Conservative allies. A Liberal rebellion soon followed, and US troops quickly returned. This time, the occupiers took dollar diplomacy to the next level, creating a new, nonpartisan military they hoped would guarantee a stable, US-friendly government. They arranged a truce between the Conservatives and the rebel Liberals, allowing a Liberal candidate to win a US supervised election in 1928. And they began to organize and train their new proxy, the *Guardia Nacional.*

The Guardia was an odd hybrid, "at once powered by U.S. technology and resources and profoundly shaped by local actors and local political culture." Rather than an apolitical, nonpartisan institution subordinate to civilian authority and defending a democratic state, the Guardia became "a masked and modernized form" of personalized rule and patronage.[42]

One group of Liberals refused the deal. "The sovereignty and liberty of a people are not to be discussed, but rather, defended with weapons in hand," announced Sandino, who gathered and led a guerrilla army aimed at ousting the occupiers. The US Marines and the Guardia spent five years fighting a classic counterinsurgency war in which the entire population in regions where the guerrillas operated—especially in the northern Segovia mountains—became the enemy. "U.S. forces used tactics that would become familiar during the Vietnam War—the aerial bombardment of 'hostile' towns and hamlets, the creation of what amounted to 'free fire zones' in rural areas, and the forced resettlement of peasants to what, later in the century, would be called 'protective hamlets.'"[43] US sources variously described Sandino "as a bandit, outlaw, and communist."[44]

The Guardia's identity was thus forged in a "brutal counterinsurgency campaign" against Nicaragua's civilian population.[45] The war was formative for the Nicaraguan state, which operated in the service of the Guardia.

When the United States deemed the Guardia firmly established and trained, the Marines withdrew, leaving the institution in the hands of Anastasio Somoza García. Governance now consisted of "an elitist dictatorial system based on a symbiotic relationship between the now corrupted and thoroughly politicized National Guard and the Somoza family . . . This system was to plunder, degrade, and bring agony to the Nicaraguan people for more than four decades."[46]

The nominal civilian government signed a peace treaty in 1933 with Sandino's rebels, offering them land and refuge in a northern mountain redoubt. Just a year later, the Guardia assassinated Sandino and most of his staff as they left a meeting with the country's civilian president. The hegemony of the Guardia was made official two years later when Somoza overthrew the civilian government and held the first of several decades' worth of elections under military rule, all of which were won by him or close family members.

HONDURAS

As elites in Guatemala and El Salvador were consolidating their control of the state and the military in the interest of the coffee economy in the late nineteenth century, Honduras remained geographically and politically fragmented. "The Honduran oligarchy was rich only in land, and lacked the necessary capital to develop an export crop," writes Alison Acker. "Honduras had profited little from exports like indigo and sarsaparilla. Its more promising cattle industry had been ruined by civil disturbances and foreign invasions. A poor transportation network, a shortage of labour, and a lack of experience in foreign marketing hampered the national capacity for export development."[47] Historian Walter LaFeber called Honduras "less a nation than a customs house surrounded by adventurers."[48] Between 1824 and 1933, Honduras had 117 different presidents.[49] But it was clear to all that real power lay with the banana companies.

BANANAS

Migration and trade have long connected Central America's eastern Atlantic coast and the Indigenous populations there more to the Caribbean world than to the mainland. British rather than Spanish influence predominated. In 1797, the British deported Afro-Indigenous peoples from the island of St. Vincent to the mainland. Known as Garifuna, they became the main population along Honduras's long coastline.

Even today, ground transport from the Pacific lowlands and central highlands to much of Central America's Atlantic coast is spotty to nonexistent. Isolated from the coffee economy, coastal peoples remained fairly autonomous until US banana companies arrived at the end of the nineteenth century.

Before the late nineteenth century, bananas were virtually unknown in the United States. A ship captain and an entrepreneur in Massachusetts paired to bring bananas from Jamaica, develop a market in Boston, and then create the United Fruit Company (UFCO). It soon became notorious as "the octopus" in Central America as it snapped up land in the Atlantic coast rainforests and brought workers from the Caribbean islands and the central highlands and developed virtual states-within-states. The company acquired or built railroads and developed shipping and marketing into a vertically integrated operation, swallowing up its competitors along the way.

In 1915, the company owned over a million acres of land in the Caribbean and Central America, including 252,000 acres in Costa Rica, 141,000 acres in Guatemala, 62,000 in Honduras, and 193,000 in Nicaragua. The low figure for Honduras only reflected the fact that two other US companies, Standard Fruit and the Cuyamel Fruit Company, owned most of the one million acres of foreign-held banana land there; Cuyamel was later folded into United. Much of the companies' land was not actually planted but held in reserve.[50]

By the time the Great Depression hit, US investors, led by United Fruit,

had become paramount in Central America . . . In Guatemala they . . . controlled all but a few miles of the railroads, one-fifteenth of the total land area, the leading bank, a number of major industries, and the great utility company (American and Foreign Power owned by General Electric). In Honduras, United Fruit and its subsidiaries controlled the rail system, port facilities, and nearly all the banana and rubber-producing lands. North Americans owned the prosperous silver mine. In Nicaragua, United Fruit and Atlantic Fruit claimed 300,000 acres. North Americans owned and/or managed the leading mines, the railroads, the lumber industry, and banks . . . In

Costa Rica . . . the dominant company in the nation was unquestionably United Fruit.[51]

By 1950, United owned 565,000 acres in Guatemala and was the largest landowner in the country. It was also among the largest in Honduras and Costa Rica.[52] "To Hondurans living on the coast, Tegucigalpa [the country's capital] might have been another world. English was the language of authority. Company lawyers became powerbrokers in Honduran affairs, and the banana companies decided the outcome of Honduran political battles."[53] Most of the country's wealth was siphoned off to New Orleans, New York, and Boston. National politics was essentially subordinated to the machinations of the companies.[54]

Chilean poet Pablo Neruda captured the relationship in his celebrated poem "The United Fruit Company." Jehovah, he wrote, "parceled out the earth to Coca Cola, Inc., Anaconda, Ford Motors, and other entities: The Fruit Company, Inc. reserved for itself the most succulent, the central coast of my own land, the delicate waist of America. It rechristened its territories as the 'Banana Republics.'" There in the "delicate waist" (i.e., Central America), the company unleashed "the dictatorship of the flies, [Rafael] Trujillo flies, Tacho [Anastasio Somoza] flies, [Tiburcio] Carías [Andino] flies, Martínez flies, Ubico flies." The names refer to the long-lived, US-imposed or supported dictators of the Dominican Republic, Nicaragua, Honduras, El Salvador, and Guatemala during the 1920s and '30s. Exemplifying the workings of dollar diplomacy, "Among the blood-thirsty flies the Fruit Company lands its ships, taking off the coffee and the fruit."[55]

In addition to Neruda's "The United Fruit Company," Central American authors ranging from labor activists on the plantations to noted intellectuals denounced the company in literary works. Costa Rican author Carmen Lyra published *Bananos y hombres* in 1931. Her book was followed by Costa Rican labor organizer Carlos Luis Fallas's *Mamita Yunai* (1941), which decried the conditions on the Costa Rican plantations, and Joaquín Gutiérrez's *Puerto Limón* (1950), which centered on a strike on a Costa Rican plantation. Union organizer Ramón Amaya Amador's *Prisión Verde* (1950) chronicled life in the Honduran plantations. Guatemalan Nobel Prize–winner Miguel Ángel Asturias published a trilogy set in the company's plantations in the 1950s. Beyond Central America, Colombian Nobel Prize–winner Gabriel García Márquez penned an unforgettable description of the army's massacre of striking banana workers in Santa Marta in 1928 in his classic *One Hundred Years of Solitude*. These authors, many of whom were leftists and some Communist Party members, used literature as a powerful tool for resurrecting suppressed histories and encouraging revolutionary alternatives.

TANGLED HISTORIES: COLONIALISM AND "PROGRESS"

As Central American elites sought to build their nations in the decades after independence, many saw the United States as their model. Like their US counterparts, Central American government and economic power holders believed that Indians were an obstacle to progress and modernity. But for the United States, Central America as a whole embodied the political and economic backwardness they attributed to Indians and sought to overcome by US-imposed "progress."

For the United States, Central America represented an extension of the American West: a land inhabited by savages that had to be subdued. "That the stewardship of the more civilized United States would benefit these savages whether or not they recognized it were points of such impressive consensus that, from the mid-nineteenth century onward, the border ceased to have much meaning when it came to determining the national interest and the right to pursue it," explained historian Matthew Frye Jacobson.[56]

Bolívar had warned of the threat of direct US intervention in Latin American affairs. Less visibly, but perhaps just as insidiously, the United States example infiltrated the minds of elite Latin Americans who were trying to build nation and state, as well as poor majorities who labored for elites in the export economies, for subsistence, or for access to the consumer goods that came to symbolize US prosperity for many.

Comparing their own realities unfavorably to the US example, some sought to mimic or adopt US ways. Central American elites often invited US economic or even military intervention in pursuit of their own goals. They taught their children English and sent them to study at US institutions. Some also resented US racism, blamed US imperialism for their countries' problems, and fought against it.

William Walker's 1855 invasion of Nicaragua spurred a violent and united rejection, and a long memory. It also "paradoxically strengthened elite Nicaraguans' infatuation with the U.S. road to modernity," according to historian Michel Gobat. With the gold rush traffic, "Nicaragua eagerly adopted a wide array of new U.S. goods and cultural practices as well as U.S. ideals of technological progress and enterprise." But Walker also brought "a highly exclusionary and bellicose strand of U.S. Manifest Destiny that claimed Latin Americans could not be Americanized through the 'civilizing' force of U.S. culture and trade but had to be violently subordinated if not physically exterminated."[57]

The much longer US occupation between 1912 and 1933 had similarly paradoxical effects. The occupation brought bankers and Protestant missionaries as well as Marines. Nicaraguan elites aspired to the kind of capitalist progress and national strength that the United States seemed to embody. But by taking over Nicaragua's finances and challenging the Catholic Church, occupiers unsettled the power of these same elites and turned many of them against the occupiers.

Central America's governing elites thus juggled adherence to Eurocentric and white supremacist ideas, idealization of US versions of "progress" that required eliminating or assimilating their own Indigenous populations, and nervous resentment against US arrogance that lumped all Central Americans into the "savage" category.

Tensions over the nature of their countries and their relations with the United States were deeply racialized. Would Euro-descended Central American elites identify *with* the Indigenous majorities of their countries in challenging US colonial attitudes and structures? Or would they ally with US power holders who identified Indians (and Central Americans in general) as backward threats that needed to be exterminated—either literally, or culturally, through assimilation into Euro-dominated culture?

Disappearing Indians

As in the United States, racism against Central America's Indigenous populations existed on multiple levels and was expressed in policies ranging from genocide, erasure, coerced assimilation, legal exclusion, forced labor, and myths about "disappearing Indians."[58] Because Central America's Indigenous population was much larger, the plantation and extractive economy there relied more heavily on Indigenous workers than did that of the United States, which exploited far more enslaved African workers. Postslavery forced-labor policies in Central America also fell more heavily on its Indigenous population than did those in the United States, where they targeted the Black population.

A series of overlapping and sequential myths accompanied the land and labor grabs in both places. Indians were backward, relics of the past, racially inferior. Their institutions were communistic and must be destroyed in the interests of progress. They used their land inefficiently and retarded the national economy. Assimilationists hoped that cultural genocide could remake Indians as productive citizens, while exterminationists believed that the only solution to the Indian threat was physical elimination. Others hoped that Indians would naturally disappear, swept away by "progress." These ideas frequently blended and overlapped.

The career of US Army brigadier general Richard H. Pratt illustrates the overlap. He oversaw some of the worst of the genocide in the US West. After the Indian military threat was crushed, he promoted forced assimilation (or cultural genocide) and the Indian boarding school system that he hoped would "kill the Indian, and save the man." Left on their own, he believed, Indians would remain in historical stasis. But if Indians were forcibly integrated into Anglo-American society, he believed, they could join the march of progress.[59]

Elites in nineteenth-century Guatemala agreed with Pratt that Indians "represented the past in a timeline—the timeline of historical progress." The country's 1894 census explained that "the Ladinos and Indians are two distinct classes; the former march ahead with hope and energy through the paths that have been laid out by progress; the latter, immovable, do not take any part in the political and intellectual life, adhering tenaciously to their old habits and customs. The Indians do not cooperate actively in the progress of civilization."[60] In Nicaragua, a Managua newspaper opined in 1919 that "Indians retard national progress . . . [they] live hermetically . . . they conserve their racial tradition . . . and the stamp of primitive sovereignty. But at the center everything stagnates and petrifies."[61]

The US State Department echoed these sentiments with respect to Guatemala in 1955, stating that "the illiterate majority has continued to live separated from the main currents of modern life, entrenched in ancient customs of the Mayan era." One briefing claimed that Indians "have little ambition and less opportunity to rise above a subsistence level . . . they throw away what little they can on liquor and fireworks and often prevent their children from attending school lest they forsake the ways of their forefathers."[62] Such attitudes justified the whole range of genocidal policies, including but not limited to dispossession and forced labor.

Comments by a German immigrant showed the extent to which Guatemala's domestic social hierarchy was embedded in a global structure. "The inhabitants of Guatemala are Indians, the native people, who belong to different tribes and speak different languages," he wrote in 1892.

> They are small, dumpy figures who occupy the lowest rung on the plantation, the so-called *mozo*, or worker, and eke out an existence on one mark a day. The second kind are the *mestizos*, mixed breed people who are tradesmen or servants and tend to the cattle and horses. The descendants of the Spaniards are the owners of the plantations, and most of the trading houses are owned by Germans. An enormous disadvantage for this country is that the Indians won't work more than just enough to fill their basic needs, and these are very few. The only way to make [an Indian] work is to advance him money, then he can be forced to work. Very often they run off, but they are caught and punished very severely.[63]

Coffee planters' need for land and for labor coincided nicely, because when Indian communities lost their land, they could no longer grow the food they needed and were forced to work for wages. In the coffee-producing middle altitudes, what Jeffrey Gould described in Nicaragua could apply to all of Central America: "[B]etween 1880 and 1950, the Indians suffered dramatic losses of land, language, and identity. Those losses were codified in census returns that reported the virtual disappearance of the Indians into the ladino populations." With the destruction of community institutions, "it took but a short leap of faith to declare the Indians dead on the arrival of the twentieth century." In El Salvador and Honduras, as well, "Indians were gradually eliminated as a social category, assimilated to the numerically dominant mestizos, even as white Creoles continued to hold power." The states were built on myths of mestizaje and assimilation.[64]

Guatemala was slightly different because its highlands were too cold for coffee. There, planters could also benefit from allowing peasant subsistence agriculture to provide cheap food for plantation workers, and a pool of potential workers to be recruited or forced onto the plantations during the harvest or for temporary projects like road building. Thus, in Guatemala's highlands, Mayan languages and traditional homemade dress, especially women's *corte* [woven skirt] and *huipil* [embroidered blouse], continued to be strong ethnic identifiers. Along with myths of mestizaje and assimilation, Guatemala's coffee economy and state rested on the myth of racial difference.[65]

Latin American nationalists struggled to define themselves and their countries in opposition to US imperialism in the 1920s and '30s, promoting ideas of *hispanismo*, *négritude*, transculturation, mestizaje, and the "cosmic race." In Guatemala, intellectuals of the "Generation of 1920" celebrated archaeological discoveries related to ancient Mayan civilization and called for the study of ancient and contemporary Mayan cultures. In Nicaragua, Sandino promoted a radical version of mestizaje with his definition of the "Indohispanic race." Yet from his redoubt in the heavily Indigenous mountains of the Segovias in northern Nicaragua, Sandino still saw Indians as backward people to be uplifted through assimilation so that they could contribute to the national, anti-imperialist fusion rather than as peoples to be recognized with rights of their own.[66]

Indians also articulated their own anticolonial ideologies, as in El Salvador in 1932. As the twentieth century unfolded, Indians and communists (and other leftist movements) engaged in complex and sometimes fraught alliances. Communism might not seem like a foreign or an academic ideology: dispossession and capitalist exploitation made up the fabric of communities' own experience. For Central American elites and their US sponsors, anti-communism and anti-Indian racism often melded.

BANANA REPUBLICS AND THE "REIGN OF THE FLIES"

Neruda's "reign of the flies" that dominated Central America in the 1930s held firm until World War II, and the Cold War opened some new avenues for protest. The violence and repression of Central America's incorporation into the world's modern industrial economy left unhealed wounds, whose festering contributed to new revolutionary uprisings in the 1960s and '70s. For Gould, "the suppression of indigenous communal identity throughout the twentieth century has played a major role in the creation of a culture of repression whose long-term effects became visible to the world in the region's violent conflicts of the 1970s and 1980s."[67] In a related way, the settler colonial nature of the United States and its violent and ongoing cultural/ideological suppression of Indigenous peoples inside its territories contributed to the culture of repression and erasure that sustained the US militarization of Central America and the US southern border over the past fifty years.

CHAPTER 3

THE COLD WAR, TEN YEARS OF SPRING, AND THE CUBAN REVOLUTION

This chapter shifts the lens to the United States and its policies toward Central America in the post-WWII period. It zooms in on the first major Cold War intervention, in Guatemala in 1954, and then looks more generally at the evolution of US policy as the United States attempted to impose its postwar developmentalist vision and Cold War counterinsurgency on the brewing revolutionary struggles in the region through the 1980s. US policy was made in the halls of Congress, the White House, and the Pentagon, but also through US investors and corporations, private and public financial institutions, and the Catholic Church. This chapter focuses on US policy toward Central American countries in the second half of the twentieth century. Part II of the book, which follows this chapter, looks more in depth at events inside each of four Central American countries (Guatemala, Nicaragua, El Salvador, and Honduras) during this same period.

THE GOOD NEIGHBOR

Franklin D. Roosevelt proposed a major overhaul in US relations with Latin America when he initiated the Good Neighbor Policy in 1933, renouncing the armed intervention that had dominated US policy during previous decades. Given the long US occupations in Nicaragua, Haiti, and the Dominican Republic, and the militarized police forces and dictatorships trained and established there, the sudden profession of friendly relations was seen by cynics as a way to legitimize the repressive results of these earlier interventions. Roosevelt has been quoted as lauding Nicaraguan dictator Anastasio Somoza, saying, "[H]e may be a son of a bitch, but he's our son of a bitch."[1] Whether accurate or apocryphal, the story took hold because it captures something fundamental about the Good Neighbor era.

The Good Neighbor Policy signaled close US relations with Neruda's "reign of the flies" in the 1930s in Central America. For US corporations in Guatemala, historian Paul Dosal argues that dictatorship was a boon. Too much democracy had allowed workers, peasants, and the government to challenge their dominance: "United Fruit discovered that it was much more profitable to do business with a dictator than with a democratic president."[2]

The Good Neighbor era aligned with the New Deal at home. The nominal recognition of Central Americans' right to govern themselves mirrored the 1934 Indian Reorganization Act that encouraged tribal self-governance for Native Americans. As US banks collapsed during the Depression, the government stepped in both at home and abroad, where it took over their funding of Central American development projects. Roosevelt created the Export-Import Bank in 1934 to provide credit to US exporters and loans to Central American governments. Trade pacts supported US recovery by facilitating the sale of US goods and especially agricultural products to the region. Finally, the United States tightened its military relations with Central American governments. Roosevelt's commitment to supply arms, training, and advisers benefited US industrial recovery as well as Central American dictators.[3]

WORLD WAR II AND THE COLD WAR

During World War II, the United States and the Soviet Union were allies in the fight against fascism and German and Japanese expansion. The USSR bore the brunt of Nazi aggression, with over 25 million deaths and massive physical destruction. Much of Europe, China, and Japan also lay in ruins. The United States, with four hundred thousand deaths and no material damage on its mainland, emerged the world's undisputed superpower, and it intended to keep things that way.

The United States oversaw the reconstruction of Europe and Japan and the emergence of a new array of international institutions, including the United Nations, the World Bank, and the International Monetary Fund (IMF), the latter two aimed at fostering market-based economies and capitalist institutions worldwide. The United States was to be a showcase for social peace and prosperity based on economic growth. Students are often taught that the Cold War was a struggle between two superpowers, the United States and the USSR. But those two countries never fought each other. Instead, the bloody battles of the Cold War took place in the Third World.

In Southeast Asia, Africa, and Latin America, the United States came to see nationalist movements that sought their own, independent forms of economic development as existential threats. Cold War counterrevolution targeted not only communism but virtually any movement for social change. "By the end of the Cold War," writes Greg Grandin, "Latin American security forces trained, funded, equipped, and incited by Washington had executed a reign of bloody terror—hundreds of thousands killed, an equal number tortured, millions driven into exile—from which the region has yet to recover."[4]

ANTI-COMMUNISM AND US ECONOMIC INTERESTS

The first major Cold War US intervention in Latin America, which ended the Good Neighbor Policy and began a renewed era of direct US interventionism, took place in Guatemala in 1954. Three intertwined factors motivated the US decision to overthrow Guatemala's independent, reformist government: Cold War anti-communism, lobbying by the United Fruit Company, and US policy makers' belief that Guatemala's reforms threatened the larger US economic plan for Latin America. The United Fruit Company enjoyed an almost ludicrous level of influence in the US government. Eisenhower's secretary of state John Foster Dulles and his brother, CIA director Allan Dulles, both had close ties to the company, which sponsored a huge public relations campaign in Congress and the media to prove that Guatemala's democratically elected government was controlled by communists. But the consistency of the Guatemala intervention and its aftermath with the long sweep of US policy in Latin America suggests that its causes transcended those individual relationships. The United States opposed and feared communism in Latin America because social reforms threatened US companies, hegemony, and economic interests there.

In some ways, it was ironic that the United States framed its Cold War policies in terms of anti-communism. Latin America's Communist Parties were small and jostled with many other players on the left. While they may have been officially incorporated into the Comintern, they were made up of local activists and responded to local conditions, generally with little interaction with Moscow. They did follow the official Soviet postwar line, though, in their commitment to working within democratic institutions, insofar as they existed, and in coalition with noncommunist opposition groups, where they did not. While other leftist groups took up the cause of armed revolution, Latin America's Communist Parties held to their commitment of working within the system. The supposed Soviet threat that dominated public and official discussion in the United States bore little relation to Latin America's realities.

GUATEMALA, 1944–1954

Guatemala's General Jorge Ubico was a classic "Good Neighbor" partner. He won an uncontested election in 1931 and ruled as a military dictator until 1944. He subjected Indians to forced labor with a national Vagrancy Law and compulsory military service. While savagely suppressing Guatemala's Communist Party and any sign of rural organizing or protest, Ubico maintained friendly relations with US corporations and government, providing tax exemption for the United Fruit Company and inviting the United States to establish its first military base in the country and send advisers to direct Guatemala's military academy.[5]

Three American companies dominated US investment in Guatemala. The United Fruit Company operated banana plantations on Guatemala's Atlantic and Pacific coasts and was the country's largest landowner. International Railways of Central America, owned partly by United Fruit, controlled the country's rail system, and American and Foreign Power operated the country's electrical grid.

By the early 1950s, about 70 percent of Guatemala's exports went to the United States, which in turn provided 64 percent of Guatemala's imports. It was an unequal relationship because the United States loomed so large in Guatemala's trade panorama, while Guatemala played only a tiny role in the much larger US trade system. Furthermore, Guatemala exported primary goods (coffee and bananas, but also sugar and cotton, and strategic resources like abaca, lead, zinc, and chrome) and imported higher-value manufactures.[6]

In 1944, a group of young, reformist army officers backed by widespread popular protest overthrew Ubico and then the military junta he left in his wake and began to establish democratic institutions. A teacher, Juan José Arévalo, won the country's first-ever truly free election in December of that year. Arévalo abolished the Vagrancy Law and passed a moderately progressive labor code, guaranteeing minimum wages and basic health and safety conditions. He released political prisoners. The labor movement, including communist-led unions, flourished.

Another reformist, Jacobo Arbenz, won the 1950 election with over 60 percent of the vote. Arbenz was a military officer who had participated in the 1944 uprising, served as minister of defense under Arévalo, and was committed to deepening the country's democratic reforms and modernizing the economy. The centerpiece of his goals was a major land reform as part of "a New Deal-style economic program" to grant rights to workers and peasants and modernize the repressive plantation system.[7] For the United Fruit Company, the US government, and the Guatemalan landed elite, the land reform, and the role of Communist Party members in the government, constituted an unacceptable threat. While the Guatemalan oligarchy opposed Arbenz, it was the CIA that orchestrated the bloody overthrow of the president, his government's democratic reforms, and democracy itself.

Land Reform

Arbenz's Agrarian Reform Law, Decree 900, like the Liberal reforms of the previous century, sought to spur rural production and development. But its vision for doing so was fundamentally different: it was to take lands *out* of the hands of large plantations and put them in the hands of land-hungry peasants, to draw them into capitalist production not through compelling them to labor for others but through granting them access to their own land. The reform outlawed all forms of forced labor and redistributed 1.4 million acres of land to some five hundred thousand Guatemalan peasants, in plots averaging ten acres.[8]

The reform targeted large properties and uncultivated lands. It thus aimed particularly at the United Fruit Company, the country's largest landholder and one that kept much of its land in reserve. The reform expropriated over half of the United Fruit Company's vast holdings, offering payment based on the value of the land declared by the company in its tax returns. But the company now claimed that was a drastic undervaluation, insisting that the lands were worth ten times as much.[9]

The law also attempted to overturn rural power structures. The initiative for land expropriation would come from below. Peasants and rural workers were encouraged to organize unions to present claims to the land. The explosion of rural organizing became part of what Arbenz called "an earthquake in the consciousness" of Guatemalans, making the agrarian reform "the most precious fruit of the revolution." The campesino league became the largest organization in the country, and rural unions replaced the military as the key institution mediating between Indigenous communities and the state. This threat to the military's local power in rural areas unsettled its relationship with the Arbenz government.[10]

The law brought to the surface conflicts that had been simmering for years. Land scarcity had afflicted the Guatemalan countryside since the Indigenous population began to recover demographically in the late colonial era. Population growth continued in the nineteenth century just as coffee plantations took over more communities' land. This meant that struggles between communities and landowners, and also among and within communities, all sharpened.[11]

The agrarian reform became embroiled in these conflicts. When the law divided plantation lands, it gave priority to workers on the plantation. But many of the workers were recent migrants, and the plantation lands were also claimed by local Indigenous communities. Municipal lands were often the object of long-standing disputes between or within communities, or between Indians and Ladinos. "In many cases the decisions of the agrarian department marked only one more turning point in a long struggle between various municipios or between parts of municipios over land."[12]

The United States

Arbenz's policies challenged three important US companies' interests in multiple ways. They all, and especially the United Fruit Company, exerted their full lobbying and propaganda power to press for a US intervention to topple Guatemala's elected government.

But the US power structure looked beyond the individual interests of particular companies. For State Department officials, anti-communism, particular corporate interests, and larger economic and geostrategic interests melded together. One warned, in late 1953, that Guatemala's democracy could threaten US interests in El Salvador and Honduras as well: "[I]ts agrarian reform is a powerful propaganda weapon; [and] its broad social program of aiding the workers and peasants in a victorious struggle against the upper classes and large foreign enterprises has a strong appeal to the populations of Central American neighbors where similar conditions prevail." Another worried that a successful land reform in Guatemala might have the effect of "fomenting destructive unrest among the rural peoples of the other American republics." A post-coup intelligence report worried that "the example of Guatemala was in itself infectious" because "Guatemala propaganda against 'feudalism' and 'colonialism' appealed to the prejudices of a wide audience" elsewhere in the America.[13]

Until mid-1952, the United States contented itself with diplomatic pressure and cutting off economic and military aid to Guatemala. With the passage of the Agrarian Reform Act and the prominence of several Guatemalan communist leaders in its implementation, the US anti-Arbenz campaign accelerated. Dwight D. Eisenhower, elected in November 1952, vowed to replace President Harry Truman's "containment" policy against communism with one of "rollback," and tasked the CIA with orchestrating Arbenz's overthrow. In the summer of 1953, the CIA's Operation PBSUCCESS was launched "with little internal debate and a heartening unanimity among the few policymakers involved."[14]

Eisenhower appointed the fervent anti-communist John Peurifoy as his new ambassador to Guatemala. Peurifoy and the CIA launched an anti-communist propaganda campaign and began to recruit allies in Guatemala's military. The US press and Congress eagerly joined the hysterical chorus, as did Guatemala's archbishop. The CIA began to train an exile force in Honduras and Nicaragua.

In the midst of the agitation around Guatemala, in May 1954 a huge strike broke out on Honduras's north coast banana plantations. *Business Week* reported that until then Honduras had been "an employers' paradise" with no unions and little labor legislation. Both Honduras and the United States blamed Guatemalan communists.[15]

Tensions rose as US planes dropped antigovernment leaflets on Guatemala City and Arbenz arrested suspected coup plotters. The Guatemalan military, already uneasy about Arbenz's undermining of its authority in the countryside, wavered. On June 17, a ragtag rebel force, trained and armed by the CIA and led by Lt. Colonel Castillo Armas, entered the country from Honduras. The rebels posed little military threat, but "fear defeated [the army]," one officer explained. "They were terrorized by the idea that the United States was looming behind Castillo Armas."[16] With the army unwilling to defend the government, Arbenz bent to Peurifoy's incessant demands and resigned.

Guatemala After the Coup

The wave of repression that followed the coup was framed in anti-communist terms, as supporters of the Arbenz government and political activists throughout the country were rounded up, killed, jailed, tortured, or disappeared. The Catholic Church, led by the anti-communist arch-bishop Mariano Rossell y Arellano, called on Catholics to "rise up as one man against the enemy of God and the Nation."[17] Thousands of Guatemalans across the country were imprisoned; many more took refuge in foreign embassies or fled the country.

In one coffee plantation town, a resident recalled: "Three or four days after the fall, soldiers came to La Igualdad to arrest people. They had a long list of people who were communists—the mayor, the municipal officers, the union leaders. They took them to the San Marcos jail. They were going to shoot them, but a counter-order came to stop the executions. That was the end of the unions in the plantation. Afterwards, no one dared try to unionize again."[18]

El Salvador's Counterpoint

In El Salvador too, a new generation of modernizing military officers, some of them trained in the United States, challenged the oligarchy's hold on the country in the 1950s. A new constitution implemented social reforms including labor rights, a minimum wage, and social security, although rural workers were excluded. International loans funded the Pacific coastal highway, infrastructure, and industrial development. But El Salvador's modernizers, unlike Guatemala's, stayed firmly in the US anti-communist camp. El Salvador also invited the US union federation, the AFL-CIO, to develop anti-communist unions through its regional organization, the American Institute for Free Labor Development (AIFLD). "Alongside the modernizing oligarchy and the technocratic colonels, the U.S. government was preparing to make El Salvador its showcase," concluded one study.[19]

The Alliance for Progress Decade

The successful 1959 Cuban Revolution accelerated US Cold War concern with Central America. On the campaign trail, Senator John F. Kennedy explained that the United States had made three mistakes in Cuba: "First, we refused to help Cuba meet its desperate need for economic progress . . . Secondly, in a manner certain to antagonize the Cuban people, we used the influence of our Government to advance the interests of and increase the profits of the private American companies, which dominated the island's economy . . . The third, and perhaps most disastrous of our failures, was the decision to give stature and support to one of the most bloody and repressive dictatorships in the long history of Latin American repression." Now, "the same poverty and discontent and distrust of America which Castro rode to power are smoldering in almost every Latin nation."[20] As president, Kennedy proposed an Alliance for Progress to reorient US policy.

The Alliance would promote capitalist economic development while gently pressing Central America's oligarchies for reforms to address the region's devastating poverty and inequality. "Those who make peaceful revolution impossible," Kennedy proclaimed, "will make violent revolution inevitable."[21] He did not, however, renounce the use of subversion and military force to supplement the reforms and suppress any hints of "violent revolution." Reform and repression were two sides of a single coin of counterinsurgency.

The Alliance and the new US Agency for International Development (USAID) brought twenty billion dollars to the cause, as well as a new role for the US military in economic development programs aimed at winning hearts and minds. Kennedy saw El Salvador's modernizing military as a model, "the most effective in containing communist penetration in Latin America." By the mid-1960s, "the soft side of the Alliance was everywhere" in the country, as "schools and clinics bore the message of American largesse; labor unions and rural workers' organizations were molded in the image of the AFL-CIO; and a dramatic increase in U.S. investment . . . lent new steam to the stalled industrialization scheme."[22]

But economic development projects paled before the US emphasis on security. Over the course of the 1960s, "military funds inundated small economies, transformed government budgets, and created a large military group trained by U.S. officers in such special schools as the Southern Command's School of the Americas in the Panama Canal Zone." Tens of thousands of Latin American soldiers went through US military centers and schools every year. Police forces "learned to use gas guns, helicopters, and other anti-riot equipment. For this newly powerful elite, it proved to be only a short step to controlling dissent through sophisticated methods of torture." When Lyndon Johnson took over the presidency in 1963, funding for social welfare projects dropped precipitously, leaving the emphasis of the alliance on economic growth and military strength.[23]

Paths to Economic Growth: Industrialization and Economic Integration

The Alliance promoted economic growth through development of agriculture and industry. But how could Central American countries, where the rural poor majority struggled to fill their basic needs and had little disposable income to purchase manufactured goods, promote industrialization? As neither the United States nor the oligarchies had little interest in redistributive policies that could create stronger domestic markets, regional integration offered an alternative. During the 1960s a new Central American Common Market (CACM) reduced trade barriers and created larger markets for nascent industries like textile and shoe production. For US investors, the CACM offered an incentive for by granting investors in one country tariff-free access to markets throughout the isthmus. Despite Honduras's withdrawal in 1971 and the CACM's virtual collapse with the oil crisis of 1973, it continued to exist until the early 1980s.

Industrialization, along with the spread of export agriculture in the countryside, brought hundreds of thousands of peasants to the cities. The new industries couldn't employ anywhere near their numbers, nor could the urban infrastructure or government institutions support them. Government programs incentivized the importation of advanced machinery and technology, which meant that the new industries created fewer jobs than some had hoped. Rural-to-urban migrants swelled new shantytowns, where they built informal shelters and scrabbled for work in informal economies. In Guatemala, the portion of the population living in urban areas grew from 25 percent in 1950 to 40 percent in 1980.[24]

Modernization and urbanization as the solution to social problems had a domestic counterpart in US postwar policy toward its own Indigenous population. In the 1950s tribal sovereignty was dismantled and tribes "terminated." Indians were relocated from reservations to urban areas with the goal of modernizing and assimilating them.[25]

Paths to Economic Growth: Export Agriculture and the Crisis

A second proposal for economic growth was increasing and diversifying agricultural exports. USAID brought pesticides and fertilizers to Central America and contributed to a major expansion of Central America's export economies. It also brought new markets for US petroleum and chemical industries, and new inputs for the growing US fast-food industry. And the spread of industrial agriculture with its heavy machinery and chemical use left landscapes deforested and poisoned.

Green revolution technologies—new seeds, pesticides, fertilizers, and farm machinery—poured into Central America, funded by governments and agencies eager to create markets for US products and to illustrate the benefits of capitalist economic development. International agencies funded the construction of the Pacific coastal highway, which opened that region to export production. These same agencies promoted central banks and agricultural development banks to expand access to credit and loans. These went overwhelmingly to large landowners rather than small peasants, and "played a leading role in facilitating the concentration of land in the postwar era."[26]

First came the cotton boom. "From several thousand acres to more than a million, cotton came to claim the best farmland along the Pacific strip, bringing with it the most advanced applications of science and technology."[27] For peasant farmers, cotton meant eviction and proletarianization under some of the worst working conditions possible—not only forced recruitment through debt and low wages but child labor, brutal heat, pesticide exposure, and inadequate shelter.

"Cotton workers are typically recruited from the most destitute of the peasant households, from the families with the least land and livestock, and from the poorest and most remote of the mountaintop villages," one economist found. "The living conditions they face on the coast are worse than those on coffee and sugar plantations: they have more meager rations, no pay for legal holidays or Sundays, inferior lodgings, and poorer sanitation facilities. The cotton workers face a higher risk of catching malaria and suffering from dysentery, and they often suffer from symptoms of cotton [pesticide] poisoning."[28] Hundreds of thousands of peasants from Guatemala's western highlands made this seasonal trek; Guatemala led the world in percentage of its population engaged in migratory labor by the 1970s.[29]

Rigoberta Menchu described her first experience descending to the coast at age ten: "It was very, very hot. After my first day picking cotton, I woke up at midnight and lit a candle. I saw the faces of my brothers and sisters covered with mosquitos. I touched my own face, and I was covered too. They were everywhere; in people's mouths and everywhere. Just looking at these insects and thinking about being bitten set me scratching. That was our world."[30]

But worse was yet to come. A new wave of US funding built the infrastructure for a rapid expansion of Central America's cattle industry. "The beef boom," one analyst wrote, "was greedier for land than any of the export booms that preceded it . . . Each of the previous export booms had profound effects on peasant life, but each was restrained by natural boundaries. The beef-export boom was different. Cattle could be raised wherever grass would grow."[31] And unlike cotton, the cattle industry provided few jobs.

Governments and international agencies tried to respond to growing peasant dispossession and landlessness by promoting colonization of new areas. Peasants who could no longer survive on shrinking plots went, or were sent, to cut down forests and prepare them for planting. Peasant colonization only compounded the already-devastating environmental effects of export agriculture: the region lost two-thirds of its primary forest in the development decades.[32] Once peasants had done the backbreaking work of clearing the land, landlords—or in some cases, the military—often moved in to claim it.

The land crisis was exacerbated by population growth. Central America's population grew from 11 million in 1950 to 27 million in 1990. The reasons were clear: medical and sanitary measures had cut the death rate by half, while an extremely high birth rate had not budged.[33] By 2000, the isthmus's population grew to 36 million, in 2010, 43 million, and in 2019, 50 million.[34]

As peasant landholdings shrank, so did per capita food production. Malnutrition afflicted over half of the population in every Central American country except Costa Rica during the cotton and beef export booms of the 1960s and '70s.[35]

Agricultural exports, while successfully enriching certain sectors (including multinationals and Central American elites), did not bring in enough revenue to repay the loans that governments received. After 1960, debt increased more quickly than export earnings, and by the early 1980s, all five Central American countries held debts significantly larger than their annual earnings.[36]

THE CATHOLIC CHURCH AND THE MARYKNOLLS

Diplomatic historians sometimes overlook another important piece of the Cold War puzzle: the Catholic Church. Since the Liberal reforms of the late nineteenth century, the official church had lost much of its political and cultural power in Central America. Instead, a popular religion called *costumbre*, which infused Catholic symbols with Indigenous meaning and connected spiritual with political power at the local level through cofradías, comprised the heart of religious life, especially in Indigenous communities.

In the 1940s, the US Catholic Maryknoll order, encouraged by Roosevelt's approach to developmentalism in Latin America, sent its first emissaries to the Indigenous highlands of Huehuetenango, Guatemala. Guatemala's highlands soon became "the epicenter of an institutional expansion reminiscent of the early colonial period," and the Maryknolls expanded from there throughout Central America.[37]

Maryknoll work in Guatemala coincided uneasily with the Arévalo-Arbenz government's goals. Both believed in modernization, and sought to displace traditional Indigenous authority and autonomy and integrate Guatemala's Indigenous communities into national life.[38] Local election of mayors, support for the formation of labor unions and cooperatives, literacy projects, rural bilingual education, and ending vagrancy laws were just a few ways that the revolutionary constitution and government extended their reach into Indigenous villages in tandem with the missionaries.

The Maryknolls agreed that Indigenous communities needed modernizing, but they diverged from the government in their adherence to anti-communist US ideology and foreign policy. Guatemala's conservative church authorities initially supported the Maryknoll project as a counter to both traditional Mayan costumbre and what the church saw as the growing communist threat in the Arbenz years.

US Maryknoll and other foreign priests formed chapters of the lay organization Catholic Action to collaborate in extending their mission. Catholic Action challenged costumbre and cofradía hierarchies,

developed new leadership, and promoted community improvement projects. By 1958, the Maryknolls estimated that they had trained a thousand
lay catechists; by 1963, they claimed there were seventeen thousand.[39]

The Maryknolls' activities had some unexpected effects. The missionaries themselves shifted and expanded their goals as they learned more
about the lives and realities of the villages they were working in. As part
of their challenge to traditional authority, many became involved in development initiatives to address villagers' material as well as spiritual
needs. Missionaries became more sympathetic to religious syncretism,
and more critical of the social and economic order that maintained Indigenous poverty and exclusion. Then Arbenz was overthrown, and the
church hierarchy, the new military government, and the United States
became more suspicious of these trends in the church.

By the mid-1960s, Latin America's Catholic bishops developed a
radical new Liberation Theology. The church, they argued, should have a
"preferential option for the poor." Religious commitment demanded that
practitioners work to bring about social justice on earth. New Christian
Base Communities reinforced the idea that the church was a community
of equals, and lay Delegates of the Word could help use Bible study to
raise peasants' consciousness about the causes of their poverty. The Maryknolls, along with Spanish Jesuits and others, brought this new outlook
to every corner of Central America. The church became revolutionary.

In Nicaragua, too, the church responded to the twin threats of Protestantism and communism by establishing Catholic Action to promote
church lay participation and social doctrine in the 1940s.[40] There too, the
newly activist church came into conflict with traditional religious practice, especially in Indigenous communities where traditional religious
and political authority had retained a fair degree of local control.[41]

Campesinos describe their participation in Base Communities and
popular education projects in similar terms throughout the region. "I was
seeing everything in a different way . . . I felt an awakening to a different world," explained one catechist from Morazán, El Salvador, after attending a church-sponsored *universidad campesina.* "Through such
conversations," historian Molly Todd explains, participants "noted striking similarities across [El Salvador's] regions and concluded that campesinos throughout the country faced the same oppression and misery,
the same adversaries and challenges. Such a realization formed the basis
of a new sort of class consciousness."[42]

Consciousness-raising, a Nicaraguan Sandinista educator explained, was essential to political and social revolution. "As long as people are ashamed and blame themselves for their poverty, things cannot change. All of our work is to change that view of themselves . . . We try to take people through three steps. First, they must see the real injustices that keep them poor . . . Second they must understand *how* this came to be— that it wasn't always this way and doesn't have to always be. Third, we show that their situation is national—that they are not alone. Theirs are the problems of the majority of our people." "Before we were blind, sleeping," recounted one community leader. "It's as if they had a blindness," another confirmed, "And then the scales fell from their eyes."[43]

CRISES OF THE 1970S

Central America's problematic postwar economic development model revealed more weaknesses in the 1970s. The global oil crisis sharply raised prices for petroleum-based imports that Central America now depended on and reduced demand for the region's agricultural exports as its trading partners fell into recession. The oil crises were followed by raised interest rates, which made the debts the countries had been encouraged to incur for development projects virtually unpayable.

On top of these economic challenges came a series of natural disasters. In Managua, a 1972 earthquake virtually flattened the city, leaving over ten thousand dead, twenty thousand injured, and hundreds of thousands homeless. In 1974, Hurricane Fifi struck Honduras's northern coast, and another major earthquake shook Guatemala in 1976. These disasters, and the governments' utter incapacity to respond to them except through scandalous corruption that sucked international aid into the pockets of politicians and elites, spurred both disillusionment and mobilization.

The Nixon Era (1969–1974): Unsinkable Aircraft Bases

The new Nixon administration had little interest in the Alliance for Progress development programs of its predecessors. Nixon's outlook was shaped by the US experience in Vietnam. The failure of the US war there, and the growing domestic opposition to the war and especially the draft, led Nixon to "Vietnamization": pulling back its ground troops while escalating the air war and arming the South Vietnamese. The "Nixon Doctrine" advocated arming and aiding proxies to carry out US foreign policy goals and avoiding direct intervention.

In Latin America, this meant support for military governments like those in Brazil and Central America, especially that of Anastasio Somoza Debayle (son of Somoza Garcia) in Nicaragua. It meant arming Chile's military to overthrow elected socialist president Salvador Allende in 1973. Arms streamed into Central America through sales and via loans and credits. Central America's already-impoverished governments fell more deeply into debt, while the region's militaries became more powerful.

The Ford Era (1974–1977)

Nixon was forced to resign in 1974, replaced by his vice president, Gerald Ford. Although Ford kept on many of Nixon's personnel, in particular Secretary of State Henry Kissinger, he was also forced to deal with the fallout of the Watergate scandal and widespread public disillusionment with US aggression in Vietnam.

Although Ford had little to say about Central America, military aid and training continued apace. US aid and advisers helped prop up Somoza in Nicaragua and the military-controlled governments in El Salvador and Guatemala.

The Carter Era (1977–1981): Human Rights?

President Jimmy Carter's name is inevitably associated with the phrase "human rights." Carter promised "a clear-cut preference for those societies which share with us an abiding respect for individual human rights."[44] To many Latin Americans, his election signaled a distinct shift in policy.

It wasn't just Carter. Congress and the US public were also feeling skeptical about allowing the State Department to operate without oversight. Concern increased as Vietnam, Watergate, and the Pentagon Papers were followed by a 1975 Senate investigation of illegal CIA involvement in assassination attempts against foreign leaders including Fidel Castro in Cuba. As news trickled into the United States about the official violence and repression in Central America, Congress attempted to exercise some restraint over the foreign policy of what seemed to be an out-of-control executive. A series of laws in the mid-1970s required the State Department to report on human rights conditions of countries around the world, and prohibited arms sales to countries that violated human rights.

The new requirements were less effective than they might have been. State Department human rights reports were often tainted by politics, exonerating right-wing allies while excoriating left-wing enemies. Arms prohibitions simply transferred US aid to economic purposes, freeing up other government funds to buy arms, and third parties stepped up to sell them. Israel, for example, became an important source of aid to Guatemala during the time when the United States was prohibited from selling arms there.[45]

Carter regarded Central America's growing revolutionary movements uneasily. After the triumph of the Nicaraguan revolution in July 1979, he made it clear that he would not allow another social revolution to occur in Central America and renewed the US commitment to the military government in El Salvador.

The Salvadoran military's human rights abuses were not random— they were inherent in the military and the elite's desperate bid to hang on to power in the face of a population demanding change. Despite mounting evidence of massacres, torture, and repression, it took the murder of four US churchwomen by Salvadoran National Guardsmen in December 1980 for the Carter administration to hesitate, demand an investigation and threaten to cut off aid. These deaths were followed in January by those of two US advisers and the top Salvadoran land reform official, gunned down in San Salvador's Sheraton Hotel. However, that same month, El Salvador's guerrilla movement began its "Final Offensive" against the Salvadoran government, and Carter shelved his concerns and restored all-out support for the government.

With respect to human rights violations in Guatemala, Carter's policy was more consistent. Direct military assistance was cut between 1978 and 1984, and arms sales also declined during this period. One reason the United States was willing to take a stronger human rights stand in Guatemala was that the revolutionary movements there never came close to actually taking power. In El Salvador, human rights concerns were subordinated to the goal of preventing a revolutionary victory. Still, despite the arms restrictions, the United States continued to send economic aid to Guatemala and train Guatemalan troops.

Regarding Nicaragua, Carter's policy vacillated. When he took office, Nicaragua's revolutionary struggle was intensifying, and the corrupt Somoza dictatorship and the National Guard were engaging in a full-scale onslaught of repression against the civilian population. Even conservative Nicaraguan archbishop Miguel Obando y Bravo finally condemned the Guardia and its atrocities. Carter pressed Somoza to open the political process and rein in Guardia violence, yet continued military aid. As the insurrection gained strength during 1978, repression spiraled, with the government bombing and massacring whole villages and poor neighborhoods. The Sandinista National Liberation Front (FSLN) set up a government in exile in Costa Rica and began to receive international recognition.

Finally, in early 1979, the United States stepped back from its support of Somoza, cutting the aid spigot. Yet it continued to support international funding for Somoza and, as in Guatemala, encouraged third countries like Israel and Argentina to step in to fill the gap.

At the end of May, FSLN troops in Costa Rica reentered Nicaragua for their final offensive. As the Somoza regime tottered, Carter made a last-ditch effort to prevent the FSLN victory that appeared imminent: he called on the Organization of American States (OAS) to send in a "peacekeeping force" to prevent the FSLN from taking power. The OAS, since its founding in 1948, had served as a platform for the United States to project a multilateral facade for its goals. But this time the OAS stood up to the United States and refused.

As in El Salvador, the death of an American jolted the US public and government. Tens of thousands of Central American peasants could be killed with little notice. But on June 20, 1979, the Guardia grabbed ABC reporter Bill Stewart from his car, forced him to kneel in the street, and shot him in the head as his camera captured everything. ABC's broadcast of the murder brought the Guardia's brutality into American living rooms.

Finally, on July 17, the United States persuaded Somoza to resign and shuttled him and his family to Florida. (Somoza soon left for Paraguay, where he was assassinated in 1980.) The FSLN government in exile in Costa Rica returned to a jubilant country and a series of US demands, including that it add US-approved "moderates" to its governing junta and preserve the National Guard. Nicaragua refused, and openly declared its independence from US policy. The Sandinistas proffered friendship to revolutionary Cuba, joined the Non-Aligned Movement, and opposed US intervention in El Salvador.

In mid-1980, the CIA began its effort to reorganize the Guardia for an eventual overthrow of the Sandinistas and, by the end of the year, was funding Nicaraguan opposition press, unions, and political parties. After Ronald Reagan's election in November, US aggression accelerated.

The Reagan Era (1981–1989): The Return of Anti-Communism

Ronald Reagan took office in 1981 with a radical anti-communist, interventionist, and what we would today call neoliberal economic agenda—then termed Reaganomics or "trickle-down economics." Like his predecessors, he preferred to fight the Cold War against small, weak countries. Central America became his staging ground. "Control of Central American policy was a payoff to militant conservatives," Walter LaFeber suggests. The administration "had to throw a bone to the right-wingers," in the words of a Senate staff member. "They can't have the Soviet Union or the Middle East or Western Europe. All are too important. So they've given them Central America."[46]

Some of Reagan's staff came from universities and right-wing think tanks, while others like Oliver North, Richard Secord, John Singlaub, and Richard Armitage belonged to "a generation of Vietnam vets politicized by their time in Southeast Asia." They stood out for their lack of knowledge of Central America. While Reagan pursued a more nuanced policy of detente elsewhere in the world, in Central America he let "his administration's most committed militarists set and execute policy."[47]

Jeane Kirkpatrick, Reagan's ambassador to the United Nations, came to Reagan's attention with an article she published in 1979 entitled "Dictatorships and Double Standards," criticizing the Carter administration's Central American policy. She argued that Carter had failed to comprehend that despite their human rights violations, "traditional autocrats" like Anastasio Somoza in Nicaragua were not really so bad. They were anti-communist and supported American interests.

"Traditional autocrats leave in place existing allocations of wealth, power, status, and other resources which in most traditional societies favor an affluent few and maintain masses in poverty," Kirkpatrick admitted. But the United States should not be put off by these facts. "Because the miseries of traditional life are familiar, they are bearable to ordinary people."[48] Any protests by these ordinary people were simply evidence that they were being manipulated by Soviet-backed communists bent on global domination. Central America, Kirkpatrick insisted, was "the most important place in the world for the United States."[49]

Of course Kirkpatrick ignored the fact that her so-called "traditional" autocrats were not traditional at all but rather US creations, imposed on unwilling populations to protect US interests. And Central America's revolutions unleashed massive popular support, suggesting that its populations were perhaps not so content with the "miseries" they endured. But to the Reagan administration, the revolutions were just Soviet plots.

Reagan justified his Central America policy as a way to overcome the US loss in Vietnam. "For too long, we have lived with the Vietnam Syndrome . . . Over and over they told us for nearly 10 years that we were the aggressors bent on imperialistic conquests . . . It is time we recognized that ours was, in truth, a noble cause," he proclaimed.[50]

Vietnam figured prominently in the imaginaries of Reagan's opponents, too. Antiwar activists argued that "El Salvador is Spanish for Vietnam" when they opposed sending US advisers there, suggesting that the United States was taking steps that would drag it into another unjust and immoral war.

Over its eight years in office, the Reagan administration fervently fought to prevent the revolutions from winning in El Salvador and Guatemala, and to overthrow the revolutionary government in Nicaragua. In the process, Honduras was turned into a virtual US base for training and arming the counterrevolutionary army the United States hoped would bring down the Sandinistas.

Low-Intensity Warfare and US Public Opinion

Reagan's preferred approach updated Nixon's Vietnamization, renaming it "low-intensity conflict" (LIC, or "low-intensity warfare," LIW). To prevent the kind of antiwar mobilization provoked by the draft and by American casualties in Vietnam, LIC would avoid sending US troops. Instead, wars would be fought by local allies and proxy armies, supported by military aid and programs to "win the hearts and minds" of the population, based on those developed in Vietnam. For Central Americans, there was nothing low intensity about it.

Outside of his far-right circles, Reagan's wars remained a hard sell despite their supposed low intensity. "I have not succeeded in explaining to the public why they should care about Central and South America," Reagan bemoaned in 1983. An interagency strategy paper the same year agreed: "The present U.S. policy faces substantial opposition, at home and abroad." So the wars were accompanied by a simultaneous campaign "to persuade the American public that the communists are out to get us."[51]

Some of Reagan's talking points were accurate, but not very meaningful. "El Salvador is nearer to Texas than Texas is to Massachusetts," he warned in 1983. "Nicaragua is just as close to Miami . . . and Tucson as those cities are to Washington."[52]

Others were simply absurd. "The Soviets' plan," he intoned, "is designed to crush self-determination of free people, to crush democracy in Costa Rica, Honduras, El Salvador, Guatemala, and Panama. It's a plan to turn Central America into a Soviet beachhead of aggression." "Hundreds of thousands of refugees fleeing Communist oppression" or perhaps "tens of millions . . . streaming in a human tidal wave" would flood into the United States. It would have been more accurate to replace "the Soviets" and "Communist" with "the United States" in these statements, given that it was the US aggression that crushed democracy and created floods of refugees in the region and that the Soviets had no presence there at all. But for Reagan, the US-sponsored Nicaraguan Contras (short for *contrarrevolucionarios*, counterrevolutionaries) were "freedom fighters" and "the moral equivalent of our founding fathers."[53]

Public opinion never came to support US intervention in Central America. Approval for US involvement in El Salvador never surpassed 35 percent.[54] In Nicaragua, Reagan increasingly resorted to covert war carried out behind the backs of Congress and public opinion.

Covert War in Nicaragua

US and international law prohibited unprovoked invasions of other countries and overthrows of sovereign governments. So Reagan's war against Nicaragua was illegal, and he tried to keep it secret. He used the CIA to covertly create and fund a proxy army, the Contras, to overthrow the Sandinistas. A simultaneous propaganda campaign was aimed at the US public and Congress. To justify US aid, Reagan claimed that Cuba and Nicaragua were sending arms to the rebels in El Salvador. Military aid, he insisted, was aimed solely at halting the arms flow, not overthrowing Nicaragua's government.

Paradoxically, while the Reagan administration sought vainly to uncover Cuban military influence in Nicaragua, the CIA relied on anti-Castro Cuban networks to run its illegal operations in support of the Contras. Cuban Americans, some of them veterans of the Bay of Pigs invasion, raised funds for the Contras, served as military advisers, organized weapons shipments, and ran a secret air resupply operation out of El Salvador.[55]

Battlegrounds in Honduras, Nicaragua, and the United States
In November 1982, *Newsweek* published an explosive investigation revealing that

> there are now almost 50 CIA personnel serving in Honduras . . .
> supplemented by dozens of operatives including a number of retired
> military and intelligence officers. . . . [These US operatives oversaw
> a fighting force] drawn from 2,000 Miskito Indians, an estimated
> 10,000 anti-Sandinistas in Nicaragua itself and an assorted group of
> former Nicaraguan National Guardsmen and supporters of deposed
> dictator Anastasio Somoza. They have set up 10 training camps divided between Honduran and Nicaraguan territory. Their hit-and-run
> forays against Nicaraguan bridges, construction sites and patrols are
> designed to harass the Sandinistas while CIA operatives cast around
> for a moderate new Nicaraguan leadership.[56]

Congressional sources "wondered pointedly whether the administration had used approval for plans to cut off the flow of Cuban arms to rebels in El Salvador for a more reckless plot to topple the Sandinistas." "While US officials maintain that the primary objective of the operation remains cutting off the supply routes, they also hope that a threatened Sandinista government will bring itself down by further repression of its internal opposition, thereby strengthening the determination of moderate forces to resist," *Newsweek* reported. Read that statement carefully. US officials "hope" that the Sandinistas will become more repressive. Their policies aimed at achieving that goal.[57]

US ambassador in Honduras John Negroponte facilitated—and covered up—the establishment of illegal US Contra training and military camps there. He also worked to hide the Honduran government's abysmal human rights record in order to maintain friendly relations and the flow of military aid.[58] The influx of aid bought the loyalty of the Honduran military and also helped to supply the Contra forces.

Congress and the Boland Amendments
Try as it might, Reagan's team could not find evidence of significant arms flows from the USSR or Cuba into Nicaragua, or from Nicaragua into El Salvador. As it became clear that Reagan's real goal was to overthrow

the Nicaraguan government, Congress stepped in. A series of budget amendments sponsored by House Representative Edward P. Boland, known as the Boland Amendments, tried to explicitly prevent the Reagan administration from using US funds for that purpose. But they all had loopholes.

The first, in December 1982, restricted only CIA or Department of Defense funds. And it authorized military aid as long as it was aimed at preventing arms from Nicaragua entering El Salvador, not at overthrowing the Nicaraguan government.[59]

In 1984, CIA operatives planted mines in Nicaragua's harbors, under instructions from the president but without informing Congress. It was a flagrant violation of both US and international law, and when the US media reported it in April, Congress and the international community were outraged. The United States vetoed a UN resolution condemning the mining. Nicaragua took the case to the International Court of Justice in The Hague, which ruled that US support for the Contras violated Nicaraguan sovereignty. The United States must immediately cease its war on Nicaragua and pay reparations for the damages it had caused. Reagan responded by denying the court's jurisdiction and ignoring its ruling.

In October 1984, journalists based in Honduras discovered a secret CIA Contra training manual. Entitled "Psychological Operations in Guerrilla Warfare," the manual offered instructions on torture and on how to "neutralize" (i.e., assassinate) Sandinista leaders. The manual recommended infiltrating Nicaraguan civil society organizations in order to "manipulate the groups' objectives" and encourage them to "become involved in a fury of justified violence."[60] The *Washington Post* wrote that "the CIA's murder manual" taught "Nicaraguan guerrillas how to kidnap, assassinate, blackmail and dupe civilians," in explicit violation of US law prohibiting such activities.[61]

Congress responded to the outrage over the mining of the harbors and the torture manual with a strengthened version of the Boland Amendment in late 1984 that banned all military aid to the Contras. Reagan retaliated with an executive order banning all trade with Nicaragua, because of the "unusual and extraordinary threat to the national security and foreign policy of the United States."[62] When Nicaraguan president Daniel Ortega made an official visit to the USSR, Reagan pressed his advantage, and the House approved his new "humanitarian" Contra aid package. A third Boland Amendment, in December 1985, reiterated the authorization of humanitarian and nonmilitary assistance. In 1986, Congress voted to allow even military aid.

The secret war was further unveiled in October 1986, when Nicaragua shot down a CIA military supply plane and captured its captain, Eugene Hasenfus. His public and highly reported confession unveiled a long-running US operation to supply arms to the Contras from US bases in Honduras and El Salvador, in explicit contravention of Congress's restrictions.

National Security Council (NSC) adviser Robert McFarlane and his assistant, Lieutenant Colonel Oliver North, immediately dismantled the El Salvador operation and destroyed incriminating documentation. Two weeks later, lulled by more lies, Congress approved further funding for the Contras. Then an explosive report in a Lebanese magazine, quickly confirmed by the Iranian government and then by Ronald Reagan himself, revealed that the United States had been secretly selling weapons to Iran and diverting the profits to buy arms for the Contras.

The Iran–Contra Affair

Almost immediately after the first Boland Amendment, Reagan had turned to the CIA and the NSC's North and MacFarlane to seek covert sources of funding. By May 1984, they had obtained a million-dollar donation from Saudi Arabia and established a secret bank account to funnel it to the Contras.[63]

Through the fall of 1985, North arranged the sale of US weapons to Iran through Israel, in exchange for the Iranians' promise to pressure Hezbollah in Lebanon to release US hostages. In the spring of 1986, the operation brought in North's private Contra finance and supply network. The pattern was set:

[Iranian arms broker Manucher] Ghorbanifar deposited funds, borrowed from Saudi businessman Adnan Khashoggi, into a Swiss bank account controlled by [retired Air Force Major General and North's collaborator in the illegal Contra supply operation Richard] Secord. Secord transferred the price fixed by DoD [Department of Defense] to a CIA account. The CIA purchased the TOW missiles from the U.S. Army. Secord then arranged for Southern Air Transport, a

Miami-based aircraft charter company, to ferry the missiles from the United States to Israel. An Israeli charter carried the weapons on the last leg to Iran.[64]

By charging the Iranians more than it paid to the Department of Defense, North's operation was able to divert significant amounts to the Contras.

While journalists, the Reagan-appointed Tower Commission, Congress, and the independent counsel who led the legal investigation slowly uncovered the story, the White House stonewalled. North shredded documents, and he and his associates lied to Congress. Reagan and many of his cabinet members claimed ignorance and memory lapses. Of fourteen administration officials eventually indicted, eleven were convicted. Some were granted immunity, and others pardoned by incoming president George H. W. Bush. A number were brought back to serve in the administrations of George W. Bush and, later, Donald Trump. Impunity prevailed, and Reagan's illegal, undeclared war on Nicaragua was whitewashed out of the history books.

El Salvador

Reagan's new secretary of state, Alexander Haig, soon clashed with Carter's ambassador to El Salvador, Robert White. Haig demanded that White make a public statement lauding the Salvadoran government's investigation into the murder of the four churchwomen. White had been close to the nuns—two of them had been eating dinner with him only hours before the four were kidnapped and murdered. "I will have no part of any cover-up," White wrote in a cable that was classified and only released years later. "All the evidence we have . . . is that the Salvadoran government has made no serious effort to investigate the killings of the murdered American churchwomen." Haig soon had White removed and forced out of the Foreign Service.[65]

From the beginning of Reagan's administration until the signing of the peace accords in 1992, the United States would pour six billion dollars into El Salvador. The tiny country's military grew from fifteen thousand to sixty thousand, and new counterinsurgency rapid deployment infantry battalions were created. The most infamous, the US-trained Atlacatl Battalion, would later be implicated in a torrent of human rights violations ranging from the massacre of close to a thousand civilians in the village of El Mozote at the end of 1981 to the slaughter of six Jesuit leaders at the Central American University along with their housekeeper and her daughter in 1989.[66]

Congressional action on El Salvador was minimal. Despite some loud protests from Democrats, one journalist wrote, "[I]t was clear that, come what may, there would not be the votes to cut off aid to El Salvador, for that, as everybody knew, would mean 'losing' the country to communists. At root, nearly everyone tacitly agreed . . . that the eventuality was too intolerable even to contemplate, and that in the end the Salvadoran government, by whatever means, *had* to win the war . . . And so, because of this underlying agreement, the entire debate, loud and angry as it appeared at first glance, was not a debate. It was an exercise for the cameras."[67]

Honduras

While Honduras attracted much less international attention, the country was profoundly transformed during the 1980s as it became the staging ground for the US war against Nicaragua. The US military flooded the small country with some seven thousand personnel and took over hundreds of square miles, expelling twelve thousand peasants to build new bases. Some forty thousand Contra forces were quartered there, including twenty thousand Miskitu Indians, to create a "New Nicaragua." After Congress cut off lethal aid to the Contras, the United States funneled more aid through Honduras.[68] In 1988, the United States began to build permanent air and port facilities. Some began to call the country "the USS Honduras."[69]

The Contadora Peace Process

While much of the world cringed at the Reagan administration's violent and exaggerated response to Central America's revolutions, a group of Latin American nations took the initiative to bring peace to the region. In January 1983, representatives of Panama, Mexico, Venezuela, and Colombia met on the Panamanian island of Contadora. In September, the group released its proposal, and all five Central American countries indicated their support. The plan called for an end to foreign military intervention, reduction in foreign military advisers, arms reduction, and democratization.

The plan didn't mention the United States specifically. But it was no secret to anyone that the United States was the country engaging in foreign intervention and supplying foreign military advisers and arms. A classified US national security directive fretted about "possible negative consequences for U.S. strategic interests and policy objectives." If the agreement was implemented, "U.S. interests and objectives would be seriously damaged," the directive concluded.[70] The United States would simply not tolerate a solution that recognized Nicaragua's government, and that prohibited US intervention. In publicly rejecting the Contadora proposal, Reagan announced that he would not be content until the Sandinistas were forced to "say uncle."[71] Under US pressure, Costa Rica, El Salvador, and Honduras withdrew their support and the plan faltered.

A year later, following the initiative of Costa Rican president Óscar Arias, the five Central American countries signed their own peace plan (the Esquipulas Agreement) in 1987, agreeing to seek negotiated solutions to the ongoing wars. After the electoral defeat of the Sandinistas in Nicaragua in 1990, the United States retreated from its war there. Final peace agreements were signed in El Salvador in 1992 and Guatemala in 1996.

DEEPER POLICY

Beyond official and stated policy, US influence in Central America had deep and wide roots. US corporate interests played a role. So did numerous agencies like the CIA, USAID, and AIFLD. And so did the many forms of military training like the US Army School of the Americas and the military advisers on the ground. Then there were unintentional impacts. The presence of US investors, advisers, tourists, military, products, and media all brought messages with them.

In 1983, Reagan announced the Caribbean Basin Initiative, a set of trade preferences granting duty-free entry to the United States for textiles, apparel, and other products manufactured in Central American and Caribbean countries, as well as tax concessions for US companies investing, relocating, or holding conventions there.

The Caribbean Basin Initiative was an early "free trade" agreement that was really less about free trade than it was about helping out foreign investors. Manufacturers flocked to take advantage of the new guarantees, low wages, and duty-free access to US markets there, setting the roots of the export processing or *maquiladora* industry. US food aid also grew from ten million dollars between 1954 and 1979, to six hundred million dollars between 1980 and 1988. Food aid mostly helped US farmers and Central American militaries, which took larger and larger portions of the countries' budgets: over half in El Salvador, and a quarter in Guatemala and Honduras.[72]

There were some profound contradictions at the heart of US policy. The United States claimed to promote democracy—but it refused to accept election results, as in Guatemala in 1952 or with the Sandinista electoral victory in Nicaragua in 1984. Counterinsurgency required winning hearts and minds, but also harsh and bloody repression. Finally, there was an inherent "contradiction between counterinsurgent and neoliberal goals."[73] Winning hearts and minds required support of social democratic programs including social welfare policies, land reform, and the cooperative movement. Neoliberalism required dismantling those same projects in the interests of foreign investors and economic growth.

The grim results of the decade of intervention could be tallied in deaths: thirty thousand Nicaraguans (on top of fifty thousand killed during the war against Somoza), two hundred thousand (or more) Guatemalans, and seventy-five thousand Salvadorans killed. A culture of impunity followed that allowed US administrations, Congress, and the public to evade accountability and bury the history of how Central Americans paid the price for US Cold War prosperity. This culture of impunity profoundly shaped the region's uneasy peace in the 1990s and beyond.

PART II

REVOLUTION
IN THE
1970s AND '80s

CHAPTER 4

GUATEMALA

Reform, Revolution, and Genocide

This chapter surveys the repression that followed Guatemala's 1954 coup and how new forms of US intervention, new trends in the Catholic Church, and Marxist revolutionary organizations brought land and labor struggles, repression, and resistance in the 1970s and 80s. It looks at Christian Base Communities, worker and peasant organizations, the armed guerrilla movement, and the Communities of Population in Resistance (CPRs), as well as the civil patrols, death squads, massacres, and disappearances. It asks why the horrific repression in Guatemala remained largely invisible in the United States, even as human rights violations elsewhere gained more media attention.

AFTER THE COUP: ELIMINATING THE "COMMUNIST" THREAT

After the 1954 coup, the first order of the day for the United States was to crush the political and social movements that had threatened its goals in Guatemala. Doing so required a bloodbath. The CIA helped Guatemala's new government create a blacklist of seventy thousand suspected communists, which grew until it included some 10 percent of the adult population. Mass firings, arrests, torture, and disappearance followed. The US Embassy noted approvingly that such measures were "an accepted means of restoring what owners and managers consider the necessary agricultural labor discipline."[1]

Yet the embassy's own research shed doubt on the nature of the "communist" threat. An anthropologist the embassy itself contracted to investigate the politics of Guatemalans imprisoned by the new regime found that not a single one was a member of Guatemala's Communist Party, and few had even heard of Karl Marx. They were activists, but local activists involved in local issues. Seventy-five percent had participated in political parties, labor unions, peasant leagues, and agrarian committees.

The ten-year revolution had brought not communism but a "sociological awakening" that allowed poor people to believe that they could organize for their rights, "the realization that certain of the previously accepted roles and statuses within the social system were no longer bounded by the same rules, and that new channels were suddenly opened for the expression and satisfaction of needs. The heretofore established series of relationships between political leader and countryman, between employer and laborer, between Indian and Ladino, were not suddenly changed, but it abruptly became possible to introduce some change into them."[2]

It was precisely that awakening, and threat to the exploitative social order, that the United States sought to crush after the coup. Within months, the United States was tightening its relations with the Guatemalan military and police, providing aid and training to support the government's "ability to maintain internal order" and to shape the military's "ideological orientation." Yet it tried to remain discreet, because "it would be disastrous . . . if it became known that we called the plays on domestic political matters."[3]

The logic behind US antipathy to Arbenz and its decision to overthrow him played out in the way the United States sought to remake Guatemala after the coup. Popular mobilizations and land reform threatened the interests of foreign investors and the landed elite. The United States sought a favorable investment climate in which US companies could make profits. This meant undoing the reforms of the Arbenz years that sought to grant rights to and share wealth and power with the poor majority and restoring these benefits to the oligarchy and foreign investors. Doing so required the massive use of terror over several decades to convince poor people that they could *not* "organize for their rights" and to restore "heretofore established series of relationships between political leader and countryman, between employer and laborer, between Indian and Ladino."

A SHOWCASE FOR FOREIGN INVESTMENT

After the coup, the Eisenhower administration sought to "transform Guatemala into a showcase" by "channeling foreign capital into new areas of investment," especially in strategic raw materials like petroleum, mining, timber, and profitable sectors like manufacturing and banking. US experts descended on Guatemala to rewrite the country's laws governing foreign investment. "Tax exemptions, the investment guarantee law, and currency convertibility helped lure U.S. businesses to Guatemala," explained historian Stephen Streeter.[4]

To make sure the new laws would fulfill their every need, the United States paid potential investors to write them. A US petroleum industry consulting firm shaped Guatemala's new petroleum code to permit fully-foreign ownership, repatriation of profits, and lower taxes, while allowing US companies to call upon the State Department to arbitrate any disputes with the Guatemalan government. The new code led to "a scramble by foreign oil companies to secure the most lucrative exploration and drilling concessions." Guatemala soon awarded dozens of new concessions covering 3.8 million hectares. A Bank of America representative advised the government on revision of the banking code and became the first foreign bank to open branches in Guatemala. US government geologists surveyed northern Guatemala's mining potential.[5]

The US Export-Import Bank extended fifteen million dollars in loans to the Guatemalan government and to private firms, most of which were used to purchase US-made machinery from firms like International Harvester and General Motors.[6] For US businesses, then, the coup brought magnificent windfalls.

FOREIGN AID, REFORM, AND CORPORATE PROFITS

New Sunbelt industries in the real estate, petroleum, and defense sectors formed a Guatemala lobby that promoted US foreign aid that would facilitate their own expansion into Central America. By 1961, the United States had provided over one hundred million dollars in foreign assistance to the new Guatemalan regime, including fourteen million dollars for rural development and twenty-seven million dollars for the construction of the Inter-American Highway. (US companies received most of the highway construction contracts.) The United States worked closely with Guatemalan government ministries to develop a series of five-year plans for economic development.[7]

Much of the foreign investment pouring into the country only exacerbated the long-standing problems of poverty and landlessness. To keep these from exploding into a new wave of mobilization, the United States added a spectrum of reforms that it hoped would ease social tensions by bettering the lives of the poor and land hungry, without threatening the interests of elites and investors. But each was laden with contradictions. Given Guatemala's extreme inequality, any mobilization by or concessions to the poor inevitably threatened those who relied on exploiting them.

Peasants' lives could be improved through access to land, through inputs like credit, machinery, and fertilizers, or through legal and institutional improvements like labor rights or cooperatives. The Arbenz land reform was an attempt to redistribute power and resources to do this. In the anti-communist reforms that followed, the idea was to mollify peasants *without* challenging the entrenched interests of elites. USAID as well as nongovernmental and religious aid projects flooded Guatemala in the aftermath of the coup.

Vaccination, public health, and sanitation measures seemed an intervention that could help the poor without threatening the powerful. But these measures exacerbated population growth and land pressure. After the massive demographic collapse following the Spanish conquest, it took four centuries for the Maya population in the Cuchumatán area to recover its preconquest numbers, which it did by 1950. Then, between 1950 and 1980, the population doubled. Between 1950 and 1970, the number of families trying to survive on *minifundia* too small to provide for their subsistence increased from 308,070 to 421,000, while the average farm size in the central and western highlands shrank from 3.2 acres in 1950 to 2 in 1975.[8] So even reforms designed to refrain from threatening elite power could in fact increase social tensions. Other reformist measures proved just as contradictory.

The Green Revolution

One anti-communist solution to population growth and land scarcity was the Green Revolution. Instead of a "red" or communist revolution involving a redistribution of land and resources, technology would provide solutions to poverty and hunger. The US government partnered with the Rockefeller Foundation to develop Green Revolution high-yielding seeds, chemical fertilizers, and pesticides. Peace Corps volunteers and Maryknoll missionaries introduced them into the rural villages where they worked.

Initially, Green Revolution inputs enabled increased production and helped reduce the desperation that was pushing peasants into seasonal migration and radical political demands. However, the changes also pulled more peasants into reliance on a cash economy. When fertilizer prices rose sharply with the oil crisis of the 1970s, many small farmers became indebted, were forced to sell their land, and were pushed further into seasonal labor migration.[9]

Green Revolution changes could also contribute to political radicalization. One Guatemalan anthropologist argued that for peasant farmers, the move into commercial crops meant "renouncing an ancestral form of thought and the elaboration of new ways of seeing the world . . . It was in this new space that a young generation of Indians began their [political] work."[10]

In the bigger picture, the Green Revolution in the highlands was only part of a much larger technical aid program aimed at large farmers producing export crops.[11] In the Pacific lowlands, pesticides, fertilizers, and roads opened the area to cotton production. Peasants in the Pacific suffered mass expulsions as the lands were taken over by cotton growers; by the late 1980s, the region had the highest levels of land concentration in the country.[12]

COLONIZATION AND COOPERATIVES

Capitalist reformers offered another alternative to land redistribution: colonization. Breaking up plantations to return land to peasants who had been displaced harmed investors and smacked of communism. The capitalist solution was to open new lands for cultivation, especially in the forested north and east of the country.

Colonization of new lands as a way of defusing popular claims against the rich echoed the long history of "settlement" of the US West and subsequent US foreign policy. The United States also has a long history of removing Indians from lands coveted for resources and economic development. Guatemala's colonization schemes differed from US settler colonialism in that many of the "colonizers" were Indigenous peasants. But as in the US West, small farmers and the big corporations that followed them had very different visions of how the land should be distributed and used.

For land-stressed peasants of the highlands of Huehuetenango and El Quiché, the northern rainforest was touted as a relief valve. It was an escape, among other things, from cotton: villages in these regions sent over half of their working population to the Pacific coast for the harvest. Small farmers had been seeking land in the rainforest informally since the 1960s, and it became a key site for the colonization projects sponsored by the Catholic Church, USAID, and the Guatemalan government by the early 1970s.[13]

"Before 1966, Ixcán was uninhabited jungle," explained Guatemalan Jesuit anthropologist Ricardo Falla.

> That year, the first settlers arrived with [a] Maryknoll priest . . . to take possession of the lands in a joint Church and [government] project to buy private lands and receive allotments of certain state properties. The colonizers settled on the banks of the Ixcán River and began to clear the jungle and sow crops, battling against the heat and intense rains (six meters a year), the impenetrable vegetation, snakes, mosquitos, bogs, lack of roads, the great distances from towns and commercial centers, loneliness, and isolation. They were pioneers hungry for lands and tired of selling their labor on the large coffee, sugarcane, and cotton estates on the coast and coastal lowlands.

Over the next few years "the jungle gradually filled with people."[14]

Many new colonists organized into cooperatives to facilitate access to aid and resources. In the repression following the coup, the Arbenz government's cooperative program had been dismantled. But a new 1956 constitution reinstated the role of cooperatives and provided for state bank funding and credit. A few years later, the US government explained that "the disbandment of the communist-led 'cooperatives' of the Arbenz era" enabled "a new stage of development" for noncommunist cooperatives "assisted by the USAID Mission and by the many independent development groups working in the rural areas of Guatemala."[15] But it was often hard for their sponsors to keep the cooperatives under control, especially as oil and cattle interests followed them into the rainforest.

Anthropologist Beatriz Manz accompanied one of the colonies trying to carve a life out of the rainforest. The Catholic Church had recruited campesinos who came from different municipios of El Quiché department. "The settlement did not happen in a vacuum," Manz explains. "Only the most energetic and optimistic went to the Ixcán . . . The colonization was part of a major mobilization and activism . . . They knew the governments were undemocratic; they knew about work in the plantations and the privilege of the land-holding elite; and they knew how Mayas were treated and perceived by society. Many of them had short-wave radios and listened to Radio Havana Cuba or news about Allende's Popular Unity in Chile."[16]

DEVELOPMENT ZONES: THE NORTHERN TRANSVERSAL STRIP AND THE PETÉN

Low-population areas in the north and east of the country were also resource-rich, and at the same time they attracted peasant colonists, the government and multinationals eyed their potential for large-scale export development. The Northern Transversal Strip (Franja Transversal del Norte or FTN) development project targeted highland villages that suffered land loss and forced labor during the coffee boom, as well as lowland frontiers of peasant migration and colonization, for export-oriented investment. The resource-rich rainforests exposed the fraught interactions between new and old peasant communities, on one hand, and large-scale economic development, on the other.

Just a few years after the colonization project began in the rainforest, Guatemala's Agrarian Reform Institute declared the FTN an agricultural development zone. USAID and the Guatemalan government embarked on highway construction and opening the land to domestic and foreign mining, ranching, cattle, and logging interests. In 1979, journalist Alan Riding reported in the *New York Times* that "[i]n the past five years . . . partly stimulated by the discovery of oil in the western jungles near the Mexican border, the Government has begun penetrating the area, improving the road into the northern province of Petén and building [a] new east-west road across the narrow waist of the country that is the Northern Transversal Strip."[17]

Liza Grandia explains that "inspired by Mexico's oil bonanza and fueled by the petroleum embargoes and the world energy crises of the 1970s, the Guatemalan government awarded exploration contracts across Petén and the Franja Transversal to a long series of U.S. and other foreign oil companies . . . Colonization planners similarly welcomed national and foreign logging interests in Petén and nickel mining operations in the eastern Franja."[18]

Guatemalan general Fernando Romeo Lucas García acquired major landholdings in the area and, as defense minister in the 1970s, took charge of an oil development project there. After being elected president in 1978, he oversaw both the development of the region and the extraordinary violence that accompanied it.

The Exmibal nickel-mining company obtained a concession for the eastern edge of the strip in 1973, and by 1978 seven international oil companies were operating in the northern and western portions. In 1974, the Guatemalan government obtained a loan for its largest-ever public infrastructure project, the Chixoy hydroelectric complex along the river of the same name, followed by other extractive projects. "The combined package of oil, nickel, hydroelectricity, and beef justified the financing of the largest road-building program of the 1970s and 80s," the Transversal Highway and a network of roads to connect the lowland rainforest under development to highland villages. "For the multinational corporations, the main attraction of the roads was in facilitating the exploration, extraction, transportation, and processing of minerals. For army officers, government officials, and other Guatemalans close to the government, the roads meant the opportunity to become cattlemen." Roads connected petroleum producers in the west to nickel mining in the east.[19]

In the far northeastern Petén region, the population density was very low, although Q'eqchi' Indians from neighboring provinces had migrated there in search of land for decades. In the mid-1960s, the government launched the National Company for the Development of the Petén (FYDEP) to encourage further colonization. The agency's development plans, including infrastructure and roads, favored cattle ranching and logging. It proceeded to allot land primarily to large, often absentee, ranchers and plantation owners, including members of the military. Indeed, despite the stated goals of colonization to provide land for the landless, the social structure of newly colonized lands in the Petén came to replicate the unequal system of the highlands, and many peasant colonists became landless workers.[20]

Conflict between peasant cooperatives and megaprojects plagued the region. A 1976 article called the Northern Strip "the site of the most immense and controversial investments in the country, in nickel and petroleum . . . It is also the site of frequent land conflicts between campesinos who have cultivated their parcels for years and new landowners buoyed by temporary titles." Rumors began to circulate about guerrilla presence in the area.[21]

The United States provided 5.6 million dollars for one resettlement project of four thousand peasants in the strip in the late 1970s, near an oil exploration project run by the Texas company Shenandoah.[22] "Even before the resettlement program is under way," wrote Riding in his 1979

New York Times account, "the Strip has suffered the same fate as Petén, with the new settlers ending up working as peons on the large farms that are now appearing in the area. Guatemala's President, Gen. Romeo Lucas Garcia, who in 1977 was in charge of development of the Strip, is reported to own three estates totaling 130,000 acres. Several other army officers, including Defense Minister Otto Spiegler, have also been given land to 'colonize.' One district near Sebol is known as 'the area of the generals.'"[23] These conflictive areas in the north became one key site of popular organizing, guerrilla activity, counterinsurgency, and genocide by the late 1970s.

CHALLENGES TO TRADITIONAL RELIGION

Religious and political power were intertwined in Mayan communities through costumbre, cofradías, and principales. The cofradías created a system of social control that tied villagers to the institution and its leadership and justified the entrenched patriarchal authority of principales. Elders also wielded power through their ability to pass their land on to their sons. Inequality was built into the system, but so was reciprocity.

Traditional leaders had a stake in maintaining the system that they benefited from. During the Arbenz years, rural organizing challenged the power structures in Indigenous communities. Many principales felt threatened and had opposed both the political opening and the agrarian reform.[24]

The repression and the post-Arbenz development decades offered principales new opportunities to restore their status. Some became labor contractors, moneylenders, and shop owners.[25] Even if they succeeded in recuperating power, it was harder to regain their legitimacy. Population growth and the consequent land pressure also weakened the foundations of community hierarchies.

Despite the repression, youth who came of age in the 1960s and '70s continued to be drawn to the ideologies and politics that had mobilized their communities under Arbenz. Some of these ideas reemerged in religious developments that drew community members away from the cofradías, like Catholic Action and Liberation Theology, or new evangelical Protestant sects.[26]

Although Guatemala's church hierarchy remained conservative, Liberation Theology began to permeate the lower levels, many of them US Maryknolls, Spanish Jesuits, and other foreign parish-level priests. If they initially sought reforms to counter the appeal of communism, by the mid-1960s these religious radicals began to work for social justice for its own sake, and some became Marxists and revolutionaries.

Liberation Theologians trained catechists, organized study groups to use biblical texts to analyze and raise consciousness about local realities, and organized credit and other cooperatives to free campesinos from the control of local principales, landlords, and moneylenders. They established hospitals, health clinics, and barefoot doctors' training programs. They founded local radio stations that created popular education projects through "radio schools."[27]

This religious revolution was particularly deep in the Indigenous highlands of El Quiché and Huehuetenango, the poorest and most land-deprived area that supplied most of the migrant labor for cotton plantations. The region lay at the western end of the FTN, opened by new roads and coveted by military officers, foreign multinationals, and local elites for cattle, mineral, and oil development. By 1968, over 50 percent of youth and adults in El Quiché were participating in Catholic Action.[28]

Traditional village institutions and authorities were profoundly threatened by the new religious activism through Catholic Action and the cooperative movement. "In some communities this unleashed a long and bitter conflict, at times extremely harsh and not without violence. There were near-lynchings, confrontations with machetes, rocks, and knives among members of a community as they sought to control the local church and to command the loyalty of community members."[29]

In early 1973, members of the traditional leadership of the town of Nebaj in the Ixil region of northern Quiché called upon the army to intervene there, claiming that "there is now among us a bad seed, the communists, who are fighting against us with cooperatives and other idiocies." This was, according to one study, the first time that Indian authorities directly appealed to the army to intervene in their own community. In January 1976, the leaders drew up a blacklist and turned it over to military intelligence officers. Two months later, the army occupied the town and began to target leaders of cooperatives, Catholic Action, and development committees.[30] The Ixil soon became the epicenter of the country's genocide.

Radicalized Jesuits and Maryknolls steeped in Liberation Theology also led the colonization projects that took land-poor peasants down from these highlands into the northern rainforest. The colonization projects brought together Mayan people from different regions and languages and were fertile ground for religious change. The absence of traditional authorities and structures opened space for colonizers to develop new, more democratic institutions.

YOUNG OFFICERS REBEL IN THE EAST: THE 1960S

The Cold War took another turn in Guatemala in 1960, when the CIA went over the head of Guatemala's army to establish several bases to train and arm Cuban exiles in preparation for an invasion of the island, hoping to overthrow Fidel Castro. Military officers and troops—many of them admirers of Castro's revolution and resentful of Guatemala's subordination to the United States—rose up in the capital and in Zacapa in the east. The rebellion inspired a significant following among Ladino peasants in the east, though local Indian populations showed little interest.

The United States sent warships, bombers, and an aircraft carrier, and the uprising was quickly ended. Some of the leaders escaped to the mountains where in the following years they reorganized into the FAR (Revolutionary Armed Forces), a guerrilla force of several hundred fighters that carried out several small-scale actions.

The savage repression that followed such actions aimed mostly at noncombatants. The military, allied with paramilitary death squads, killed between three and eight thousand peasants, mostly in the eastern Zacapa department, between 1966 and 1968. The defense minister who led the operation, Colonel Carlos Arana Osorio, known as "the butcher of Zacapa," was then elected president in 1970.

"Why did the military recruit people to settle the frontier and then kill them?" asks geographer Megan Ybarra. She answers her question this way: "By the mid-1970s when the military's counterrevolutionary project to colonize the lowlands did not seem to go according to plan, the military enacted counterinsurgency violence as part of a larger development project."[31] The events in the east prefigured the violence that would sweep the mostly Indigenous western and central highlands as the decade progressed.

THE 1970S: RESISTANCE GROWS

In the 1970s, some 60 percent of Mayan peasant farmers migrated seasonally to labor on the coast.[32] Seventy-five percent of children were malnourished.[33] Several different strands of organizing in the 1970s mobilized the urban poor, migrant workers on the coast, highland villages, and the new cooperatives. By the middle of the decade, ties were also growing with the nascent guerrilla groups that, like those in Nicaragua and El Salvador, believed that the time was ripe for armed revolution to overthrow the unjust order.

In 1976, a massive earthquake shook the highlands of Guatemala. Over twenty thousand were killed, and seventy-five thousand injured, and a million left homeless. For Arturo Arias, "[T]he earthquake provided a true trial by fire for the local leadership in the affected rural communities . . . From that moment, the literacy work, the work of the Christian communities, the work of political discussion, began truly to be transformed into organizational work" that became more explicitly politicized, and sometimes brought connections with the armed leftist groups.[34]

Earthquake relief brought together progressive Catholic organizations, urban labor unions, Indians from different communities, and activist Ladinos. "Secondary and primary students organized to demand the rebuilding of their schools, factory workers fought for relief aid from their employers, and neighborhood committees, which were often started by students or trade unionists, flourished everywhere in the city as residents mobilized" to provide basic services. "The aftermath of the earthquake was an experience in local power in the face of state corruption" that nourished further revolutionary organizing.[35]

Union Organizing in Guatemala City

Guatemala City grew rapidly as export agriculture displaced rural dwellers and the Central American Common Market prompted the growth of manufacturing and new opportunities for foreign investors, who controlled close to 50 percent of the country's industries by 1975. "Workers often used the image of a concentration camp or a prison to describe factories, which were usually surrounded by barbed wire, guarded by armed men and police dogs, and patrolled inside by armed supervisors."[36] Despite massive repression, labor unions formed especially in the capital's large, foreign-owned factories producing goods for local and regional consumption like shoes, textiles, cigarettes, canned foods, and Coca-Cola. Most migrants worked in the informal sector, but they too participated in urban popular organizing.

Like Catholic Action in the countryside, the Young Catholic Worker (JOC) movement began with the goal of rejuvenating the Catholic

Church to pose an alternative to communist organizing. With the rise of Liberation Theology, the JOC's clubs and programs began to focus on how "people had the power to transform life," and move into trade union organizing. Conditions radicalized many activists, who moved away from the centrist Christian Democratic Party and to an analysis "inspired by Christian notions of social justice and a Marxist analysis of capitalism."[37]

Armed Guerrilla Movements

In the 1960s, the FAR had, like many Latin American guerrilla groups, subscribed to the *foco* theory, popularized by Che Guevara, proposing that a small guerrilla organization carrying out spectacular attacks would spark a widespread revolutionary uprising. In addition to the FAR in the east, several other armed guerrilla organizations formed inside Guatemala including the Guerrilla Army of the Poor (EGP) and the Revolutionary Organization of the People in Arms (ORPA). By the mid-1970s, all agreed that the foco approach had failed, and that instead they needed to work to build grassroots organizations and build support for revolution step by step. Their approaches differed in that the FAR sought a base in the urban working class, while ORPA focused on the rural Indigenous population and the EGP sought to build ties between rural Indigenous, plantation workers, and the urban poor. Guatemala's Communist Party, the PGT, like most of the continent's communist groups, emphasized legal organizing within the system rather than armed struggle, though a group of party dissidents also took up arms. By the end of the 1970s, the EGP, after years of quietly building support in the cooperatives of the Ixcán rainforest and the nearby villages of the Ixil region, had become the largest group and was operating in two-thirds of the country's territory.[38] In 1982, the guerrilla organizations united to form the Guatemalan National Revolutionary Unity (URNG).

Mayan Cultural Rights

Connections among different Mayan communities through church activities, schools, and migrations contributed to growing consciousness of shared material conditions and exploitation, and shared cultural experiences of racism and marginalization. *Leftist* or *classist* Mayan organizations focused on structural or class issues that united poor Indians and Ladinos, while *culturalist* organizations emphasized Mayan identity and rights. For many activists, the two were intertwined and complementary, given the racialization of class in Guatemala, as in most colonial and postcolonial societies.

In 1974, Mayan activists formed the Coordinadora Indígena Nacional to sponsor a series of workshops bringing together activists from around the country. In 1977, with the support of the Maryknolls, they founded a monthly newspaper, *Ixim: Notas Indígenas*, aimed at fostering a pan-Maya consciousness that transcended regional, language, and rural-urban divides. A 1978 editorial renamed October 12, officially Columbus Day in the United States and the Día de la Raza in Guatemala as elsewhere in Latin America, as the Día de Desgracia—the Day of Misfortune.[39] Events like the 1976 earthquake and the 1978 Panzós massacre (discussed below) spurred criticism of state-sponsored "folklore" promotion that exoticized and exploited Mayan culture while covering up official racism. Many young people graduated from cultural activism to the ranks of the leftist Committee for Campesino Unity (CUC) and the EGP.

Traditional village authorities tended to be dubious about the pan-Mayan activism that sought to create new politicized understandings of indigeneity that transcended the village level and the cofradía system. Local Ladinos too benefited from and had reason to preserve Indigenous political and religious hierarchy. When one Ladino mourned the decline of traditional Indigenous customs, a highland youth responded, "Yes, it is sad . . . *for you!*"[40]

Linking the Highlands and the Plantations: The CUC

Plantation workers in the new cotton export economy on the southern coast came from many different Indian communities and shared the grueling work with poor Ladinos. Many also migrated seasonally from their highland villages, creating new webs of connections and identities among different Indian communities, and between highland communities and coastal workers.

Many Indians came down from the highlands to observe the May 1, 1977, International Workers Day demonstrations, and national rallies on October 20, 1977, commemorating the 1944 revolution. The following month, Indian and Ladino mine workers from Huehuetenango marched 351 kilometers over nine days along the Pan-American Highway through much of the Indian highlands, arriving in Guatemala City "accompanied by 150,000 people, including students, settlers, government employees, workers, and campesinos." Sugar workers on the southern coast also demonstrated and joined them. The march brought the coastal peasant leagues and the highland Christian Base Communities together for the first time, and "created a growing feeling of euphoria in the mass organizations."[41] A Maryknoll priest who had supported the miners' organizing wrote that "never before had workers and peasants, Indians and Ladinos, the Indians of different ethnic groups showed such solidarity with each other."[42]

This activism coalesced in the CUC, which made its first public appearance the following May 1 with slogans including "No more forced recruitment by the Army," "Lack of land," "No to repression," "No to discrimination," "No to the high cost of living."[43] Though the CUC never openly affiliated with the EGP, the organization was or quickly became "tied to national politics and the revolutionary Left" with significant overlap with the EGP in membership and in its vision of a revolution based on the common interests of highland Indigenous peasants, coastal plantation workers, and the urban poor.[44]

In January 1980, twenty-seven CUC activists from northern Quiché, including Vicente Menchu, father of Rigoberta, traveled to Guatemala City to demand that the government investigate the repression in their region. When the Congress refused to meet with them, they carried out a peaceful occupation of the Spanish embassy. Over the protests of the Spanish ambassador, Guatemalan security forces assaulted the building. The attack culminated with the burning of the embassy, killing the occupiers and their hostages, a total of thirty-seven people. The ambassador and one demonstrator survived, the latter only to be kidnapped from the hospital later that night, tortured, and killed, his body dumped on the university campus the next day.

Horror at the massacre contributed to bringing together culturalist and classist sectors of the unarmed left. Out of their meetings came the Declaration of Iximché, a statement "from the indigenous peoples of Guatemala before the world." The declaration offered a framework for the leftist CUC and the more culturalist *movimiento indígena* to link Indigenous with class-based issues. The EGP, with its strong overlap with the CUC, also took its cue from the declaration.

THE MASSACRE AT PANZÓS

One army response to the country's growing mobilization took place a month later in the east of the country, in the village of Panzós, Alta Verapaz. On May 29, 1978, a group of Q'eqchi' Indians gathered to deliver a document to the mayor presenting their land claims. Local landowners, Guatemala's Truth Commission later concluded, "not only requested the presence of the army, but also favored the creation of a hostile environment against the peasant population."[45]

Soldiers fired into the crowd, killing dozens, while army helicopters pursued those who tried to flee. Unknown numbers were killed or drowned as they fled into the river or died later in the mountains. It was the beginning of what was to become an avalanche of military and paramilitary savagery against the rising popular organizations, unarmed civilians, and especially against Indigenous communities.

Most accounts of the massacre focus on the horrifying events of the day: perhaps over a hundred unarmed men, women, and children gunned down, hunted, and chased to their deaths. But Panzós's history shows how its conflicts were the result of Central America's brand of economic development. Panzós is one of a cluster of communities in the valley of the Polochic River, at the southeastern corner of the Northern Transversal Strip. In the middle of the nineteenth century, the land was filled with corn plots planted by dispersed Q'eqchi villages. Then came the coffee plantation system that "literally enveloped Q'eqchi's." New plantations took over village lands and replaced corn with millions of coffee trees, displacing thousands of campesinos. By the 1920s, nearly 40 percent of the department's population had lost their land and lived as peons on coffee plantations.[46]

Like so many in Guatemala, these workers organized and received land during the 1952 land reform and lost both land and the right to public voice after the coup. "When Jacobo [Arbenz] died," one elder told the later truth commission, "the mayor called us to a meeting. He said we were not going to work together like we had been. That is where our work in committees ended and our work on *haciendas* began again."[47]

Both cattle ranchers and peasant colonizers moved into the area in the 1950s and '60s, and as local coffee planters too expanded their cattle holdings, they clashed with the remaining peasant farmers. In the 1970s, when the mining road connected the region to the highlands and to the meatpacking plant in Guatemala City, cattle ranchers moved there in full force.[48]

The Panzós massacre, argues historian Greg Grandin, "marked a watershed in Guatemala's war . . . Perhaps no other event had such far-reaching

political and symbolic consequences."[49] The massacre galvanized dispa-
rate forces in the urban and rural left to unite and drove many Mayan
campesinos to give up on reformism and hope that the state would protect or defend them. When Victoria Sanford went to interview massacre survivors twenty years later, her team was overwhelmed by relatives
of people disappeared during and after the massacre in the plaza. "That
year many people died," one survivor told them. "It was a year of death."[50]

Just months after the Panzós massacre, General Romeo Lucas García,
a major architect and beneficiary of the land grabs in the east, won a
fraud-ridden election and became president of Guatemala. Under his
regime, what happened at Panzós began to be repeated throughout the
Indigenous highlands.

GUERRILLA WAR IN NORTHERN QUICHÉ:
THE IXCÁN AND THE IXIL REGION

The Ixcán rainforest and highland Ixil region of northern Quiché became the epicenter of both guerrilla organizing and the genocide against
Guatemala's Mayan population that began to unfold in the months after Panzós. The growing violence there coincided with the construction
of the Northern Strip road and the encroaching oil exploration in the
region.

EGP guerrilla leader Mario Payeras described how a few survivors
of the 1960s guerrilla uprising and its repression regrouped in Mexico
and decided to return to Guatemala and "do things right" this time by
building a strong base of support before relaunching an armed struggle. The small group crossed into Guatemala in early 1972, in the Ixcán
rainforest region where the first colonizers had only recently established
settlements.[51]

The cooperatives proved fertile ground for organizing. "The insurgents spoke in terms similar to those of the priests, the nuns, the students,
the social promoters, and the political activists back in the highlands.
These experiences could be uplifting, hopeful, and inspiring." The villagers cooperated cautiously with the ragged men who entered the village
asking to buy food.[52]

Slowly, at the end of 1973, the group approached the older highland
Ixil villages. As in so many villages in the highlands, Catholic Action and
peasant organizations had brought new ideas and new economic pros-
pects to the villages, which engaged many of the youth.[53]

By early 1975, according to Payeras, "a constant stream of peasants sought out our local cells, bringing with them their ancient burden of grievances." After two years, the EGP began "armed propaganda actions," meaning small-scale military operations, "limited so that the enemy's reaction would not exceed either what the people were prepared to understand or what we were capable of withstanding and defending at the local level."[54]

The EGP chose a spectacular action to publicly declare its existence: the assassination of Luis Arenas, the Tiger (or Jaguar) of Ixcán, a large coffee grower who established his plantation there after the 1954 coup and who was notorious in the region for his expropriation of village lands and his exploitative and cruel treatment of his workers. Payeras described how a small guerrilla group infiltrated the plantation on payday, as the workers gathered to collect their wages. "Standing in front of the manager and looking like a bird of prey, the lord of the land was counting his coins and unfolding some crumpled bills" as the guerrilla contingent startled and instantly shot him.

> Not believing what they had just seen, the crowd nervously listened to the explanation, in their own language, that we offered then and there. As the indictment progressed, recalling Arenas' injustices and depredations, voices began to be heard among the crowd, interrupting the speaker and adding justifications of their own for the man's execution. Finally shouts of joy burst from throats accustomed to centuries only to silence and lament, and with something like an ancestral cry, with one voice they chanted with us our slogan, "Long live the poor, death to the rich."[55]

That's how Payeras saw it. Anthropologist David Stoll points out that not all of the plantation's workers were local villagers who had lost lands to the plantation. Some were Ladino and Indigenous migrants, for whom the plantation was their only source of income. These migrants "are more likely to recall Don Luis with nostalgia . . . Instead of joining the revolution, the [migrant workers] became a mainstay of the army's counterinsurgency drive."[56]

The army reaction was fierce and directed against the entire population of the region as village after village was occupied and suspected collaborators tortured, beaten, and killed. Campesinos fled their villages, some making their way to the guerrilla camps, where, Payeras wrote, "in less than a week we tripled our membership," and "four or five different dialects were suddenly heard."[57] Fortified with the influx of local people, the armed propaganda campaign expanded to "taking" a village, gathering together the residents to explain their struggle and denounce army atrocities, then disappearing again into the countryside.

Payeras reported calmly that "although the guerrillas in the mountains suffered no losses, these were considerable among our organized supporters in the villages."[58] Counterinsurgency sweeps between 1981 and 1983 killed thousands, while tens of thousands fled as their homes were burned and villages destroyed. "The army burned down all hamlets and homesteads outside the three towns" of the Ixil, reported Stoll. In village after village, "army units shot, hacked, or burned to death thousands of unarmed men, women, and children." The population of the region shrank to half its size.[59]

Survivors' accounts recall beatings, rapes, torture, and gruesome violence. Many fled towns that were occupied and put under military rule. Massacres were followed by scorched-earth tactics that burned homes and cornfields, making return impossible. "The army burned everything. So we stayed in the mountain," one survivor recalled.[60]

Some of those who fled eventually reorganized themselves into Communities of Population in Resistance (CPRs) in the areas outside of government control. Tens of thousands lived for years in hiding and almost permanent flight and under relentless army pursuit. "They bombed the entire mountain. Many people died from these bombs. Many people died from hunger," another reported simply.[61]

Farther north in the rainforest of the Ixcán, in the Santa María Tzejá cooperative where anthropologist Beatriz Manz worked, over 50 people out of the 116 families that formed the village joined the EGP in the 1970s. When the military and the death squads descended on the cooperatives, some of the foreign priests fled the region. Most villagers had little choice. As one recounted to Manz, "Some even thought of returning to the highlands, but how could they, given the poverty there? So no one returned."[62]

By the time the EGP arrived in the southern Quiché in the late 1970s, reported the official church-sponsored truth commission later, "a large percentage of the population was waiting for it . . . The EGP's political cadres and combatants were increasingly astonished by their overwhelming reception and the speed with which the population organized itself." Popular organizations like the CUC mobilized in support of guerrilla actions. Through 1980 and 1981, "guerrilla triumphalism" grew as popular uprising spread around the country, and many believed that a revolutionary victory was imminent or at least possible, despite the viciousness of the army response.[63]

Victoria Sanford, who investigated massacres in dozens of communities, wrote that in every case, there was a history of organizing, through Catholic Action, cooperatives, and earthquake response projects, among others. In some but not all cases, guerrilla organizers participated clandestinely or openly in the village. But the pattern of army attacks against village activists, followed by occupation, massacre, then burning of the village and its fields, prevailed in almost every case.[64]

"Villagers did not have to be suspected of sympathizing with guerrillas to be attacked," explained Richard Wilson. "The plan was to terrorize the entire indigenous population and separate it from guerrilla troops. Villages with developed local institutions such as cooperatives or schools were especially targeted . . . The army believed that such villages had the potential to become sympathetic to the revolutionaries, and this was enough to warrant their destruction. In its raids, the army set fire to houses, burned or cut down crops, and killed livestock . . . The army created a no-man's-land, depopulated and devoid of crops and domestic animals, between militarized towns and the guerrillas' jungle."[65]

THE COUNTERINSURGENCY: MODEL VILLAGES

For the army, Indigenous villagers, massacre survivors, and those who found refuge in the mountains were automatically subversives. Beginning in the Ixil region, tens of thousands were captured and reconcentrated into new "model villages" eventually established in four "development poles" throughout the highlands, to "militarize rural communities based on an exorbitant level of control . . . over populations considered to be the social base of the guerrillas." The resettled villages were strengthened with new roads and bases that attempted to establish an army presence in the guerrilla-controlled countryside.[66]

General José Efraín Ríos Montt, a devout evangelical Christian with close ties to the military hierarchy and large landholdings in the north, took power in a 1982 coup. Ríos Montt reduced the more internationally visible violence in urban areas but escalated the assault on the Indigenous highlands. He institutionalized and expanded the model village system, implementing what he called the "guns and beans" program. Villagers were given work, housing, and food, but virtually imprisoned in their villages under military control.

From northern Quiché, the counterinsurgency spread through the Indigenous regions to the south and west. By 1983, some 80 percent of the Indigenous population of the highlands in Huehuetenango, Quiché, Chimaltenango, and Alta Verapaz had been forced to flee their homes at least temporarily. By the time the bloodletting receded later in the decade, over 600 villages had been destroyed, 200,000 people killed, and 1.5 million displaced. Some 150,000 fled to refugee camps over the Mexican border, others to the guerrilla-held territories in the mountains.[67] In 2013, Ríos Montt was convicted of genocide against the Mayan population.

TURNING VILLAGES AGAINST THEMSELVES: THE ARMY, THE DEATH SQUADS, AND THE PACS

Many of the army troops were also Mayans, forced to attack villages similar to their own. Kidnapped or forcibly recruited as teenagers, they were brutalized and indoctrinated with anti-Indigenous racism. "The army kills part of your identity," explained one former recruit. "They want to break you and make you a new man. A savage man. They inspired me to kill."[68]

In village after village, the army organized Civil Defense Patrols (PACs) that quite literally forced villages to attack and destroy themselves. Military commissioners (sometimes large landowners) were armed and empowered in village after village, and all adult men forced to participate in newly organized patrols under their control. The PACs "transformed a war between rebels and the army into a civil war among indigenous peasants . . . It was these ad hoc groups . . . that began an escalating campaign of torture, murder, and rape . . . Politically divided communities . . . turned on themselves."[69] By 1983, a million men around the country had been mobilized into the PACs—virtually the entire adult male population.[70]

Two anthropologists studied in depth how a death squad functioned in one highland village. After the ORPA guerrillas appeared briefly to explain their cause in a public meeting, the military moved in. An army post appeared nearby, and the army expanded the local military commissioner's power by providing arms and enlarging his force. As more villagers were forced or chose to join, the commissioners became a violent and arbitrary authority and a spasm of bloodletting followed: kidnappings, murders, and disappearances that went on for two years.

"It may be tempting to blame the outbreak of violence in San Pedro on social divisiveness and the settling of old scores," the authors warn, "but the temptation should be resisted. Religious competition and vigorous political in-fighting were features of [village] life in the decades before 1980 without producing violence. The same can be said for interpersonal antagonisms. They arose in the past and were settled by means short of murder. What disrupted the peace . . . was not the presence of differences and divisions but the army's recruitment of agents and spies that had the effect of exploiting these cleavages."[71]

In the new cooperative of Santa María Tzejá in the Ixcán, too, Manz reported that "it became common practice for a patrol chief to spread rumors about an individual he did not like, hoping for some personal gain for himself while causing fear, military punishment, or even death for the victim." One PAC leader told a relative that "[n]ow there are no uncles, no parents, no cousins, it's all the same, so watch out." He believed that if he did not inform on his relatives, he would be accused and punished himself.[72]

Jennifer Burrell summarized the literature and her findings in Todos Santos: "Personal and community-based conflicts were politicized by both Maya Indians and the military to fuel the intensification of warfare during the early 1980s. People almost always knew who was behind a denunciation that led to the death of a loved one and often could identify the conflict that likely precipitated the accusation. Conflicts commonly occurred over land disputes, water rights, unpaid debts, and internal tensions produced by class differences."[73]

The nefarious web of terror spun inside isolated Indigenous villages could be traced all the way to the United States, which provided counterinsurgency ideology, training, and techniques. "Militaries quickly learned not only to terrorize the population to dry up guerrilla support but to incorporate it into new ideological and political structures of authority" including "destabilization, psychological operations, internal policing, and low-intensity warfare." Repression was delegated to "quasi-autonomous death squads staffed by army and police officers supplied with information by rationalized military intelligence agencies and often trained by the United States."[74]

In one village in El Quiché, the civil patrol was ordered to murder all of the men of a neighboring village and rape the women or be killed themselves. "The idea seems to be that, once these people become involved in the crimes, they become accomplices and allies in the government counterinsurgency campaign."[75]

REPRESSION AGAINST THE RELIGIOUS

Sectors of the Catholic Church, especially among the Maryknolls and the Jesuits, were deeply involved in Liberation Theology, consciousness raising, cooperatives, and other movements that challenged the social order and the government. In some cases, they developed ties to armed guerrilla movements. Catechists, members of Christian Base Communities, and lay religious involved in radio, education, and other activities quickly became suspect.

Priests, including foreign missionaries, were kidnapped, tortured, and murdered. Church meetings and facilities were attacked. But the main victims were peasants who had become mobilized into church activism. The United Nations documented 1,169 religious who were killed, disappeared, or tortured, 921 of them lay catechists.[76]

The church shuttered the entire diocese of El Quiché in 1980 because of the unremitting repression and the killing of several priests. Bishop Juan Gerardi wrote that "[f]or four years, a situation of extreme violence weighs upon us in El Quiché, aggravated by the military occupation of the northern part of the department . . . We find the fundamental cause of this in a system of economic, social, and political development, supported by a doctrine of national security, that doesn't take into consideration the interests of the poor, forcing people to live under a reign of terror."[77] The number of priests in Guatemala fell from six hundred in 1979 to three hundred by 1981, as many were killed or fled.[78]

The Maryknolls closed their centers in Huehuetenango in 1979 after participants started to appear on army lists. In all, some four hundred of the fifteen hundred students who had participated in the programs were disappeared or killed. Their Centro Indígena in Guatemala City shut its doors in 1980 after being sacked by the army. Over eighty people connected to the Centro were killed, and its founder fled Guatemala.[79]

Well after the violence had begun to diminish, there were two more well-known religious victims. In 1989, a US missionary working in Huehuetenango, Sister Dianna Ortíz, was abducted, raped, and tortured by the Guatemalan military. Before her abduction, she received several threats accusing her of working with subversives.

Ortíz was released after twenty-four hours. Not so Bishop Gerardi, who had led the diocese of Quiché during the war years and coordinated the church's Recovery of Historical Memory (REMHI) project after the war's end, filled with anguished testimonies and concluding that the military had been responsible for 80 percent of the atrocities committed during the war. Two days after the report, *Guatemala: Nunca Más* (*Guatemala: Never Again*), was released in 1998, Gerardi was found bludgeoned to death outside his home.

DISAPPEARANCE AND RESISTANCE: GAM AND CONAVIGUA

In Central America, as under the dictatorships in Argentina and Chile in the late twentieth century, "disappear" became a transitive verb, and "disappeared" the noun that named the victims of disappearance. It referred to people who were kidnapped from their homes, workplaces, or the streets. Government security forces denied any culpability or accountability; sometimes they claimed that the person had never existed to begin with. In vain, loved ones searched for their relatives in police stations and army bases. Sometimes their tortured bodies were discovered, but most of the time they simply vanished without a trace. By the end of the war in 1996, Guatemala counted some forty-five thousand disappeared.

In 1984, relatives of the disappeared formed the Mutual Support Group (GAM), and later the Association of Relatives of the Detained-Disappeared in Guatemala (FAMDEGUA) and the National Coordination of Widows of Guatemala (CONAVIGUA). These organizations have continued to play a key role in the campaign for justice and accountability in postwar Guatemala.

THE UNITED STATES AND THE GUATEMALAN GENOCIDE

Grandin described the United States as "a distant but still involved patron during the Guatemalan genocide."[80] The United States organized the 1954 coup, and US government agencies (including the military), businesses, and nongovernmental organizations (NGOs) shaped the development model that underlay Guatemala's violent modernization in its aftermath. These facts constitute the mostly invisible underpinnings of Guatemala's holocaust.

US military aid was officially ended in 1977 because of Guatemala's human rights violations. But aid continued through back channels, including through US allies and aid recipients like Israel.[81]

Ronald Reagan, who had been pressing for renewed US assistance to Guatemala, greeted Ríos Montt's 1982 coup enthusiastically. He visited Guatemala at the end of the year and declared that Ríos Montt was "totally dedicated to democracy in Guatemala" and had gotten a "bum rap."[82] In 1983, Reagan lifted the embargo on arms sales to Guatemala. Both the United States and the United Nations provided aid for the model villages that Sanford described as having "more in common with Nazi concentration camps" than any supposed "development" project. Private US organizations including evangelical and other NGOs followed.[83]

DID THE GENOCIDE END?

In 1985, Christian Democrat Vinicio Cerezo won the presidency, the first civilian elected since 1966. It was clear, though, that the military remained the real source of power in the country. Cerezo's elected successor carried out a self-coup in 1993, dissolving Congress and the Supreme Court, and was eventually replaced by former Human Rights Ombudsman Ramiro de León Carpio. The latter oversaw negotiations with the URNG guerrilla coalition leading to Guatemala's peace accords signed in 1996, making Guatemala the last Central American country to end its war.

For urban Guatemalans, "*la violencia*" generally refers to the period between 1978 and 1982. For rural Guatemalans, the "violencia" did not end in 1982 but continued for a much longer period, through the final bombings against the CPRs and refugees in the Ixil mountains in the 1990s, or through the 1996 peace accords that finally ended the PACs. In this "decade-long campaign of genocide," the massacres were only the beginning. Genocide continued with the scorched-earth campaign that eliminated villages and crops, the bombing of civilians who had fled to the mountains, the concentration of survivors into model villages, and the long-term military occupation and coercion that continued to be enforced by the PACs after the army withdrew. Even after the peace accords were signed and the PACs officially dismantled, what Sanford calls "the living memory of terror" continues to dominate the lives of those who endured it.[84]

CHAPTER 5

NICARAGUA

*"Luchamos contra el yanqui,
enemigo de la humanidad"*

ORIGINS OF REVOLUTION

The overwhelming presence of the Somoza family dictatorship in Nicaragua shaped Nicaragua's history in the twentieth century. The Somozas ruled through a combination of patronage, co-optation, neglect (especially of the northern interior and the Atlantic coast), and repression. During the last years of the dictatorship, repression reigned supreme, and resistance gained more and more moral legitimacy. The Sandinistas inspired many with their youthful, idealistic leadership; their revolutionary commitment to social justice, popular mobilization, and participatory democracy; and their David-and-Goliath struggle against the United States. In the euphoria surrounding their 1979 victory, some of the complexities and conflicting interests in Nicaraguan society were submerged. These conflicting interests weakened the revolution from within even as they created fodder for the Reagan administration's vicious counterrevolution.

The FSLN

The Sandinista National Liberation Front (FSLN), founded in the early 1960s, drew on and drew together different strands of popular organizing, the popular church, and nationalist, anti-imperialist, and Marxist analysis. Its goal, reviving the words of Augusto C. Sandino, was "free homeland or death": a new Nicaragua liberated from the Somoza dictatorship, the Guardia, and US imperialism. Much of its formal ideology was elaborated by Carlos Fonseca during his time in Cuba, where he studied the history of Sandino, and his battle against US occupation. Marxism, the Cuban Revolution, and Liberation Theology all contributed to Sandinista thought. But the Sandinistas' critique of their country's situation was sui generis: it grew out of their own history and everyday realities. Some of these realities were shared with the rest of Central America, like rural landlessness and poverty, the expansion of cotton and cattle, and the influx of reformist groups like USAID and radical strands of Catholicism. Some were particular to Nicaragua, like the long US military occupation, the personalist form of corrupt rule under the Somozas, and deep memories of the popular guerrilla struggle of the 1920s and '30s.

While the origins of the FSLN were urban, just over half of Nicaragua's population was rural in the 1970s. In western, Pacific-facing Nicaragua, the countryside was taken over first by coffee, and then by cotton and cattle. Much of the rural population migrated during the mid-twentieth century: to the cities, to labor in the new agro-export industries, or to frontier areas in the north and east where they established new settlements. One historian described them as "peasants who reside in the maelstrom of agrarian capitalism rather than in their ancestral villages."[1] Meanwhile along the Atlantic coast, Caribbean-facing Indigenous and Afro-descended peasants remained almost completely isolated from the national economy.

In contrast to Guatemala, in Nicaragua, the United States played an overwhelming role in shaping the state. Rather than representing the oligarchy, Nicaragua's state and military represented the personal interests of the Somoza family. Nicaragua's elites resented their marginalization and were potentially more open to anti-imperialist nationalism and opposition.

During the development decades of the 1960s and '70s, presidents Luis and then Anastasio Somoza Debayle continued the family tradition, serving as reliable US allies (or puppets) in the international sphere. Access to aid-sponsored agro-export development depended on loyalty to the regime. When aid poured into the country after the 1972 earthquake that killed ten thousand and destroyed the center of Managua and tens of thousands of homes, relief funds flowed into the pockets and companies of the regime and its allies. The glaring corruption in time of disaster helped to solidify popular outrage and unify the opposition, including members of the upper classes who were not part of Somoza's inner circle. The Sandinista guerrillas called for revolution in utopian, moral, nationalist, and Christian terms that could unite broad sectors of the population against Somoza and the Guardia. This unity was the revolution's strength, but also its weakness.

Liberation Theology

As in Guatemala, the popular church and Liberation Theology played a major role in Nicaragua's revolutionary movement. "Between Christianity and revolution, there is no contradiction!" proclaimed the revolutionary slogan. Indeed, Sandinista thought explicitly fused Christian ethics and social doctrine with Marxism and patriotism.

Liberation Theology's belief in bringing about social change and social justice in this world drew activist Catholics to work with Nicaragua's rural poor and to learn about their struggles for land and labor rights. The priest Ernesto Cardenal, who established a meditation community on the island of Solentiname in Lake Nicaragua in the 1960s, wrote that "union with God led us first of all to union with the country people, all of them poor . . . It was the Gospel which had the most radical political effect on us." Enacting God's will meant "the establishment on earth of a just society, without exploited or exploiters, with all possessions shared, like the society in which the first Christians lived." Cardenal's *The Gospel in Solentiname* became a classic account of consciousness raising through Bible study.[2]

Student radicalism flourished at the Jesuit Central American University (UCA).[3] In 1969, Jesuits created the Educational Center for Agrarian Advancement (CEPA). Their widely circulated *Cristo, Campesino* pamphlets challenged Nicaragua's unequal land tenure and urged peasants to organize to defend their rights. As in Guatemala, the church sponsored *cursillos* that brought together campesinos from different communities. Radio schools reached into distant campesino homes. Christian Base Communities provided ongoing spaces for education, reflection, and organizing. Thousands of lay Delegates of the Word brought these ideas to remote communities, and many joined the Sandinistas. The Sandinista Rural Workers Association (ATC) "drew on local union traditions, the appeal of radical Christianity, and the growing understanding that the FSLN represented the only alternative, since the Guardia repressed peaceful forms of popular protest."[4]

In 1976, Carlos Mejía Godoy's "Misa Campesina" called on Jesus to "have solidarity with us, the oppressed." The same year, his "Cristo de Palacagüina" placed the story of the Christ's birth in rural Nicaragua. The infant's mother, María, hopes that he will follow in his father's footsteps and become a carpenter, but outraged with the contrast between the landlord's wealth and his parents' struggle, "the little kid thinks, tomorrow I want to be a guerrilla."

Even Nicaragua's Miguel Obando y Bravo, named archbishop of Managua in 1970 and cardinal in 1985, while a critic of the popular church, eventually raised his voice against the Somoza regime. After the revolution succeeded, he moved steadily rightward, refusing to condemn Contra atrocities and, in 1986, calling for increased US aid to the Contras. Other prominent church figures remained deeply committed Liberation Theologians and Sandinistas. Solentiname's Ernesto Cardenal served as Sandinista minister of culture. His brother, the Jesuit priest Fernando Cardenal, led the revolutionary literacy campaign. Maryknoll priest Miguel D'Escoto was foreign minister. Nicaragua offered the world a very different sort of Marxist revolution from those in Russia (1917), China (1949), and even Cuba (1959), one deeply inflected with popular Catholicism.

THE SANDINISTAS AND THE ARMED REBELLION

After a decade of underground and rural organizing, the FSLN burst into the national scene with several dramatic actions in the 1970s. In December 1974, a group attacked a Christmas party in Managua where Somoza ministers had gathered. One guest was killed in the scuffle, and the group took the others hostage, freeing them in exchange for the release of Sandinista political prisoners, publication of an FSLN communiqué, and a million dollars in cash.

The attack jolted the Somoza government and the United States out of their complacency. Somoza declared a state of siege that lasted for three years. The United States nervously began to pour resources into modernizing and reforming the Guardia. A revolution in Nicaragua threatened the United States' global Cold War order, and suddenly the Guardia had a new role to play and needed modern arms and techniques.

The Guardia's foot soldiers, like those in the Guatemalan army, were mostly poor campesino youth whose humiliating training indoctrinated them into a culture of cruelty. Their operations were small-scale and local: "centered on vice, quotidian violence, and criminal impunity." In the

1970s, the Guardia's long-standing "culture of masculine brutality" was mobilized in the interest of crushing the growing Sandinista movement. Within a few years, its mission "shifted . . . to one in which political violence and gross human rights violations would become its primary, daily function." But instead of crushing the revolutionary movement, the escalation of state terror alienated and disgusted growing numbers of Nicaraguans and increased the revolution's appeal.[5]

After 1975, the Sandinistas split into three tendencies. The Prolonged Popular War faction advocated continued rural organizing, while the proletario, with a more traditional Marxist orientation, wanted to focus on organizing urban workers. The terceristas believed the time had come for major urban insurrection and called for a broad national front including the anti-Somoza or "patriotic" bourgeoisie. In January 1978, well-known Conservative opposition journalist Pedro Joaquín Chamorro was murdered, apparently on Somoza's orders. His assassination galvanized the Sandinista bases, and also signaled a shift among the mainstream opposition to the regime. Traditional political parties and even the Chamber of Commerce began calling for Somoza's ouster. The Sandinistas recruited business and political leaders who formed the group of "The Twelve" (*los Doce*) in support of the uprising.

On August 22, 1978, a group of Sandinistas stormed the National Palace. In a recap of the Christmas 1974 events, they held over fifteen hundred Somocista government officials hostage until the regime agreed to free Sandinista political prisoners, grant them free passage out of the country, make concessions to striking health workers, and publish a Sandinista manifesto in the national press. On September 9, the FSLN called for mass insurrection in cities around the country. Guerrillas, supported by civilians, threw up barricades and burned government offices. The Guardia responded with massive bombardment and the invasion of rebel neighborhoods. The revolutionary stronghold of Estelí held out the longest.

The Sandinista retreat was followed by *Operación Limpieza*, with "full-scale massacres of unarmed men, women, and children" aimed at "draining the proverbial sea in which the guerrillas swam."[6] But the repression only caused more people, especially youth, to flee to the mountains and join the guerrillas. In March 1979, the three Sandinista tendencies united. In April, their incursion from Honduras into the northern Segovia mountains and the city of Estelí provoked a mass uprising in support there, again bloodily put down. Carlos Mejía Godoy captured the utopian mood of the insurrection in his homage to the city: "Estelí, you are an implacable guerrilla, indomitable, sweet, and ferocious combatant of love."

In June, the Sandinistas launched their final offensive, in cities around the country including the capital, Managua. A symbol of the rebellion became the concrete *adoquines* or tiles made by a Somoza-owned factory that paved the streets of Managua and other cities. Sandinista fighters tore them out of the streets to build barricades as the fighting intensified. After the victory, the new Sandinista newspaper took the revolutionary name *Barricada.* On July 17, 1979, Somoza fled the country, and on July 19, the Sandinistas arrived triumphantly in Managua as the remnants of the Guardia surrendered.

THE SANDINISTAS IN POWER

The new revolutionary government confronted the near-insurmountable poverty and chaos of their country with a utopian idealism, voluntarism, and passion. Nicaragua was very poor to begin with, made more so by the corruption and siphoning off of aid money by the Somoza regime. Out of its population of about 2.5 million, some 50,000 were killed and 100,000 wounded during the war.

The capital city was barely rebuilt after the 1972 earthquake, and infrastructure was further destroyed by government bombs and by neglect during the war. A decade after the earthquake, Managua "was still a wasteland . . . Only a few buildings had survived the quake . . . The rest of Managua was a random patchwork of unconnected neighborhoods scattered over a vast area of what had once been prairie and farmland."[7]

Upon taking power, the Sandinistas immediately set about making it clear that this was the beginning of a new, revolutionary society. They invited representatives of business and elite sectors to join them in a National Reconstruction government. The widespread outrage against Somoza allowed patriotic unity to transcend very different visions of what the new Nicaragua should look like, at least temporarily.

Managua's central plaza was rechristened the Plaza of the Revolution. Somoza was gone, and the Guardia and the Congress disbanded, and the Somocista Constitution of 1939 discarded. Somocista properties were confiscated, and names and imagery removed. In contrast to Somoza's human rights violations, the new Nicaragua would be a humane Nicaragua: the death penalty was abolished, and special tribunals set up to try former Guardia members and collaborators. Those found guilty were subject only to prison terms, while many were granted amnesty for low-level crimes. A new Sandinista People's Army and Sandinista Police were created.

Social programs and education took top priority, beginning with a literacy campaign modeled on that of the Cuban Revolution. Symbols of Somocista vice and corruption, including brothels and cantinas, were shut down. Massive redistribution of confiscated Somoza properties and mobilization of human resources and international aid dramatically increased access to social services and reduced inequality.

The gains of the first years of the revolution were close to astonishing. Land reforms transformed the agricultural structure and increased productivity, both in basic grains like corn, beans, and rice and in exports like sugar and coffee. The population was eating more—significantly more— and imports of basic grains dropped to close to zero. Public health campaigns reduced or eradicated malaria, polio, measles, and tetanus, and the infant mortality rate dropped by a third. Hundreds of new schools were built, and the literacy campaign cut illiteracy from over 50 percent to less than 15 percent.[8]

The country's material scarcity was compensated by the revolution's extraordinary mobilization, voluntarism, flexibility, and optimism. The Sandinista government combined a fierce commitment to radical mobilization and restructuring in the interest of the poor majority with a pluralistic desire to maintain friendly relations with the capitalist as well as the socialist world, and with Nicaragua's private sector.

Land Reform

A centerpiece of the revolutionary program was land reform. Rural poverty, unequal land distribution, exploitative working conditions on plantations, and landlessness characterized rural Nicaragua. The campesino struggle for land underlay the revolutionary movement in the countryside, and agricultural workers organized into the ATC formed a pillar of the insurrection. The ATC took a leading role in pressing for and carrying out the land reform, even as peasants' radical vision of reform came up against the Sandinista commitment to alliance with the patriotic bourgeoisie.

Immediately after the triumph of the revolution, lands belonging to the Somoza family and its allies were confiscated—some 20 percent of Nicaragua's farmland. Almost all of these were large, export-oriented enterprises dedicated to coffee, sugar, cotton, or cattle. Breaking them up, the Sandinistas believed, would cripple their much-needed export earnings. So instead of distributing the land to peasants, the Sandinistas turned them into state farms.

Landless campesinos continued to agitate for access to their own land. On the revolution's second anniversary in 1981, the government responded with an agrarian reform law that initiated a more profound change. The law made large landholdings subject to productive use. Large holdings that were abandoned, idle, and decapitalized would be confiscated for redistribution. The law was intended to address the increasingly urgent campesino demands for land, while encouraging production by reassuring large landowners that as long as they used their land productively, it would not be confiscated. About 4 million acres, 30 percent of the country's agricultural land, was affected by the new law.[9] A third reform in 1986 encompassed *all* nonproductive land, even that held by smaller owners. By 1988, large private landholdings had shrunk from covering 2.1 million hectares to 350,000 hectares.[10]

The agrarian reform was "a balancing act" that tried to maintain national unity by answering the demands of the campesinos for food, land, and rights, while also trying to keep export production flowing and large landowners loyal to the new national project. The Sandinistas needed export earnings to fund the redistribution and social programs the revolution had promised. And they needed the expertise and capital of large landowners to keep export production going.[11]

But the demands of the rural poor—for better working conditions, better wages, access to credit, land, machinery—seemed to come into direct conflict with what landed elite wanted. "One of the government's biggest headaches," wrote one study, "was trying to resist the demands of peasants in order not to threaten the well-off landowners."[12] Landlords wanted to charge high rents to peasants and sharecroppers and use their labor; peasants and sharecroppers wanted the land for themselves. Plantation workers wanted better wages and conditions; landowners did not want to have to pay more. The new state farms turned the Sandinistas into employers, who sometimes clashed with workers over issues like discipline, productivity, and wages. And when peasants got access to their own land, they didn't want to work in the export economy.

The Sandinista ATC represented agricultural workers. Campesinos who owned or wanted their own land soon formed the National Union of Farmers and Ranchers (UNAG) to push for different kinds of reform. In addition to land, they needed state aid in the form of credit, access to markets, and agricultural inputs, and they wanted to be able to sell their produce for high prices. The government had limited resources and wanted to keep food prices low for urban workers and the poor. The balancing act was a tough one.

Among the Sandinistas, "developmentalists" advocated the eventual incorporation of the peasantry into larger, state-run industrialized units, while "campesinists" supported small-scale subsistence farming. The first few years of the land reform tilted toward the developmentalists. Peasant resistance and demands led to a shift toward titling small plots to individual peasants over the course of the 1980s, but still privileging those who organized into cooperatives for access to credit, technical assistance, and machinery.

In the north of the country, many small and medium-sized coffee and cattle farmers had supported the revolution but hesitated when the land reform and the formation of state farms threatened their holdings or their independence. Some priests, evangelical churches, and the Contra forces being organized by the United States in Honduras bombarded them with propaganda claiming that the "communist" revolution wanted to take their lands. Some formed antigovernment militias that joined with the Contras.[13]

The Contras targeted the state farms, destroying infrastructure and killing and terrorizing workers. Labor shortages became chronic as workers retreated, fearing for their safety. Others took advantage of land they'd gotten through the reform to withdraw from plantation labor altogether. And the Sandinista military draft, implemented in response to Contra attacks, diverted even more campesinos from farm labor.[14]

The first five years of the land reform increased agricultural production, unlike most countries' experiences. The war, the US suspension and blocking of international loans and aid, and the 1985 US trade embargo all contributed to an economic collapse in the late 1980s. Even as land distribution accelerated after 1986, agricultural production decreased.

The Mixed Economy

Like previous Latin American revolutions, Nicaragua's confronted profound economic dilemmas. How could the government redistribute the country's resources in a world where the owners of land and businesses could simply take their money elsewhere? How could investors be convinced to support a redistribution—allowing their profits to be used for the benefit of the many—rather than a purely market logic of investing where they could make the most profit? And how could a revolution based on anti-imperialism and redistribution avoid provoking the wrath of the United States?

The Sandinista project called for a mixed economy—expanding the public sector while leaving much of the economy in private hands. Regulate and tax the private sector enough to expand government programs and services, but not so much that businesses stopped producing. Regulate and tax wealth, but not so much that the wealthy just decided to send their money abroad. Key sectors including banking, insurance, export, mining, and forestry were nationalized, but much of the economy remained in private hands.

The Sandinistas hoped that what they termed the "nationalist bourgeoisie" would be motivated by their commitment to their country and be willing to contribute more to society as a whole. One researcher wrote, "After talking with many [businessmen], I'm convinced that their fears for the future were what caused them to dig in their heels against the new government. Knowing that the countryside was alive with the demands of hundreds of thousands of people who had been ruthlessly exploited for generations, it was *la Revolución* that threatened them. And perhaps it was inevitable that at the beginning of a revolution the fears of the rich affect their behavior so that their fears are self-fulfilling."[15]

Wary Nicaraguan business leaders used their Permanent Council for Private Enterprise (COSEP) to advocate for their interests. COSEP became a major platform of opposition and straddled an uneasy space between loyal opposition to the Sandinista government and alliance with foreign (US) aggression against Nicaragua. After Reagan's election, COSEP moved more firmly into alliance with those seeking to undermine and overthrow the government.

Instead of investing in keeping production going, many land and business owners began a process of decapitalization. They sold their machinery, let their workers go, and sent their money abroad where they felt more confident that it would not be taxed or requisitioned. When the Sandinistas tried to incentivize them to stay, and keep producing and investing, they sometimes accepted the government loans and credits and left anyway. "A vicious circle of self-fulfilling prophecies was at work. The more landowners decapitalized, the more they were denounced by work-ers and by the government, and the more insecure all landowners felt (and were). Thus the circle starts again, but this time with more people."[16]

There were contradictions in the socialized government sector, too. The new state farms that produced crops for export had to compete in a capitalist world market in which other poor countries were also selling these products. If Nicaragua raised wages and improved working condi-tions, how could its products compete on the world market? If it sold its products cheaply, how could it bring in the revenue it needed to pay its workers a decent wage and provide basic services?

The government and a large majority (though not all) of Nicara-guans wanted the country to produce more, export more, and to distrib-ute better. But it proved very, very hard to do all these things at the same time. By bending over backward to promote the mixed economy and not alienate large producers, the government had even less to redistribute to the poor.

No matter how much the government tried to reassure the private sector, it couldn't guarantee that plantation and business owners could keep making the profits they made before the revolution—or that they could make elsewhere. It couldn't guarantee professionals they could keep making the same salaries and enjoying the same privileges. Those profits, salaries, and privileges had been based on a system that exploited the poor for the benefit of the rich, and the whole point of the revolution was to change that system and provide more for the poor. Some members of the elite were willing to sacrifice their privilege for the cause of build-ing a more just and equal society. But not all were.

Once the United States began to take decisive action to overthrow the revolution, more of the landed and moneyed sectors decided to throw their lot in with the counterrevolution. Nicaragua lost the US aid and World Bank loans that the economy had depended on. Farm machinery couldn't be repaired; fertilizers couldn't be purchased. Much worse, once the United States began to organize and fund the Contra war, more and more of the country's resources had to be devoted to defense, which meant even less to fulfill the promises of the revolution to make people's lives better.

Food for the People

Another aspect of the balancing act of the mixed economy was the cre-ation of ENABAS, the National Basic Foods Corporation, to create a kind of public option to work alongside the free market in food provision. ENABAS would stimulate peasant production of basic grains by guaranteeing farmers that it would purchase supplies at fair prices, and would sell or distribute them at subsidized prices. "Three years' experience has raised deep doubts whether the free market can serve the poor majority, at least in times of scarcity," concluded one study. "It has also shown how difficult it is for a new government to set up an efficient, low cost alternative system."[17] Indeed, many peasants resented what they perceived as forced sales to ENABAS.[18]

"Nicaragua's economy was heavily based on what development specialists call 'micro-businesses,' the mechanics, knife sharpeners, bakers, seamstresses, and others who earn their livelihood from day to day, working out of their homes or tiny shops," explained another observer. "Sandinista leaders viewed the existing system of food production in Nicaragua as anarchic, and so it was. But by trying to transform it so completely and so suddenly . . . the result was predictable. All over the country, many peasants decided that farming was no longer a good business, and abandoned the land altogether. In Managua and other cities, most of them found work as middlemen or market vendors, joining the network of speculators and hoarders who were steadily pushing prices higher and making life more and more difficult for everyone."[19]

The Atlantic Coast

The history of Nicaragua's Atlantic coast differed from the rest of the country's. Little Spanish presence and little economic potential meant that the people there were not truly colonized, but rather developed trade relations with the British Caribbean, and were ruled as a British protectorate during much of the nineteenth century. In the twentieth century, US companies flooded the region to export hardwoods, seafood, and bananas, bringing a sort of prosperity and an influx of US consumer goods. The Indigenous Miskitu and smaller Sumo (or Mayangna) and Rama populations in the north coast region were joined by Caribbean migrants including Garifuna (descendants of African and Caribbean Indigenous who were deported to Central America by the British) and Creole (Afro-descendants from the British Caribbean) peoples. German and then US Moravian missionaries formed the most important church presence.

The United States maintained a strong presence in Miskitia even after US Marines withdrew from Nicaragua in the 1930s. The Moravians

> acted quickly to bring their Miskitu worshippers into the circle of US
> influence. Missionaries—other Protestants in addition to the Mora-
> vians, as well as US Catholic orders—poured into the region, bring-
> ing US consumer goods with them. By 1961, the United States was
> so confident of its position there that it used Miskitia as the launch-
> ing point for the failed Bay of Pigs invasion of Cuba. After that failed
> mission, the United States sent in the Peace Corps, and set up a local
> radio station to teach the natives about the evils of communism, the
> horrors of Cuba and, of course, the values of that wonderland, the
> United States. The counterinsurgency against the Sandinistas began
> in the Miskitia even before they came to power.[20]

Coastal peoples participated little in the Sandinista uprising. Sandinista leaders shared a derogatory image of the coast as backward and
in need of development. The Sandinistas were profoundly nationalist and
anti-imperialist. For the Miskitu, ethnic militancy and "Anglo affinity"—
positive memories associating British and US influence with prosperity and autonomy from the national government—alienated them from
both elements of the revolution.[21] These same factors made the Sandinistas view coastal peoples with suspicion.

Sandinista state expansion in the coast both raised expectations and
"nettled incipient indigenous and Afro-Nicaraguan rights movements"
there.[22] Where Sandinista literacy, health, and agrarian reform initiatives
were organically connected to popular movements in much of the Pacific
region, in the Atlantic, Sandinista projects, cadres, and soldiers were perceived as unwanted "Spanish" intruders.

The local organization Miskitu Sumu, Rama and Sandinistas Working Together (MISURASATA) played an uneasy role in trying to participate in revolutionary initiatives while pressing for local interests and
identity. MISURASATA's campaigns ranged from demanding literacy in
Miskitu and English rather than Spanish, to seeking self-determination
and autonomy. After the Sandinistas jailed a MISURASATA leader, he
fled across the border to Honduras to join the CIA-sponsored Contra
army forming there. Others soon followed him.

The United States was able to take advantage of fault lines and contradictions everywhere in Nicaragua, but particularly on the coast with its history of English and US influence. The region became a major front for the Contra war. From Honduras, the Contras broadcast anti-Sandinista radio and conducted military raids into Nicaragua, encouraging others to join them.

As the Reagan administration armed and trained the Miskitu in Honduras to attack Nicaragua, Reagan portrayed the United States, improbably, as the defender of Indigenous people. Contrary to Reagan's claims, "most of the U.S.-financed action was aimed at destroying the economic infrastructure and impeding people from resuming their normal lives," reported anthropologist Martin Diskin.[23]

Sandinista responses poured gasoline on the fire. A mass forced relocation took some ten thousand Miskitu from the Río Coco along the Honduran border into a new settlement farther south, ominously named Tasba Pri (Free Land). The government claimed it was removing a civilian population from a war zone and protecting its sovereignty and its revolution. On the ground and in the press, it looked more like removal to a concentration camp. Twenty thousand Miskitu instead fled to join the refugees in Honduras; others complied with the relocation but turned even more firmly against the revolution.[24] Between 1981 and 1984, the counterrevolution enjoyed "nearly unanimous support" among the coastal population.[25]

Although the conditions in the Tasba Pri camps were, according to activist Roxanne Dunbar-Ortiz after a visit in early 1983, often materially better than in their villages of origin, the refugees "longed for their ancestral villages and they missed their neighbors and relatives who had fled across the river to Honduras when the fighting began . . . As river people, with many from areas near the Caribbean, they missed fishing and the freedom of movement it allowed."[26]

In 1984, the Sandinista government began negotiations with the various factions and populations on the coast and, in 1987, signed a new law granting autonomy to the region. The change was "in part auto-critique and visionary advance in black and indigenous rights, but in part also precocious experiment in multiculturalism as containment."[27]

Like the shifts in the land reform policy in the mid-1980s, the Sandinistas' changing policy toward the Atlantic coast evolved in response to popular pressure as well as in response to the Contra war. To the revolution's supporters, these changes showed Sandinista pragmatism, responsiveness, and flexibility. To the United States, they showed that the war was pushing Nicaragua up against the wall and should be escalated.

GENDER AND REVOLUTION

Nicaragua's revolution, like others in Central America, was led mostly by men, although it mobilized and created opportunities for many women. Some revolutionaries argued that the revolution must come first and women's rights later. Problems of poverty, landlessness, exploitation, and imperialism transcended gender, and men and women must unite to fight against the common enemies: Somoza and US imperialism, and for common goals of land reform, health care, and education. "Bourgeois" or First World feminism that put women's rights before social change would only divide and weaken revolutions. Only through social revolution could women's rights truly be achieved.

But through the 1970s and '80s, Latin American women also developed a struggle against patriarchy and for women's rights within the revolutionary left, analyzing the oppression of poor, working-class, and Indigenous women as a feminist struggle.[28] The personal, they argued, was very much political.

Patriarchy and abuse in the home expressed the culture and ills of the larger society and the world. Poor Nicaraguan men had little capacity to fulfill idealized male roles of providing for the family. Alcohol abuse, domestic violence, and abandonment all responded to the contradictions between patriarchal ideas of male dominance and structural obstacles to men's economic and social stability. Nicaragua was one of the most violent countries in the world and had the highest rates of both violence and alcoholism in Central America.[29]

The Somoza regime and its Guardia wove itself into the fabric of cities and towns around Nicaragua through the gendered control of vice: alcohol, gambling, prostitution. It was profitable for the regime, but it was also a form of social control. The Guardia "cunningly converted men from Nicaragua's most dispossessed social groups into its own violently loyal enforcers" through its "internal culture: an exaggerated personal loyalty to the Somozas and the promise of social mobility, an aggressive masculine sociability patterned around hard drinking, vice, and interpersonal violence, and a visceral anti-communist ideology."[30]

The Sandinistas challenged this culture with moral appeals also framed in gendered terms. By building on Che Guevara's concept of the "new man," they offered a version of masculinity that rejected drinking, gambling, domestic violence, and family abandonment. Instead of this "dysfunctional male sociability," the Sandinistas urged "solidarity, egalitarianism, and sacrifice." The Sandinistas' approach to gender rights, like the rest of their ideology, stretched and expanded beyond "the classic stereotype of a left-wing insurgency" to incorporate grassroots activists influenced by Catholic Liberation Theology, artisans' labor movements, and campesino women.[31]

Women also revolutionized traditional female roles like motherhood. Mothers in Nicaragua, like those in Argentina and elsewhere, argued that as women and mothers, they were being crushed by dictatorships' mass repression, torture, disappearance, and murder of their children.[32] Women took advantage of their supposedly sacrosanct cultural position to take clandestine or open political action and possibly evade the repression that their male counterparts might provoke.

The FSLN created a women's mass organization, the Association of Women Facing the Nation's Problems (AMPRONAC) in 1977 during the insurrection, directly subordinate to the FSLN. The organization later changed its name to the Luisa Amanda Espinoza Women's Association (AMNLAE), after the first female FSLN fighter to die in combat. Like other mass organizations, AMNLAE maintained an uneasy balance between representing women to the FSLN and representing the FSLN to women.

Revolutionary transformations in health, education, land distribution, and labor rights dramatically changed life for poor women. Women's consciousness was revolutionized through participation in Christian Base Communities and through the larger transformations in revolutionary consciousness. In many areas, the Sandinista relationship with Liberation Theology and the popular church made it *more* revolutionary than other revolutions. As far as reproductive rights, and especially abortion, the relationship prevented the Sandinistas from enacting the kind of reforms that greatly expanded reproductive rights in revolutionary Cuba.

THE CONTRA WAR

The US decision to destroy Nicaragua's revolutionary experiment undermined Sandinista successes and exacerbated their weaknesses. Outrage against US aggression also spurred support for Nicaragua's revolution at home and abroad.

The CIA's war on the Sandinistas was fought on multiple fronts. The Contra army had its origins among elites and ex-Guardia organized, trained, and armed by the CIA in Miami and Honduras into the Nicaraguan Democratic Forces (FDN). In Costa Rica to the south, the agency enjoyed a fraught relationship with former Sandinista Edén Pastora, who accepted aid but not orders. In the northeast, the CIA created a Miskitu force on the border with Honduras. In the United States, it launched a propaganda offensive.

By early 1982, the United States had set up military camps in Honduras and was arming and training commandos there and in Florida to attack Nicaragua. While the US government publicly claimed that the purpose was to halt Nicaraguan arms shipments to the rebels in El Salvador, as journalist Stephen Kinzer wrote, this was "an argument no sentient observer could honestly have believed . . . By accepting [CIA director William] Casey's outlandish rationale with a figurative wink, Congress gave its tacit approval to the contra project."[33] Peasants and coffee workers fled the fertile northern hills, devastating harvests there.

"Although unable to capture or hold any sizeable town or populated area, the contras have inflicted numerous casualties and caused substantial damage to the Nicaraguan economy," a 1985 investigation reported. Exhaustively vetted and fact-checked, the report interviewed over a hundred survivors of twenty-eight different Contra attacks. "The contras," the report concluded, "are directing their attacks against civilian targets—such as workers in the northern provinces attempting to harvest the coffee crop," and "these attacks have resulted in assassination, torture, rape, kidnapping and mutilation of civilians."[34]

The report described a "distinct pattern" in which the Contras assaulted "purely civilian targets resulting in the killing of unarmed men, women, children and the elderly." Attacks included "premeditated acts of brutality including rape, beatings, mutilation and torture," individual and mass acts of kidnapping especially in the Miskitu region "for the purpose of forced recruitment . . . and the creation of a hostage refugee population in Honduras," attacks aimed at "economic and social targets such as farms, cooperatives, food storage facilities and health centers, including a particular effort to disrupt coffee harvests," and attacks on religious leaders.[35]

When Pope John Paul II visited Nicaragua in early 1983, the Sandinistas hoped that he would acknowledge and denounce the war being waged against their country. He made it clear that he would not. He then went further and declared his support for Nicaragua's bishops in their conflict with the popular church, and openly criticized the religious who served in the Sandinista government. Protesters in the crowd began to chant and make catcalls. Rather than reconciliation, the events surrounding his visit only deepened divisions.

The war forced the Sandinistas to impose what became their most unpopular measure yet—a military draft—in late 1983. The United States had just invaded neighboring Grenada, and Contra attacks from Honduras were devastating agriculture and society in the north of the country. Nicaragua's bishops spoke out against the draft, claiming that the Sandinistas had turned the army into "an instrument of forced political indoctrination."[36]

By 1983, the Contras, flush and confident with US aid, "were often better equipped and supplied than their Sandinista Army counterparts." They "ranged over 34,000 square kilometers of Nicaragua's interior and within this territory they disrupted agricultural production, road traffic, and services to the population. They also established extensive networks of peasant collaborators in a number of mountain communities to provide them with food, shelter, and information." For many young men, the choice was not whether to take up arms, but merely for which army.[37]

Why Did Peasants Join the Contras?

Although the United States bears responsibility for organizing, training, and funding the Contra war against Nicaragua, many of the foot soldiers had their own reasons for joining. Besides the Atlantic coast region, the Contras successfully recruited among campesinos in the northern highlands. In some areas, "up to one fifth of young [army] recruits deserted to go into hiding or join the contras."[38] "I met many contra fighters during the course of the war," wrote one journalist, "and was always struck by how much they resembled Sandinista fighters. Both armies were made up of young boys, almost exclusively from the poorest social classes."[39] Why did some peasants oppose the revolution and decide to join a foreign-sponsored force invading their country?

Sandinista mobilization and the insurrection were concentrated in the urban, central, and Pacific regions of Nicaragua. Small and landless campesinos and urban youth and workers formed a core of the revolution's constituency and its plans for economic development, health, education, and land reform. Many of them had a history of experience in popular organizing in unions and Christian Base Communities.

In the highlands to the north and the Atlantic region to the east, more autonomous peoples and cultures had very different histories. Ethnic, regional, and patron-client relations prevailed over the kinds of class and community organizing that nourished Sandinista loyalty in the more densely populated Pacific. The incoming Sandinista government knew little about local conditions. Ninety-seven percent of the some twenty thousand Contra fighters who demobilized in 1990 came from these two regions, even though two-thirds of Nicaragua's population lives in the country's Pacific coastal departments.[40]

One area of high Contra support was the lightly populated and remote region of Quilalí in the eastern Segovias that had been one of the strongholds of Sandino's rebellion in the 1920s. The area attracted cattle ranchers and subsistence peasant colonists in the 1950s and '60s, and had developed a frontier culture with little state influence, aid, or control.[41] By the mid-1970s, the population had mushroomed.

The region differed from Pacific Nicaragua in both the larger proportion of rich and middle-class peasants, and the stronger patron-client relationships that tied the poor to the haciendas where they worked. In the mountains, "Peasants continued to view their municipality as a harmonious zone of agricultural richness, where there was ample room for all, wealthy and poor. Successful landowners . . . were not necessarily a threat, but rather a potential source of assistance and employment, as well as a model to be emulated."[42]

As one peasant explained, "Here the campesino knew nothing about strikes. He came [to Quilalí] to work however he could. There were no organizations or unions. Those things didn't exist. The campesino didn't have anywhere to look for support and didn't protest. He was submissive. It wasn't like the campesinos on the Pacific coast. There were no land takeovers in Quilalí."[43]

When the FSLN first made its appearance in Quilalí in the mid-1970s, it attracted Conservative and other landowners who resented the closed and personalist Somoza system. To the extent that poor peasants joined, it was more in alliance with these patrons than in opposition to landed elites.[44] Absent radical peasant organizing, Quilalí and other remote rural zones were also spared the growing repression and bombardment that forged Sandinista identity and support in the Pacific during the late 1970s.

As in Miskitia, revolutionary government projects were not always welcomed in Quilalí. They were brought by outsiders and disrupted local structures and systems. Both landlords and those who worked for or rented land from them resented the land reform that expropriated several large estates and created state farms. Some soon took up arms against the government, initially autonomously from the US-sponsored ex-Guardia in Honduras, but eventually linking with them.

In the words of a Sandinista from the capital, "The people here in the north have a different mentality. The soldiers say this northern campesino is an Indian [*indio*]. These are true campesinos, who have never even been to school. They've never even been to Managua!"[45]

Still, poor peasants in Quilalí had a "more complex and contradictory" relationship to the revolution than did the large landholders in the region. "Poor peasants were both drawn to certain aspects of the FSLN program such as land reform, and distanced from Sandinismo by economic and ideological dependence on elites, doubts about the model's viability, and frustrated expectations of the revolution," one study concludes.[46]

Contra attacks on what were elsewhere popular government projects like schools and health clinics meant that they could not function effectively in the region, further dissipating potential support for the revolution. Even when the Sandinistas retreated from the state farm model after 1982 and offered land in cooperatives, these "became virtual islands of Sandinista support in a countryside under the hegemonic influence of the counterrevolution." Thus, "from 1983 onward virtually the only Sandinista presence in the mountains would be a military one."[47] In 1985, the army went further and forcibly displaced and evacuated much of the civilian population to the more accessible river valleys, turning the region into a free-fire zone.

THE MID-1980S: A TURNING POINT?

The mid-1980s brought a series of significant changes in direction to the beleaguered revolution: greater dependence on the USSR; a shift in land reform away from state farms toward giving land directly to small farmers; negotiations with MISURASATA and other Miskitu groups on the

Atlantic coast; and internationally observed elections to choose Nicaragua's political leaders.

As the Contra war and associated "psychological operations" (aimed at infiltrating and influencing local organizations) escalated and the United States blocked trade with and international aid and loans to Nicaragua, the Sandinistas had no choice but to rely more on the socialist bloc. They also became more suspicious of dissent and more insistent on unity. US propaganda claimed that Nicaragua was a Soviet puppet, that its redistributive policies would destroy the country's economy, that it was mobilizing a formidable army and repressing independent organizations, the private sector, and freedom of speech. US policies then set out to force the Sandinistas to do all of those things.

Still, in early 1984, the Sandinistas announced that they would hold elections in November. Although the government agreed to implement a number of reforms, including relaxing press censorship and guaranteeing the rights of opposition candidates, the most important of the candidates pulled out before the election took place. International observers deemed the elections remarkably fair and open. Some 75 percent of the eligible population voted, and Sandinista leader Daniel Ortega won with over 60 percent of the vote.

In the Atlantic coast, the government shifted gears fairly drastically and entered into negotiations with MISURASATA. By 1985, the Sandinista leadership acknowledged the terrible effects that forced displacement had had on the Miskitu and began referring to Nicaragua as a "multi-ethnic nation," acknowledging the "just demands of the coast" and beginning a process of establishing regional autonomy there.[48] The resettled Miskitu communities were allowed to return to their river communities.

The Contra war in the north only worsened. There, too, the Sandinistas acknowledged that their own policies had contributed to rural disenchantment. At the end of 1984, state farms accounted for 50 percent of the lands taken in the agrarian reform, and cooperatives, 28 percent. The amount of land available to small farmers had barely changed.[49] The war contributed to a major reorientation of the agrarian reform toward granting land to small farmers and legalizing titles.[50]

INFLATION AND AUSTERITY

The war forced the Sandinistas to devote more and more of their national budget to defense. The military absorbed economic resources that were desperately needed for health, education, and agricultural production, while the Contras explicitly attacked these Sandinista projects. The thirty thousand Nicaraguans killed in the Contra war, on top of the fifty thousand killed during the struggle against Somoza, meant that one out of thirty-eight Nicaraguans died violently during more than a decade of war. Virtually every Nicaraguan had family members, friends, or acquaintances who lost their lives to the violence.[51] The idea that families must keep sacrificing their sons and daughters to the military draft was a bitter pill to swallow.

The combined effects of the war, social spending and subsidies, and decreased production led to rampant inflation by the late 1980s. The project of social transformation had been ground down to a project of mere survival, under the slogan "Everything for the fighters."[52]

The value of the country's currency, the *córdoba*, sank to practically nothing. In 1988, the government made a major economic U-turn by issuing a new córdoba that constituted a thousand-fold devaluation and implementing drastic austerity measures.

This meant that the jobs, credit, schools, clinics, and social services that defined the revolution were all cut back. "The revolution was supposed to make things better for the common people," a Nicaraguan friend told me mournfully in early 1988. "But things are worse."

On the battlefield, the Contras were defeated by the end of the 1980s. But the larger US goal, of preventing Nicaragua from becoming "the threat of a good example" that could encourage other poor Latin Americans to organize for profound social change had in some ways succeeded. "The most significant development in Nicaragua since 1985 has been the country's accelerating economic collapse," wrote Oxfam grimly in 1989. "After the years of suffering they have inflicted, the *Contras* no longer represent a credible fighting force. The war looks set to fizzle out once the remaining *Contras* are finally starved of U.S. government funding. But the damage has already been done. The spiraling indirect costs of the war have devastated Nicaragua's economy and with it all hopes of improving the living standards of the poor majority."[53]

PEACE?

We've seen how the United States undermined the Contadora peace process and prodded Costa Rican president Óscar Arias to propose a more acceptable alternative. In August 1987, Nicaragua and the other

Central American countries signed the Esquipulas Agreement, calling for all Central American governments to seek negotiated peace, prohibit the use of their territory by irregular forces, and end outside aid to these forces.

Despite its supposed support for the plan, the Reagan administration also immediately declared its intention to undermine it. Reagan announced that he was "totally committed to the democratic resistance, the freedom fighters." A month later, he made a new proposal to Congress for $270 million in funding for the Contras.[54] Nevertheless a few months later, the Sandinista government entered into negotiations with Contra leaders in Sapoá, signing an agreement in March 1988 to end hostilities while a definitive cease-fire was worked out.

THE 1990 ELECTION

The Sandinistas lost the next national election, held in February 1990, receiving 41 percent of the vote to the opposition's 55 percent. The opposition had coalesced into the Unión Nacional Opositora or UNO, around presidential candidate Violeta Barrios de Chamorro. It was the first time in Nicaraguan history that one elected president was replaced by another. Although the Sandinista electoral loss could be seen as a repudiation of the revolution that was so closely identified with the party, in some ways the process embodied the revolution's very success in creating democratic institutions that transcended the party.

Chamorro presented herself as the candidate of peace, promising to end both the war and the draft. Her own family symbolized this. She was the widow of *La Prensa* editor Pedro Joaquín Chamorro, whose assassination in 1978 was one of the sparks mobilizing the successful last stage of the revolution. She was a member of the original revolutionary junta. Her own family was politically heterogeneous: two of her sons edited the country's two independent newspapers, the anti-Sandinista *La Prensa* and the pro-Sandinista *El Nuevo Diario*.

One analysis of the election results suggested that a significant number of voters were either strongly pro-Sandinista or strongly anti-Sandinista, and their loyalty remained firm from 1984 to 1990. A middle or swing group, though, was exhausted and disillusioned by the war and the austerity. Daniel Ortega's campaign slogan, "*Todo será mejor* [everything will be better]," was unconvincing to many. While it acknowledged just how bad things had gotten, it inspired little confidence in his prediction. The fact that the United States vowed that only a Sandinista defeat would lead it to end its embargo on the country and the Contra war certainly swayed some voters.

For many voters, it felt like the choice was between Sandinista austerity and war, or Chamorro's austerity with peace.

Much of the country was silent and in shock the day after the election. Preelection polls had shown the Sandinistas solidly ahead. Some suggested Chamorro voters were ashamed to admit to pollsters that they intended to vote for her.[55]

The Sandinista electoral loss was followed by what came to be known as the *piñata* in which outgoing government officials grasped for whatever favors and riches their declining power enabled. One author called it "the swiftest transfer of goods in national history: farms, houses, buildings, factories, vehicles, tractors, small islands and millions of dollars in cash were taken from the state and given to the Sandinista elite." This "new class of Sandinista capitalists" became a powerful interest group of their own.[56] But others emphasize that the "piñata laws" also granted legal title to tens of thousands of poor Nicaraguans who had received land and houses during the revolution's agrarian and urban reforms.[57]

Chamorro promised reconciliation. With the help of the United Nations and the OAS, some 22,000 Contra fighters demobilized and turned in their weapons. She also ended the draft and shrank the army from 60,000 in 1989 to 15,500 in 1993.[58]

Reintegration was challenging in a country devastated by war and plagued by poverty and lack of resources. Within a year, some demobilized Contra fighters emerged again as the "recontras." Some twenty-four thousand rearmed over the course of the early 1990s.[59] Meanwhile some demobilized Sandinistas rearmed as "re-compas" (meaning "again compañeros" or comrades). Some on both sides were disillusioned with their former leaders who seemed to come out of the war doing just fine, even as austerity deepened and Sandinista social programs were dismantled. In some cases, they found that their common interests outweighed their political differences. Joined together as "rejuntos" or "revueltos," they demanded land. One Sandinista leader commented that the recontras had in fact taken up the Sandinista political program: "the contras are out there, demanding their rights as peasants."[60] Others took up arms as independent gangs or bandits. In the northern mountains, levels of violence remained high in the 1990s.

The Chamorro government responded to some of their demands. A "new distribution of land, in significant if not enormous quantities, was an exceptional policy within Central America" in the 1990s. Access to land for many of the demobilized helped Nicaragua avoid the spike in organized crime and violence that afflicted other Central American countries during that decade. Still, many campesinos and ex-combatants lost their lands to large investors.[61]

Is it possible for a small, poor, Third World country to carry out a revolution in the interests of its poor majority when the world's most powerful country, the United States, remains intent on preventing any threats to its political and economic hegemony? The examples of Guatemala in the 1950s and Nicaragua in the 1980s suggest that the odds against it are steep.[62]

CHAPTER 6

EL SALVADOR

Si Nicaragua Venció, ¡El Salvador Vencerá!

Guatemala's revolution was crushed by terror in the decades after 1954; Nicaragua's triumphed in 1979. Many supporters of revolution in El Salvador believed that "[i]f Nicaragua triumphed, El Salvador will triumph!" El Salvador's strong organizational culture and popular movements sustained the Farbundo Martí National Liberation Front (FMLN) guerrilla organization, but there was no triumph. Instead, the country remained locked in a bitter civil war. The United States pursued a dual counterinsurgency strategy of reform and repression, in alliance with an oligarchy composed of a far-right traditional agrarian elite, and a moderate right modernizing sector. Neither repression nor reform succeeded in crushing or undermining the popular and guerrilla movements, which forced the government to the negotiating table at the end of the 1980s.

El Salvador is the smallest of the Central American countries and the most densely populated. Unlike the other countries, which span the isthmus from Atlantic to Pacific, and where the eastern regions have remained fairly lightly populated up to the present, El Salvador huddles on the Pacific coast. This meant that there were no US banana companies in El Salvador, and the country's oligarchy followed a more locally led path to dependent development prior to World War II. The tightly knit group became known as the "14 Families," although it was actually more like 250 families or clans.

The coffee revolution in the early century turned many Indigenous peasants into tenants and workers. When the country implemented the first rural minimum wage in 1965, coffee planters responded by simply expelling peasants from their plantations. The cotton, sugar, and cattle revolutions after World War II concentrated more fertile land in the hands of the oligarchy and further squeezed El Salvador's peasants, as did population growth. The number of landless peasants mushroomed from thirty thousand in 1961 to over one hundred thousand in 1971.[1]

Coffee was concentrated in western El Salvador, sugar on the low hills in the center, and cotton along the southern coast. In these fertile regions, displaced campesinos scraped out a living on the margins of the plantations. Some left for the infertile and mountainous north and east along the border with Honduras. Many who settled there migrated seasonally to work on the plantations.

Other Salvadorans crossed the border to Honduras to work or to get access to a small plot of land to farm or moved to the cities, making El Salvador more urban than its neighbors. Still, in the 1960s, approximately 60 percent of El Salvador's people lived in rural areas. Economic and political power was highly concentrated nationally as well as at the local level where village landowners and elites reigned.

TWO SIDES OF COUNTERINSURGENCY

In the decade after the Cuban Revolution, El Salvador went through a period of political opening and reform. Young army officers, modernizing elites, the United States, and the Catholic Church hoped to break the oligarchy's iron grip on politics and the countryside and mitigate the inequalities that had brought revolutionary uprisings in Guatemala and Cuba.

While political reform faltered in Guatemala and Nicaragua, El Salvador became its showcase. The Alliance for Progress and the Catholic Church supported the creation of the Christian Democratic Party as a moderate reformist alternative to oligarchic rule. In 1964, party founder and leader José Napoleón Duarte was elected mayor of San Salvador, and in 1968 the party won local elections in hundreds of municipalities around the country. Duarte gained popularity as mayor for his attention to infrastructure and services in poor neighborhoods and shantytowns.

The Central American Common Market formed in 1960 brought new industries aimed at export in the region. US companies like Maidenform and Texas Instruments established the first export processing industries in El Salvador, taking advantage of the low cost of labor and other incentives.[2] Beef and cotton exports boomed, and a new free-trade zones with no taxes or unions helped the maquiladora industry grow.

The changes created more opportunities for the modernizing faction of the oligarchy tied to new industries and the burgeoning financial sector. As their interests became more diversified and international, they came to accept the need for rural reform and, within limits, democratization. Those tied to the older agro-export economy relied on the far right and the military to maintain iron control over their rural labor force and saw all reform as threatening. This split mirrored the two approaches to counterinsurgency coming from US Cold War policy. Would repression or reform best avert revolution? What the reformers failed to predict was that the reforms themselves could foster new revolutionary currents.

Reform and Popular Mobilization

Historically, El Salvador's rural poor were described as "fatally resigned to poverty and misery . . . venerating both civil and military authority, and with little potential for class consciousness." Post-WWII expansion of export agriculture weakened traditional patron-client and village ties by bringing land loss, wage labor, and migration.[3]

One analyst described the country's campesinos as "neither entirely landless nor purely wage laborers nor all renters but some combination of the three. What they share is the common experience of extreme poverty closely tied to the behavior of landowners as employers, landlords, expropriators, or holders of idle lands. That is, the semi-proletariat's experience of poverty is visibly tied to the action of human agents of the landowning class and hence easily understood politically in terms of exploitation."[4]

These changes made peasants fertile ground for the reformers who moved into the countryside in the 1960s and '70s, including from AIFLD, the Christian Democrats, and the Catholic Church. The consciousness-raising, cooperative, and union movements they promoted "were eventually led by rural people themselves, who adapted the political categories of ideologues to fit their local circumstances."[5]

The 1932 *matanza* cast a long pall over any kind of organizing in the coffee regions of western El Salvador. Elsewhere, some of the new outside forces filtering into the countryside in the 1960s contributed to the creation of peasant leagues and the Salvadoran Christian Peasants Federation (FECCAS), under the umbrella of the new Christian Democratic Party, and the more radical but still Catholic-inspired Union of

Rural Workers (UTC). Unions in the country's new industries, along with the radical teachers' union ANDES and new federations, began to make stronger demands for better wages and working conditions.

The Darker Side of Counterinsurgency

The burgeoning popular movements brought on the darker side of what one author described as "counterinsurgency without insurgency . . . at a time when no armed insurgency had yet emerged in the country." Even while pushing for reform, the United States also supported the far right's construction of "a massive counterinsurgency apparatus" that "systematically persecuted activists, public intellectuals, and members of independent political parties, as well as priests and laypeople associated with the progressive sector of the Catholic Church. In doing so, the counterinsurgency created 'an internal enemy' as radicalized activists and intellectuals joined or supported the armed insurgent groups."[6] The principal US ally in the counterinsurgency campaign was the Salvadoran military, with its long-standing institutional and personal commitment to the oligarchy and to maintaining its dominance in the countryside.

"The origins of the civil war in El Salvador are virtually unintelligible without a careful examination of the reverberations of U.S. Cold War anti-communism and counterinsurgency in that country during the three decades that preceded the conflict," writes Joaquín Chávez. US anti-communism converged with "the longstanding antidemocratic and genocidal trajectory of the Salvadoran elites" who adopted US national security doctrine. "The oligarchic military regime framed the leaders of the teachers' union, peasant organizations, and progressive Catholic priests as the 'internal enemy' in an effort to justify state repression against the emerging social movements, a counterinsurgency policy that motivated many activists to join or support the insurgency."[7]

PROJECTING TENSIONS OUTWARD: THE "SOCCER WAR"

In 1969, domestic tensions were projected outward as El Salvador and Honduras exploded into what was popularly known as the "soccer war." Dispute over a soccer match, of course, was just the spark that lit the tinder. Struggles over unequal economic development and peasant access to land and rights were turned, for a time, into xenophobic nationalism.

As agricultural modernization uprooted El Salvador's peasants, some three hundred thousand Salvadorans migrated across the border into

Honduras, where land was more accessible. One in eight people in Honduras was an immigrant from El Salvador.[8]

It wasn't just population density or even population growth that caused land scarcity in El Salvador: it was the fact that land was taken out of the hands of small, subsistence farmers and taken over by large landholders producing coffee, and later cotton and sugar, for export. The first exodus of small farmers, to the capital, the northern frontier, and across the border to Honduras, began when they lost their lands to coffee plantations at the beginning of the twentieth century. The second exodus came after World War II when the new export agriculture pushed a new wave of farmers into landlessness.

The first Salvadoran migrants to Honduras were recruited by US banana and mining companies in the early twentieth century. After a major banana workers' strike in 1954, Honduran law "nationalized" the labor force and prohibited the importation of migrant workers. Still, some 30 percent of Honduran banana workers hailed from El Salvador well into the 1960s.[9]

As export agriculture in Honduras expanded, Salvadoran-origin peasants there joined with their local counterparts to defend their lands. As in 1954, the Honduran government and landowners found Salvadoran "foreigners" an easy scapegoat to distract attention from the powerful agents that controlled the economy and began evicting Salvadoran peasants.

But El Salvador's landed elites also saw a potential influx of radicalized peasants as a threat, and El Salvador responded by closing its border and then invading Honduras. The war ended with an OAS-negotiated cease-fire just four days later.

The border area was a kind of zone of refuge, with little attraction for the old or new export or plantation economies and little state presence. While the land may have been infertile for agriculture, it was fertile for peasant activism. The very remoteness of these northern communities fostered collective identities and initiatives, and receptivity to the radical Catholic and other influences that began to filter in by the late 1960s. For peasants in the north, the Salvadoran government's invasion of Honduras owed more to the government's desire to militarize the region and crush the campesino organizing there that had begun in the 1960s.[10]

The aftermath of the brief war heightened domestic conflict in El Salvador in two additional ways. First, Honduras turned on its entire

Salvadoran-origin population, expelling hundreds of thousands back to El Salvador. This exacerbated land struggles in El Salvador. Second, El Salvador was the country whose industries had benefited the most from the Central American Common Market. When Honduras withdrew and the organization collapsed after the war, El Salvador's industries and economy contracted, putting even more pressure on the poor.

LIBERATION THEOLOGY AND PEASANT RADICALIZATION

El Salvador's Catholic Church embraced Liberation Theology enthusiastically. The Jesuits at the Central American University (UCA) became some of the continent's most prolific authors and theoreticians of the movement. As in Guatemala, most villages rarely saw a priest. Church leaders influenced by Liberation Theology labored, of necessity, to develop peasant leadership in the communities where they worked.

The work of Salvadoran Jesuit Rutilio Grande and his team in Aguilares, in the sugar region north of the capital, sparked a major upsurge in peasant organizing starting in 1973 locally and nationally. The team began a popular education process, holding small meetings in remote villages to read and analyze passages from the scripture and electing lay preachers—Delegates of the Word—to continue holding meetings when the priests were absent. These meetings formed the core of the lay-led Christian Base Communities. Observers described the meetings as "part religious service, part town hall, political forum and fiesta."[11] Although their work was "consciously, deliberately, and exclusively pastoral, never political," its impact "was profoundly radicalizing in a political as well as a religious sense."[12]

The small FECCAS organization in Aguilares flourished and radicalized under new leaders developed through the CBCs. A few months after the Jesuits' work began, FECCAS called a work stoppage at the Cabaña sugar mill, demanding that the mill pay the wage increase it had promised. The strike inspired campesinos around the country who flocked to FECCAS, many mobilized through church networks. FECCAS activists from Aguilares organized migrant workers in the coffee and cotton fields, who took the federation's ideas and tactics back to their home provinces. Landowners held Rutilio Grande "to be responsible for everything" and accused the Jesuits of spreading communism. The military-landlord alliance's drive to eliminate the progressive Catholic movement was strengthened.[13]

THE ARMED LEFT: URBAN ORIGINS

A new left-wing guerrilla organization appeared on the scene in 1971, kidnapping and murdering a prominent member of the country's oligarchy. His assassination is often seen as the beginning of the long Salvadoran civil war. The students who carried out the kidnapping went on to found one of the guerrilla organizations that later formed the FMLN, the coalition of several armed guerrilla organizations that fought an all-out war against the Salvadoran government in the 1980s. Like Nicaragua's armed liberation movement, El Salvador's took the name of a 1930s revolutionary.

The ever-popular reformist Christian Democrat José Napoleón Duarte was at the point of winning the presidency in 1972 when the military stepped in and handed a last-minute victory to his right-wing opponent Colonel Arturo Molina. When junior officers rose up in protest, the military called in international support. Somoza's National Guard and the Guatemalan military, backed by US advisers, arrested and tortured Duarte before sending him into exile in Guatemala. (He soon left for Venezuela, where he remained until 1979.) The military went on to attack the National University and Duarte's Christian Democrat Party, spreading repression throughout the country and killing some two hundred civilians. Reformism seemed to have crumbled.

In the following decade, other left-wing guerrilla organizations formed to challenge the military government and the oligarchic social and economic structure. Three main groups emerged. The Farabundo Martí Popular Liberation Forces (FPL) found fertile ground in the rural areas where priests and nuns had sown the seeds of Liberation Theology. A faction of the Christian Democrats split to form the People's Revolutionary Army (ERP). After that organization assassinated one of its best-known leaders, the poet Roque Dalton, accusing him of being a spy, it too split, with the dissidents forming the Armed Forces of National Resistance (FARN). All of the organizations were characterized by hyper-politicization and factionalism, but also by weaving close ties to the unarmed left including FECCAS, the student movement, and the radical teachers' union ANDES. By 1975, FECCAS had broken completely with its Christian Democratic origins and was calling for "total destruction of capitalism and exploitation; construction of a socialist system."[14]

The different organizations on the left debated and fought with each other and within themselves over analysis and strategy for bringing about change. Should they participate in elections or focus on armed struggle? Should they organize peasants and workers or concentrate on small military actions? What kind of relationship should the armed organizations have with the growing popular movements like the worker and peasant organizations?

It's worth noting that one organization was not in favor of armed struggle: the Salvadoran Communist Party. Until the end of the 1970s the party remained committed to working to bring change through legal means including participation in elections. As in Nicaragua and elsewhere in Latin America, El Salvador's Communist Party had deep historical roots in the early twentieth century, was affiliated with the Soviet-sponsored Communist International (Comintern), and did not believe that Latin America was ripe for revolution. The armed guerrilla movements of the 1960s and '70s were influenced by different forms of Marxism but derided the Soviet-affiliated communist parties of their countries as conservative and bureaucratic. The communist parties in turn saw the youthful guerrilla fighters as naive and adventurist. These subtleties escaped US policy makers, who threw around the word "communist" like a football, with little concern for the debates and divisions in the Latin American left.

ORGANIZATION AND REPRESSION IN THE COUNTRYSIDE

FECCAS was strongest in the region north of the capital, but campesino organizing also spread to the east, and repression followed. In the village of La Cayetana in the east, peasant activists confronted the local hacienda owner in a land dispute. In November 1974, the National Police and the Guardia descended on the community, killing several and imprisoning twenty. Local religious leaders alerted their national and international counterparts. "They have since disappeared," Reverend William Wipfler of the National Council of Churches reported to the US Congress in a strategy that was later used to great effect by the Central America solidarity movement to draw public attention to human rights violations there. "All protest has been useless."[15]

The La Cayetana massacre spurred peasant leaders in the east to form the Union of Rural Workers (UTC). Like FECCAS, the UTC followed networks already established by religious organizing. UTC members "who survived the massacre became the backbone of the insurgent army that emerged" in the region during the following decade.[16]

The victims of the escalating repression, as in Guatemala and Nicaragua, were rarely the small armed guerrilla forces, which one source described as "gnats compared to the Salvadoran army."[17] Instead, army repression turned against the civilian population and against popular organizations and religious and political activists in particular.

Campesino organizing in rural El Salvador struck at the heart of the oligarchy's power. The military and its associated policing forces had embodied that power for a century. In the 1960s, these were reinforced by a new paramilitary force, ORDEN, which was expanded as part of the militarization of the northern countryside at the end of the war with Honduras. ORDEN recruited peasants in village after village to serve as "the body and bones of the army in the countryside," and had a hundred members by the mid-1970s.[18] Peasant communities "grew deeply divided between those who supported the emerging peasant movement and those who joined ORDEN. Peasants affiliated with ORDEN, along with members of the National Guard, engaged in a terror campaign against members of the emerging peasant organizations, who often were their close relatives and neighbors."[19]

As in all of Central America's wars, poor rural people made up the great majority of those mobilized on both sides of the political divide.[20] "El Salvador is small, Salvadoran families are large, and, especially in the countryside, it was not uncommon for a single family to include both soldiers and guerrillas. Cousins—sometimes brothers—faced one another across the battlefield."[21]

Organized communities that had protested or occupied land, especially in the north and northeastern regions where peasant activism was strongest, suffered the greatest military reaction. "By 1975 many men from northern Chalatenango no longer slept in their own houses; before dusk they headed into the mountains and woods surrounding their towns where they were less likely to be caught by the military and paramilitary forces." Campesinos began organized *guindas* or flight into hiding when their communities were attacked by government forces. "By the late 1970s entire communities also began taking to the hills on temporary escape journeys."[22]

Yet repression, paradoxically, "not only failed to contain the insurgency, it helped to transform the broad-based pro-democracy movements of the 1960s and 1970s into one of the most potent insurgencies in the modern history of Latin America."[23] By the late 1970s, El Salvador's popular organizations "were unique among Latin American radical movements both due to the preponderant influence of Liberation Theology and the degree to which they aligned themselves with guerrilla groups."[24]

THE LATE 1970S: THE WAR ESCALATES

General Carlos Humberto Romero became president in a military-controlled and blatantly fraudulent election in 1977. When thousands protested in San Salvador, they were surrounded by the National Guard and other police forces who opened fire on the crowd, killing unknown numbers. The government declared a state of siege. Attacks on the church ramped up even further. One victim was Rutilio Grande, the Jesuit organizer in Aguilares, who was murdered in March 1977. He was the first in what was to become a long line of religious leaders killed.

Rutilio Grande's assassination deeply affected Óscar Romero (no relation to the general), the new archbishop of San Salvador and a close friend of Grande's. Romero had distanced himself from the popular church and politics, but this murder changed everything. He closed Catholic schools and called for mass protests, and soon became an outspoken advocate for human rights.

A few months after Grande's murder, the Salvadoran army attacked Aguilares, killing perhaps fifty and arresting three hundred. A witness recounted that "they spent all day Thursday searching the town, house to house, and beating and carrying off all the people who had Rutilio Grande's picture."[25] A flyer began to circulate in the capital urging "Be a Patriot. Kill a Priest." The Jesuits received a threat that if they did not all abandon the country within thirty days, they would be systematically executed.[26]

General Romero's administration outlawed criticism of the government or distribution of information about human rights violations. ORDEN grew into a force of some fifty thousand to a hundred thousand. It was in 1978, during Romero's brief presidency, that Carolyn Forché wrote her poem "The Colonel," capturing for US audiences the yawning contradictions between the pleasant and familiar daily lives of the oligarchy and the vicious brutality that underlay it. In the familiarity of the colonel's lifestyle, the poem also uncomfortably calls into question the innocence of its readers.

THE 1979 COUP: THE LAST CHANCE FOR THE REFORMISTS

Romero was overthrown in a bloodless coup by reformist junior officers in October 1979, three months after the Sandinista victory in Nicaragua. The junta sought one last time to create a reformist middle path. The armed left and right agreed to a truce, ORDEN was temporarily disbanded, and the far right in the military demoted. Labor and peasant organizations took advantage of the political space to mobilize and escalate from strikes to occupations and takeovers. The church radio station opined that "the land occupations occur spontaneously as the repression lessens in the countryside . . . The campesinos can only be kept silent, peaceful, and tranquil through increasingly brutal repression. When the repression stops, thus arises campesino demands, combative actions, and revolutionary spirit."[27]

Jeffrey Gould, who studied the politics of the period in depth, wrote that as the grassroots in the unarmed organizations surged forward to take advantage of the political opening, the wave of mobilization "outlined the possibility of a radical restructuring of rural society. The withdrawal of the security forces also allowed for intense synergy of radical Christian and Marxist consciousness—most notably when people seized plantations and ran them, however briefly, as cooperatives." The armed left, though, remained suspicious that the reforms were tokens aimed at undermining the revolutionary movement. "Had the radical Left remained consistently open to a practical dialogue . . . they might have posed a more effective challenge to the homicidal Right who deliberately set out to annihilate all forms of resistance within the popular classes," Gould suggests.[28]

By the end of the year, the right wing of the military reasserted its power, and the reformists in the junta were forced to resign. Repression spiraled into a "campaign of terror" against the emboldened popular movements in city and countryside, with hundreds killed. Newly unified popular organizations announced a peaceful mass mobilization on January 22, 1980 (the anniversary of the 1932 uprising). Many thousands turned out and marched to the Cathedral Plaza, where they were greeted with gunfire from the National Palace. Over fifty were killed and hundreds wounded.

The death squads came back with a vengeance. "Intelligence officers in the various security services and in the Army brigades organized the death squads, recruiting National Guardsmen, Treasury Police, and regular soldiers who were interested in 'moonlighting' for extra money, and supplying them with lists of the names of people who were to be picked up and brought back for interrogation and torture . . . There can be no doubt that the 'dirty war' was basically organized and directed by Salvadoran Army officers—and no doubt, either, that the American Embassy was well aware of it," wrote journalist Mark Danner.[29]

The Junta's Land Reform

Even as the right took control and repression rose, the junta, pressed by the popular movements and the United States, made efforts to burnish its image. It brought the Christian Democrat José Napoleón Duarte back from exile in March 1980 to become the junta's new public face and put forward a land reform, in close collaboration with US advisers.

The first phase (which was the only one actually implemented) called for holdings over 1,235 acres to be expropriated, with compensation, and turned over to peasant cooperatives under the auspices of the government's Agrarian Reform Institute. This was the soft side of counterinsurgency. "The point was to build a military and civilian counterforce in the rural areas of sufficient strength to render the organized leftist peasants less capable of mounting revolution," concluded a political scientist who studied the reform.[30] To keep the right wing on board, a simultaneous state of siege allowed the military to occupy the countryside and implement the reform.

Thus, the reform was accompanied by a rural wave of terror: the violent side of counterinsurgency. Army troops attacked peasant organizations, while land was distributed to progovernment organizations including ORDEN. One official involved in the reform resigned, accusing security forces of using the reform as a cover for destroying peasant organizations and killing their leaders.[31]

Most landowners found ways to avoid expropriation. Because they were allowed to reserve a portion of their land, they kept the best lands, and over half of what was expropriated was pastureland and not actually cultivable. Some mortgaged their land, leaving the government to expropriate their debt. Some evaded expropriation by dividing their holdings among family members into parcels under the 1,235-acre limit.[32]

In the regions of strongest peasant organizing, the reform was experienced primarily in the form of intense repression against these movements.[33] Thousands of cooperative members and close to a hundred leaders were killed during the first year of the reform, and thousands more forcibly evicted from the lands they had been granted.[34]

In May 1980, during an army incursion into the northern Chalatenango region, some sixty-five hundred peasants fled their homes, many heading for the Honduran border. The Honduran army gathered to prevent refugees from crossing. Three hundred to six hundred refugees were killed by the combined forces, many of them drowned in the Sumpul River. It was the first time Salvadoran and Honduran forces had collaborated since the soccer war, and their newfound goodwill was lubricated by big infusions of US aid to Honduras. Others who did not join the guinda were slaughtered in their villages.[35]

Even the officials who orchestrated the land reform were not immune to the wave of terror. In January 1981, right-wing assassins shot and killed two US advisers and the Salvadoran official responsible for the reform as they relaxed in the capital's Sheraton Hotel.

Three years into the reform, the *Christian Science Monitor* reported that "[m]ost of those who began the program have been killed, exiled, or have joined the rebel movement here. The Christian Democratic-military junta that designed the program in 1979 has in effect been replaced by an elected assembly controlled by politicians who oppose land reform. The [Land Reform] [I]nstitute . . . now is in the hands of the ultra-right Nationalist Republican Alliance (ARENA)."[36]

The Assassination of Romero

The Vatican initially assigned Archbishop Óscar Arnulfo Romero as archbishop of San Salvador in 1977 as a neutral or even conservative counterweight to the growth of Liberation Theology and especially to the radical Jesuits at the UCA. But like so many Catholic religious in Central America, Romero was politicized by the growing repression of the 1970s, and especially by the assassination of his colleague Rutilio Grande.

Romero became an outspoken voice denouncing military abuses against the population. He publicly begged President Carter to withhold military aid to El Salvador and called on the Christian Democrats to refuse to collaborate with the military. In weekly radio broadcasts, he listed the dead and disappeared. In his last sermon, he described some of the atrocities taking place daily in the country and reiterated his call for an end to US military aid. He described the security forces as "peasants in uniform" and beseeched them to stop the killing. "Brothers, each one of you is one of us . . . The campesinos you kill are your own brothers and sisters." He called on soldiers to listen to their own conscience if they were given orders to commit abuses. "No soldier is obliged to obey an order contrary to the law of God," he declared.[37]

A few days later, on March 24, 1980, the archbishop was shot and killed while saying mass. Thousands attended his funeral, which was in turn attacked with bullets and bombs apparently coming from the National Palace. Twenty-six were killed and hundreds wounded. The day after the funeral, a US congressional subcommittee approved a new round of "non-lethal" security aid to El Salvador.

Subsequent investigations revealed that Major Roberto D'Aubuisson, founder of the far-right ARENA party, had ordered the murder. D'Aubuisson represented the most violent and antireformist wing of the oligarchy. The US ambassador to El Salvador called him a "pathological killer." Yet he and his party continued to be a major force in Salvadoran politics in the 1980s and even after his death in 1992.[38]

Toward a "Final Offensive"

It was the right that undermined the land reform and unarmed peasants and popular movements that were its victims. The guerrilla organizations saw armed struggle further legitimized, as the failure of land reform made it clear that the right would not allow even the most meager reform.[39] The success of the Sandinista revolution, the killing of the archbishop, the end of Carter's presidency, and the likelihood that Reagan was going to win in November and throw further US support behind the faltering government all motivated the left to unify. The mass organizations joined together in the Revolutionary Democratic Front (FDR) as the political arm of the revolution, and the different armed guerrilla movements into the FMLN. Their collective political platform mirrored that being implemented in Nicaragua, calling for a radical remaking of society including land reform, dismantling the army and its replacement with a people's army, a literacy campaign, and health care for all.

Romero's assassination was followed by series of horrifying military attacks that drew the world's attention. In June 1980, government forces invaded the National University, which, like the church, had served as a refuge. Sixteen students were killed, and the university occupied.

In November 1980, six FDR leaders were preparing a press conference at the Jesuit high school in San Salvador. Several of them had recently returned from speaking tours in Europe and the Americas, where they had raised the issue of beginning negotiations with the governing junta. Instead, the building was surrounded by security forces, and the speakers were seized by heavily armed men. Their mutilated bodies were found the next day.

Only days later, four American women religious—an Ursuline nun, a lay worker, and two Maryknoll sisters, who were involved in relief and social work projects in La Libertad and Chaletenango—were kidnapped while driving from San Salvador's airport. The following day, their car was found, burned, on the airport road, and soon their bodies were found. Once again President Carter announced a suspension of aid, only to reinstate it a few weeks later. The murders of Archbishop Romero and the four US churchwomen were only the tip of the iceberg. By the end of the year some eight thousand had been killed, three-quarters of them in El Salvador's rural areas.[40]

In late December, the FMLN prepared for its "final offensive" to begin in January 1981. The organization hoped that the urban populations would join the insurrection as they had in Nicaragua. That didn't happen, partly because of the deadly effectiveness of the urban counterinsurgency in the previous months. The offensive failed. The urban popular movements were decimated, and many survivors fled to join the rural insurgency.[41]

A SHIFT TO THE COUNTRYSIDE

The FMLN retrenched to focus on its rural strongholds in the northern mountains, which became the main war zone of the 1980s. Between 1981 and 1983, the guerrillas established control over nearly a quarter of the country's territory, especially in the northern departments of Chalatenango, Morazán, Cabañas, and San Vicente. Despite repeated army incursions and bombing, the FMLN was able to establish institutions of governance there, including schools and health clinics. Local self-governance grew through popular assemblies and community councils.[42] Christian Base Communities flourished, and foreign priests and doctors supported the revolutionary communities, even as government attacks forced many residents into long-term or short-term flight to the mountains, across the border to refugee camps in Honduras or as far north as the United States.

US physician Charles Clements, who worked providing medical care in the rebel-held region from 1982 to 1983, wrote that the situation reminded him of his time in Vietnam, where the US-backed government could bomb, invade, kill, and destroy villages, but not win hearts and minds.[43] In the scorched-earth campaign, "thousands of troops scoured the countryside . . . burning crops, killing animals, destroying villages, and torturing and murdering civilians."[44]

When the army attacked, the population would flee to the hills in guinda as the guerrilla forces tried to provide cover. Once the army left, peasants would return to their destroyed homes and crops and start to rebuild. One of the most horrifying aspects of the guinda was the need for utter silence that put parents in the desperate situation of having to quiet their infants by any means necessary, sometimes leading to their deaths.[45]

Meanwhile the United States poured aid into El Salvador's military effort, including funding and training five new elite battalions. The most notorious, the Atlacatl Battalion, was responsible for some of the worst massacres and human rights abuses documented during the war. While failing to engage the guerrillas themselves, the new forces did succeed in terrorizing and expelling much of the peasant population in the guerrilla-dominated areas in the north.[46]

Massacres like the one at the Sumpul River were repeated time and again. At the Río Lempa in March 1981, Salvadoran army helicopters strafed thousands of villagers fleeing an army offensive on their villages in Cabañas. When they reached the Honduran border, at least two hundred were killed as they were trapped between the rushing waters of the river, the Honduran army on the other side, the Salvadoran army behind, and army attacks from the air. A few months later, in October, another massacre occurred at La Quesera, also along the Lempa.

El Mozote Massacre

Deep in the FMLN control or "red zone" in the north of the country lay the small town of El Mozote. "In the crazy-quilt map of northern Morazán in 1981, where villages 'belonged' to the government or to the guerrillas or to neither or both, where the officers saw the towns and hamlets in varying shades of pink and red, El Mozote had not been known as a guerrilla town."[47] Around half the population was evangelical, and Liberation Theology had not flourished there. By 1981, those who supported the FMLN there had either joined the guerrillas or left.

Four miles south of El Mozote lay a guerrilla base, where the rebels' Radio Venceremos broadcast from a cave underground. Alerted of a coming military incursion in the area, some campesinos joined a guerrilla escort to flee to refuge over the Honduran border. But most in El Mozote chose to stay, believing their town to be a safe haven. It wasn't.

In El Mozote and some surrounding villages, over the course of several days, the soldiers led by the US-trained Atlacatl Battalion ordered people from their homes, separated them, and began a terrifying orgy of torture, rape, and gruesome killing that ended with the incineration of the entire town and many of the bodies. By the time the carnage ended, over eight hundred villagers lay dead.

After the soldiers retreated, the guerrillas returned to the area and encountered the horror, and a few survivors who had escaped. The ground was littered with charred corpses, and the vultures were so thick that the villages "seemed covered by a moving black carpet."[48] The FMLN's Radio Venceremos was the first to report the atrocities. Some locals made contact with the archbishop's human rights office, which notified the US National Council of Churches, which in turn contacted the US Embassy and the US press.

For the Reagan administration, the timing was crucially important: it was set to provide its first Congress-mandated certification that the Salvadoran government's human rights practices were improving, in order to release military aid. This context bolstered the administration's desire to cover up the massacre.

The embassy staff, challenged by press reports, contacted their military allies, who told them it would be impossible to get through the supposedly guerrilla-held towns around El Mozote. The embassy dutifully filed reports explaining that it had found no evidence to support guerrilla and press accounts of the massacre. Technically, this was true.[49]

New York Times reporter Raymond Bonner, Alma Guillermoprieto of the *Washington Post*, and photographer Susan Meiselas managed to do what US Embassy officials avoided: get into the town, interview survivors, and photograph the corpses, with vivid front-page stories appearing at the end of January.

El Mozote was exceptional only in the number killed in a single event, and in the international publicity it received. From 1981 to 1983, the army killed up to a thousand a month, almost forty thousand in total.

REAGAN AND EL SALVADOR

If President Carter's approach to El Salvador was meandering and hesitant, Reagan's was anything but. For Reagan, crushing the revolution in El Salvador was a key to reasserting US Cold War hegemony. For Reagan, El Salvador was the place to "draw the line" and "send a message to Moscow."[50]

Reagan's influx of military aid facilitated the bloodbath of the early 1980s, but also provoked significant public and congressional resistance. The reports on El Mozote did not deter the Reagan administration from issuing its congressionally required certification that El Salvador's human rights situation was improving, thus enabling military aid to continue.

"Certification was this political game they were playing," an embassy official explained later. "Everybody knew, Congress knew, what [the Salvadoran government] were doing down there . . . So they beat their breasts, and tore their hair, and yelled about human rights, and made us jump through this hoop called certification. If any Ambassador wanted to keep his job, he had to jump . . . I mean, 'improvement'— what's improvement, anyway? You kill eight hundred and it goes down to two hundred, that's improvement. The whole thing is an exercise in the absurd."[51]

Meanwhile, the administration and the embassy pressured the *Times* to remove its reporter who had made it to El Mozote. Within six months, the *Times* complied. "The *Times'* decision to remove a correspondent who had been the focus of an aggressive campaign of Administration criticism no doubt had a significant effect on reporting from El Salvador," journalist Mark Danner later noted drily.[52] But it did not stop information from reaching the US public through church channels, refugees, and the growing solidarity movement.

After 1983, in part under pressure from the United States, which was in turn being pressured by Congress and the public, the death rate declined. By 1984, believing that the FMLN had been essentially vanquished and with Christian Democrat José Napoleón Duarte defeating the far right in a long-awaited election, Congress and the Reagan administration reverted to the reformist side of counterinsurgency.

Under Duarte, the death squads were reined in and the number of civilian deaths declined significantly, especially in the cities—in part because the death squads had accomplished their work so efficiently and the country's vibrant leftist movements had been effectively crushed. With Congress lulled by Duarte's election, the United States continued to pour resources into a corrupt, right-wing military that maintained control over the cities. The FMLN controlled virtual liberated zones in much of the northern countryside. The seeds of the new El Salvador flourished there through the decade, despite ongoing army bombings and incursions.[53]

REFUGEES AND REPOPULATIONS

About a quarter of El Salvador's population (somewhere between 650,000 to 1.4 million people) fled the country during the war. Hundreds of thousands, or perhaps millions, became internal refugees. (Estimates range from 10 percent to over 35 percent of the population.)[54]

Salvadoran peasants who fled their villages found refuge of a sort in the slums of the cities, especially San Salvador, and in Honduras and the United States. Thousands were housed in squalid refugee camps around the capital. Some thirty-five thousand fled across the border to Honduras, about two-thirds of them to UN-run refugee camps and the other third as "unofficial refugees" settling in rural villages.[55]

In Colomoncagua, just over the border in Honduras, some eighty-four hundred refugees arrived between 1980 and 1981 as their villages in Morazán, San Miguel, and La Unión were attacked. Colomoncagua, like the two other large camps in Honduras (Mesa Grande and La Virtud), was officially overseen by the UN High Commission on Refugees (UN-HCR), but the guerrillas had a strong presence there as well. The camp became a self-governing revolutionary oasis, a laboratory for political education where, despite occasional conflicts with Honduran authorities, social transformation and peasant organization flourished. Popular education projects helped students understand that the "conditions of misery" they lived in "were not a natural state of being; rather they were imposed by the wealthy and powerful."[56]

In the second half of the 1980s, many refugees returned to form repopulations—over a hundred of them, mostly in FMLN-controlled territory. For the FMLN, it was a way to establish facts on the ground and improve their position in the negotiations that seemed increasingly likely as the road to peace—or to strengthen what it hoped would be a true "final offensive" in late 1989.[57] International agencies and organizations, the church, peasant activists who wanted to build the new, revolutionary society, and peasants who simply hoped to return to farm collaborated and sometimes conflicted in the repopulations.

When the UNHCR attempted to begin a repatriation process in the late 1980s, the organized peasants insisted that the repatriation must be collective and under their own control. As one youth leader explained, "We lived for ten years in exile . . . We learned so much . . . If we had lived longer in [El Salvador], it would have been more difficult to become organized, to think about serving the community . . . We [youth] have come back into a capitalist system, the same one our parents lived in, but we've had the experience of being in an autonomous community, of deciding for ourselves what our values are."[58] Repatriation into the FMLN-controlled zone became a new phase of revolutionary activity for mobilized peasants in the camps by the second half of the 1980s.

Four thousand campesinos from one camp carried out a grassroots repatriation in 1987, repopulating five villages in the FMLN zone. They joined others who were repopulating from church-sponsored refugee areas in San Salvador and from populations *en guinda* who also returned. The solidity of FMLN control, new national-level pro-repopulation organizations, the Salvadoran church, and international solidarity organizations converged to provide material and political support, as well as a level of protection against renewed military incursion. For some, it was the next stage of the revolution: returning to build the new El Salvador. By 1990, some twenty thousand refugees had repopulated dozens of villages.[59]

The largest repatriation, in 1989, founded the town of Ciudad Segundo Montes in Morazán, named after the UCA Jesuit priest and scholar who had worked in the refugee camps and was assassinated just days before the return began. In 1991, the city of Cleveland, Ohio—home to two of the murdered churchwomen—created a sister-city relationship. Berkeley, California, and Cambridge, Massachusetts, also reached out to create sister relationships with cities in the rebel-held zone. But the new context was not kind to the utopian dreams nurtured under the international aid regime in the refugee camps. Creating an autonomous, collective economy based on fulfilling human needs rather than on profit proved very difficult in El Salvador's unforgiving northern hills.

THE LAST FINAL OFFENSIVE AND THE JESUIT MASSACRE

In November 1989, the FMLN launched its last attempt at a final offensive. In attacking the capital city, the guerrillas hoped once again to inspire a popular uprising. The government responded by unleashing a bombing campaign against poor neighborhoods. The death squads also turned on the Jesuit-run UCA, considered a hotbed of Liberation Theology and support for popular organizations and the unions. Jesuit scholar-priests like university president Ignacio Ellacuría, Ignacio Martín-Baró, and Segundo Montes were internationally prominent for their denunciations of government violence and human rights violations and their studies of El Salvador's campesinos and popular movements. Six of the priests, their housekeeper, and her daughter were assassinated in cold blood.

While the offensive was defeated militarily, it showed the Salvadoran military and its uneasy US patrons that the FMLN still retained significant force and support, including beyond the areas under rebel control. The virulent government reaction against the civilian population and especially against the church also showed the world that the reforms of the mid-1980s had been mostly superficial.

PEACE?

The FMLN had been calling for a negotiated peace ever since its failed "final" offensive in 1981. When the Esquipulas Agreement was signed in 1987, El Salvador's government officially committed to negotiations as well. But as long as the military—and the United States—believed that the FMLN was close to defeat, the government had little incentive to negotiate seriously. The 1989 offensive in large part was an attempt to force the government's hand. In that, it succeeded.

Other factors helped to push the government to the negotiating table. While the new Bush administration was not shaken by the flood of violence, Congress was, and revisited the issue of cutting aid for the first time in years. Even Bush pushed El Salvador's new ARENA president Alfredo Cristiani, who took office in 1989, to quickly investigate the Jesuit massacre and bring the perpetrators to justice.

Cristiani's election also reflected a new stage in the longer-term split within the country's military and oligarchy. Cristiani represented the modernizing/moderate faction, based in the new financial, commercial, and industrial sectors. These newer groups had slowly gained sway over the rural, agricultural wing of the far right and, with Cristiani, came to dominate the ARENA party. The trend was accentuated by the growth in migration over the 1980s as close to a quarter of El Salvador's population took refuge in the United States, and their remittances contributed to the reorientation of the economy toward services and commerce.[60]

The convergence of factors pushed the Salvadoran government to the negotiating table, and the UN-sponsored peace talks resulted in the Chapultepec Accord signed in Mexico in January 1992.

CHAPTER 7

HONDURAS

Staging Ground for War and Reaganomics

Honduras escaped the all-out war that ravaged its neighbors in the 1970s and '80s, but it became a staging ground for US involvement in those wars, and for US-sponsored experiments in structural adjustment and neoliberal economics. When the elected president, Manuel Zelaya, swung to the left in the mid-2000s, the United States supported yet another military coup in Central America. The 2009 coup opened Honduras to full-fledged drug war capitalism and underlay dramatic rise in refugees fleeing the country during the following decade.

A BANANA REPUBLIC

Honduras, it has been said, is the one country in Central America that can truly be termed a "banana republic." It's the poorest country in the region, with the least fertile land. Both the colonial indigo export economy and the nineteenth-century coffee boom bypassed Honduras. As in Nicaragua, the Spanish compensated early on by deporting large numbers of Indigenous people into the slave markets of Peru.

Until the spread of cotton, sugar, and cattle after World War II, land scarcity was less acute in Honduras than elsewhere in Central America. Honduras was less densely populated to begin with, and its land less fertile and apt for coffee. It did not develop the same degree of government-military-oligarchy alliance and rule as did the other countries, at least before the 1950s. Bananas, and US companies, played an outsized role.

The country's extensive tropical northern (Atlantic) coast attracted the banana industry in the late nineteenth century. Several different US-based companies moved in, at first competing with each other (and even fomenting a civil war in the country) but consolidating under the United Fruit Company by 1929. They occupied hundreds of thousands of hectares of the most fertile lands in the country.

The banana industry brought in migrant workers from the Indigenous highlands, from the British Caribbean, and from neighboring El Salvador. Bananas were exported through what became the booming city of San Pedro Sula on the north coast, and the city grew with the industry in the late nineteenth century as Samuel Zemurray's Cuyamel Fruit Company built a railroad connecting it to the port of Puerto Cortés.

International agencies joined the United States in playing a major role in Honduras after World War II. The IMF stepped in to restructure the tax system and create a Central Bank and a National Development Bank in 1950, and in 1951 the United States created and helped to staff an agricultural extension service and then a Ministry of Agriculture. Together with the US-sponsored Pan American Highway through the south of the country and new highways to the capital and the northern coast, the groundwork for the new export agriculture was laid.[1]

In 1954, some fifty thousand banana workers and their allies embarked on a sixty-nine-day general strike, just as the plotters of Guatemala's 1954 coup were using Honduras as their base. The strike brought significant gains to banana workers and catalyzed peasant organizing and the formation of peasant unions elsewhere in the country, especially as export agriculture started to expand in the south. The year 1954 also brought a permanent US military presence to Honduras.

PEASANTS AND THE LAND ISSUE

Unlike the north coast banana plantations, the postwar cotton and cattle industries were concentrated in the more densely populated southern portion of the country. In southern Honduras, a hectare that was devoted to export agriculture meant a hectare taken out of subsistence production. Small farms growing corn and feeding the population were replaced by large plantations producing for export and enriching a small elite.

Poor Honduran peasants may have had more land than their counterparts in El Salvador, but since the land was generally of poorer quality, they were no better off. Increasingly squeezed by population growth, land concentration, and migration from El Salvador, some Honduran peasants migrated to the rapidly growing urban centers of Tegucigalpa and San Pedro Sula. Others, like their counterparts elsewhere in Central America, organized to defend their lands.

The strength of the banana workers union contributed to the relative peace in Honduras in the 1970s and '80s. The banana workers made up a significant sector of the agricultural labor force with decent pay and conditions. The union helped strengthen peasant organizing and place limits on state repression in the 1960s and '70s as export agriculture expanded.

The United States, hoping to keep Honduras tranquil, pressed United Fruit and the Honduran government to enact Alliance for Progress reforms, which were more successful in Honduras than in Nicaragua and El Salvador. Jesuit priest James Guadalupe Carney believed that "Honduras is the country in Central America that has most faithfully followed the U.S. policy of making small social reforms in order to calm the revolutionary fervor of the peasants."[2] Several waves of land reform during the postwar expansion of cotton and cattle distributed a significant amount of land to peasants.

Army colonel Oswaldo López Arellano, who first took power in a coup in 1963, then after a brief hiatus (1969–1971) returned to the presidency through another coup from 1972 to 1975, exemplified the anti-communist Alliance for Progress mix of repression and reform. After first crushing the radical National Federation of Campesinos of Honduras (FENACH), the government created a more docile anti-communist alternative in the National Association of Honduran Peasants (ANACH). After the soccer war, López Arellano continued to promote a reformist agenda including land reform.

SALVADORAN MIGRATION AND THE SOCCER WAR

Just as the expansion of export agriculture was making land more expensive and scarcer for Honduras's peasant population, a similar process in El Salvador was sending tens of thousands of Salvadorans across the border into southern Honduras. Some continued north to the banana plantations. But most of the three hundred thousand migrants clustered on small plots near the southern border, becoming renters and sharecroppers on the larger haciendas there.

Honduran smallholders, tenants, and sharecroppers had few conflicts with Salvadoran migrants. Instead, it was the hacienda owners who reflected hostility. As the new highway and new packing plants created opportunities for cattle ranchers, many *hacendados* expelled their tenants to expand their cattle production. When tenants organized in protest, the hacendados blamed the Salvadorans.[3] When Honduras began to expel Salvadorans and El Salvador invaded Honduras, the war raised nationalist sentiment in Honduras. At least temporarily, many privileged national unity—and anti-Salvadoran racism—over class or revolutionary solidarity.

HONDURAS'S PATH TO LAND REFORM

Between 1962 and 1980, in fits and starts and not without both official and private repression, Honduran peasants occupied and demanded land with varying degrees of success as sympathetic officials in the agrarian reform agency frequently ruled in their favor. The expulsion of the Salvadorans did not stop Honduran peasants from organizing.

Desperation increased after Hurricane Fifi destroyed some 60 percent of the country's agricultural production in 1974. The next year, the government carried out a major land reform, Law 170. Between adjudications in their favor and the land reform, some thirty-six thousand peasants or almost a quarter of the country's landless and land-poor families had obtained land by 1980.[4]

The Honduran government and its military proved more open to peasant grievances than did those of its neighbors. The weaker oligarchy, anti-Salvadoran nationalism, and the particular role of the banana companies all helped shape this stance. The military's role in carrying out the land reform "created a much more progressive image for Honduran soldiers than for their counterparts in neighboring countries and demonstrated clearly that the armed forces were not under the control of the Honduran oligarchy."[5]

The land reform was facilitated by the large availability of public land and land donated voluntarily by the fruit companies, as well as by the expulsion of the Salvadorans after the soccer war. The center of the reform was the Bajo Aguán river valley on the northern coast. The Aguán was part of the banana region, but after a banana disease afflicted the plantations in 1935, much of this land was abandoned. Hurricane Fifi further decimated the region. The banana companies had little to lose by donating this unused land to the reform effort.

Thus, the Bajo Aguán became "the capital of the Agrarian Reform," home to over 30 percent of the land distributed.[6] Peasant farmers flowed into the region, forming government-supported cooperatives that produced primarily African palm for export, but also basic grains.[7]

Other land distributed in the reform was public land that had not previously been cultivated. Land was also taken from coastal Garifuna communities that had lacked titles to the lands they lived on and cultivated.[8]

Elsewhere in Honduras the reforms were stymied by the emerging landed elite of cattle ranchers and cotton producers, who formed the National Federation of Farmers and Cattle Ranchers of Honduras (FENAGH) in 1966 to protect their own growing interests.

During the turbulent 1980s, USAID focused on putatively peaceful Honduras, pouring agricultural research and export promotion funding into the country. Much of this went to the emerging agro-industrial elite. Even the aid directed at small farmers and those who had received lands through agrarian reform helped to promote the elite-controlled agro-export model. USAID encouraged land reform recipients to produce bananas, African palm, and sugar for sale to multinationals and export. Exporters could then shift "from direct production on their own lands to contract buying from domestic producers," freeing them from the risks of labor and peasant demands. Thus "agribusinesses have been provided by the reform settlements with a guaranteed source of supply, backed by the Honduran government and partially financed by international donors."[9]

Despite the reforms, population growth meant that the numbers of landless actually grew during the 1970s and '80s. Much of the land that was distributed was in remote regions and of poor quality. Little was provided in terms of credit or technical support, despite a $12 million USAID loan for the process in 1974. By 1982, some 40 percent of recipients had abandoned their plots. Nevertheless, the willingness of the government to respond to peasant demands kept the reform option alive in Honduras while it was disappearing in Guatemala and El Salvador.[10]

HONDURAS BECOMES THE USS HONDURAS

Although Honduras did not descend into civil war in the 1980s like its neighbors, the country became a central player in the wars going on across its borders in Guatemala, Nicaragua, and El Salvador. As the revolutions in these three countries gained strength at the end of the 1970s, Honduras became ever more important to US aims in the region, in particular, supporting the Contra war to overthrow the Nicaraguan revolution and crushing the left in El Salvador. From Honduras, US troops could operate along both borders and train both Salvadoran troops and Contra forces. "Without a war of its own," explained the *Los Angeles Times* in 1989, Honduras "has played host since the early 1980s to an uneasy mix of Contras, Sandinista spies, U.S. troops, Salvadoran refugees, CIA agents and cocaine smugglers."[11] By the mid-1980s, there were *four* different armies operating in Honduras: US, Honduran, Salvadoran, and the Contras.

US military aid poured into the country, peaking in 1985. Over a hundred million dollars went toward building hundreds of miles of roads and numerous airfields. Never-ending joint maneuvers and exercises kept US troops pouring into the country. Operation Big Pine II in 1983, for example, brought fifty-five hundred US ground troops into Honduras, with sixteen thousand providing sea and air support.[12] The Soto Cano Air Base at Palmerola, where US troops had been stationed since 1954 and which the United States operated jointly with the Honduran government, became the center of US operations.

President Reagan appointed John Negroponte as ambassador to Honduras (1981–1985), charged with turning Honduras into a base of operations to organize the Contra army to overthrow Nicaragua's Sandinista revolution. A *Newsweek* exposé in late 1982 revealed that the CIA station in Honduras had doubled to a staff of fifty and was "training Honduran intelligence and security forces in intelligence gathering and interrogation, providing logistical support for raids into Nicaragua, aiding the Honduran coast guard and helping the Argentines and other non-Nicaraguans train anti-Sandinista Nicaraguans in sabotage operations using small arms supplied by the Americans."

A key ally for Negroponte was Fort Benning–trained Gustavo Álvarez Martínez, who led the Honduran national police until 1982, then moved on to command the army until he was ousted in 1984. Álvarez "does what Negroponte tells him to," a Honduran military source told *Newsweek*. "Álvarez's G-2 military-intelligence agents act as liaisons to the *contras* and Álvarez himself reports to Negroponte." And "Álvarez's military is the main conduit for small arms being delivered to Nicaraguan exiles and is the main link to Argentine military advisers in Honduras."[13]

Nicaragua was not the only target: the rapidly expanding Honduran army also collaborated with its Salvadoran counterpart along the border in the war against the peasant populations of northern El Salvador.

For the Honduran oligarchy and army, the US war against El Salvador's mobilized peasantry melded with anti-Salvadoran nationalism and with their own class interests in preserving the rural status quo.

As US troops rotated continuously to and from Honduras, the United States "established a permanent U.S. military capability in the heart of Central America." By the mid-1980s, scholars were beginning to refer to the country as the "USS Honduras." US bases proliferated for covert and overt US operations. Honduras became "a sort of land-locked aircraft carrier" for the United States.[14]

THE USS HONDURAS AND COUNTERINSURGENCY AT HOME

As the Honduran army was drawn into the US wars in Nicaragua and El Salvador, it increasingly embraced domestic counterinsurgency. Honduras never approached the levels of violence of its neighbors, but hundreds of political dissidents were murdered and at least 180 disappeared during the militarization of the country in the 1980s.[15] Counterinsurgency and militarization nicely supported the US need to eliminate the church-based, student, peasant, and other movements that challenged its economic goal of remaking Honduras as a paradise for foreign investment.

Along with his amenability toward US foreign policy goals, Gustavo Álvarez shared the US commitment to quashing any hint of popular organizing inside Honduras. As US military aid poured into the country, the army became the seat of power, and it increasingly signed on to the fanatical anti-communism and state terrorism that characterized US policy in the region. With Reagan's support, Álvarez oversaw a new "dirty war" counterinsurgency including death squads, kidnappings, and torture, which lasted far beyond his brief presidency. Reformism became more marginalized and dangerous, tagged automatically as "communist" or "subversive."

The CIA helped Álvarez create Honduras's infamous Military Intelligence Battalion 316 that was responsible for the assassination of hundreds of Catholic and leftist activists in the 1980s, including American Jesuit priest James Guadalupe Carney. In 1995, the *Baltimore Sun* interviewed four Battalion 316 members in exile. The paper described the battalion bluntly as "a CIA-trained military unit that terrorized Honduras for much of the 1980s" and "stalked, kidnapped, tortured and murdered hundreds of Honduran men and women suspected of subversion." The former members described in detail the instructions they received from

Álvarez and their US trainers on army bases in Honduras and the United States, and the grisly forms of torture they were taught, and employed.[16]

The *Sun* concluded that Negroponte "systematically suppressed reports to Washington describing kidnappings and murders of political dissidents . . . Instead he was responsible for false reports to Washington that portrayed the Honduran regime as committed to democracy and the rule of law."[17] What was common knowledge in Honduras and amply documented in the local press, and even what was reported by Negroponte's own staff in the embassy, was carefully excised from the reports Negroponte wrote for submission to Congress. If the human rights abuses had been reported, they would have required Congress to cut aid to Honduras and undermined the Contra operation and the entire US counterinsurgency effort in Central America.[18]

FROM DEVELOPMENTALISM TO THE FREE MARKET: THE MAQUILADORA MODEL

The US development project for Central America during the 1960s and '70s had promoted foreign investment in agro-exports complemented with moderate reforms. Reagan's economic project in the 1980s, abroad as at home, emphasized the dismantling of the social welfare state, privatization, and the primacy of the free market: "Reaganomics for Honduras," according to the local press.[19] Nicaragua's Sandinista revolution, and the revolutionary movements in Guatemala and El Salvador, stymied Reagan's economic goals there. Instead, Honduras was chosen as the prime testing ground for Reagan's approach to economic development in Central America.[20]

One aspect of this was the maquiladora free-trade model, in which Central American countries were encouraged to become low-wage, low-regulation havens for labor-intensive US industries seeking to escape the regulations that limited their profits at home. Honduras opened its first industrial free-trade zone in 1976, in Puerto Cortés, and soon expanded to include other north coast cities. US taxpayers funded the draining of their jobs southward. "USAID financing paid for road construction, sewers, buildings, transportation, and the basic infrastructure for manufacturing. US companies were then wooed to either invest directly in building plants themselves, or guaranteeing work to contractors to operate factories for them." San Pedro Sula "became the industrial heart of Honduras."[21]

"The physical overlap of maquiladoras and bananas was glaringly obvious," wrote Adrienne Pine. On the north coast, "access to ports and infrastructure in place from the early United Fruit days has been improved and expanded at taxpayer expense."[22]

The same Negroponte who oversaw Honduras's counterinsurgency abroad and at home set about pushing the neoliberal economic agenda there. "Negroponte's 12-month tenure in Honduras has been a bit imperious," wrote *Newsweek* in 1982.

> At the Inauguration of President Roberto Suazo Córdova . . . a messenger handed the new leader a four-page letter from the U.S. Embassy drafted by [Negroponte]. Encouraging a prompt "revitalization" of the economy, the letter—using the imperative form of Spanish—directed the government of Honduras to take 11 specific actions, such as reducing taxes on mining companies and lifting some price controls. The government dutifully complied with many of the demands. Negroponte's influence steadily grew . . . "I'm not saying that the guy who gives all the orders here, even for covert ops, is Negroponte," says a Western source who knows. "But that guy wears Negroponte's suits and eats his breakfast. Do you get the picture?"[23]

FROM LAND REFORM TO COUNTERINSURGENCY AND DRUG TRAFFICKING: THE BAJO AGUÁN

The land reform of the 1970s had distributed significant amounts of land in the Bajo Aguán to peasant cooperatives. The Bajo Aguán was also home to the Honduran army Fifteenth Battalion's Río Claro military base, which became a center for counterinsurgency. In the spring of 1983, the United States bypassed Honduras's elected government and worked directly with the country's army to create the Center for Regional Military Training (CREM) bordering the Río Claro base to train thousands of Salvadoran soldiers and Nicaraguan Contra fighters. Over five thousand hectares that had been designated for distribution to campesinos was instead taken over by the military. The military presence there cast a pall on any nascent peasant organizing or protest.[24]

US-built airstrips and US-funded private airlines also had an unintended effect: they became key nodes in the transport of cocaine and marijuana from Colombia into the United States, and the secretive bases in Honduras proved an irresistible transit point. The US Drug Enforcement

Agency briefly opened an office in Honduras in 1981. When the office began documenting the extensive Honduran military involvement in the drug trade, the office was abruptly closed in 1983.[25]

"It is clear," a US Senate investigation later concluded, "that individuals who provided support for the Contras were involved in drug trafficking, the supply network of the Contras was used by drug trafficking organizations, and elements of the Contras themselves knowingly received financial and material assistance from drug traffickers. In each case, one or another agency of the U.S. government had information regarding the involvement either while it was occurring, or immediately thereafter."[26] The shadowy operations had much in common, and the US desire to cover up one led it to also cover up the other.

PEACE AND VIOLENCE IN THE 1990S

With the collapse of the Soviet bloc and the Central American peace treaties in the 1990s, Honduras, like its neighbors, lost its value to the United States as a pawn in the fight against communism and gained importance as a site for investment. US military aid dropped from its high of hundreds of millions in the mid-1980s to $532,000 in 1994. Honduras had its own truth commission, the National Committee for the Protection of Human Rights, which issued its report, "The Facts Speak for Themselves," in 1993. The *Baltimore Sun*'s investigation into Battalion 316 followed soon after. Several military officials were prosecuted, though Álvarez was enjoying his retirement and a Pentagon consultancy in Miami.[27] Honduras created a new civilian police force and ended obligatory military service.

But the return to peace was undermined by US refusal to release information about CIA activities in Honduras, and an amnesty for accused military officers. "Impunity for those responsible for the disappearances, tortures, and executions of people who are considered a threat to society continues to send a clear message about the acceptability of these crimes today," points out Adrienne Pine.[28] The rehabilitation of John Negroponte, who under President George W. Bush was awarded several high-level foreign policy positions, confirmed this impunity on a grander scale.

By 1998, Honduras's Committee for the Protection of Human Rights (CODEH) was reporting that death squad activity not only was ongoing but had increased significantly since the 1980s. "The military," CODEH reported, "was taking advantage of a death squad structure still intact from the 1980s to carry out a social cleansing in which the main target was no longer alleged leftists but alleged delinquents." Young men marginalized by structural violence are targeted by "street cleansing . . . carried out by men who originate from that same social class, whether they are gang members using military bullets, soldiers, private security guards, or policemen."[29]

Honduras began its Rudy Giuliani–advised zero tolerance war on crime in 2002. There were intricate back-and-forth resonances among the Central American counterinsurgencies and the multiple iterations of the wars on crime from the late 1960s on. In both the United States and Central America the defeat of the left, along with structural changes that led to the economic marginalization of whole populations, contributed to spikes in violent crime. US counterinsurgency spurred the drug trade, and the wars on drugs took place in US cities and in Central America. US military and policing tactics honed in Central America were brought back to US cities.[30] In all cases, the poor and people of color were directly enlisted, or were pushed by structural forces, into becoming the agents of violence in their own communities. "While the fault is not theirs," Pine concludes, "without the poor's active complicity, it would be impossible for the state to harm them to the extent that it has."[31]

THE COUNTERREFORMS OF THE 1990S

Honduras in the 1980s had already served as a testing ground for what would become a continentwide neoliberal agenda enforced by international lending agencies in the 1990s. The country's north coast became the prime staging ground for Honduras's neoliberal counterreforms that "sparked a massive transfer of state resources to the Honduran private sector, granting north coast-based elites unprecedented access to global markets, investment capital, and political power." The two "boom sectors" were in new export processing zones and in palm oil, both in the north of the country.[32]

One knotty area in which the reformism of the 1970s crashed against the neoliberalism of the 1990s was land reform. The World Bank now pressed for a counterreform that would break up collective titles and privatize land. In 1992, the Honduran government complied, enacting the Agricultural Modernization Law. The government also pulled back from credits, training, and other supports for cooperatives.

In the Bajo Aguán, peasants had laboriously cleared abandoned banana lands during the 1970s and '80s. When the nearby CREM closed in
the late 1980s, instead of being restored to local peasants, its lands were
taken by military officers from the Fifteenth Battalion that was stationed
there. Backed up by private security forces belonging to land-hungry
elites who saw new opportunities for profit in the region, they began a
campaign of expansion and terror against peasant activists.[33] Between
1992 and 1997, seventy-three cooperatives sold or lost tens of thousands
hectares of land there, earning the Bajo Aguán the title of "the capital of
the agrarian counter-reform."[34]

Much of the land was scooped up by Miguel Facussé, an entrenched
figure in the Honduran elite with close ties to the military, for his growing palm oil business. Promoted (somewhat disingenuously) as a healthy
alternative to hydrogenated trans fats in processed foods, and a climate-
friendly source of biofuels, a global market for palm oil boomed. International agencies provided loans to Facussé and his company Dinant
to expand the industry in the 1990s. As the peasants were pushed back,
the well-connected drug traffickers that had already established routes
through the area expanded their operations.[35]

The land counterreform was only one of a series of neoliberal structural adjustment measures of the 1990s, known as *el paquetazo*, that included currency devaluation and austerity measures for the population
and incentives for foreign investment, free-trade areas, and maquiladoras.

The maquiladora model mushroomed from its first experiments in the
1980s into the 1990s, mostly in and around the northern city of San Pedro Sula. By 1992, there were fifty factories employing over twenty thousand workers. A USAID consulting firm predicted that there would soon
be close to three hundred factories requiring over a hundred thousand
workers and recommended that more young women be drawn into the
labor force. In rural areas, USAID noted approvingly, it was common for
girls as young as ten to work. The agency set up family planning dispen-
saries in several factories to help keep women from getting pregnant.[36]
Employers subjected women to a two-month probation period, followed
by a pregnancy test, before offering them a formal job. Anything to avoid
having to pay for the maternity leave required by Honduran law.[37]

By the 2000s, Honduras was the fifth-largest exporter of clothes to
the United States and the top exporter of cotton socks and underwear.
In 2006, San Pedro Sula had grown to half a million inhabitants, and the

city alone housed two hundred factories. But like Honduras's historical export-oriented growth policies, this one was vulnerable to loss of markets during recession, as happened in 2008. Even without recession, the model created a race to the bottom as Honduras competed with other low-wage countries for factories built on the premise of flexibility. Maquiladora employment began to decline after 2000, the year it reached its peak of 125,000 workers.[38] In 2011, the city generated two-thirds of the country's GDP, but this was more a reflection of the devastation of its banana industry by Hurricane Mitch in 1998 and the collapse of coffee markets than of its prosperity.[39]

Like most natural disasters, Mitch was far more terrible for the poor than for the rich. Eleven thousand were killed and two million lost their homes. Mitch's impact on the banana industry exemplified how disaster could exacerbate inequalities: the companies were able to take advantage of the opportunity to shift to African palm production, with the added advantage of being able to lay off many of their unionized workers.[40]

Mitch was followed by a flood of development aid, both from US agencies and NGOs. The response to Mitch accelerated another aspect of the neoliberal agenda: a shift from state-led development to private- and NGO-led development initiatives.

State-led development, as we've seen, was often hijacked by powerful actors and failed to address the needs of poor majorities. But, at least, states were known, visible institutions with some degree of accountability to the public and susceptibility to popular pressure or revolution. NGOs are private organizations, accountable only to their donors. They fragment development into individual projects and channel movements for social or structural change into competition for access to the kinds of services that states should provide to all. "Their newfound power symbolizes the process of depoliticization that has occurred in rural Honduras," concludes one study. The larger project of social transformation that had motivated the Central American left in the 1970s and '80s evolved into "depoliticized social movements" that focused on "cultural rights of particular ethnic groups and environmental preservation rather than on more systemic issues of economic inequality or dependency."[41]

HONDURAS SWINGS TO THE LEFT: 2006

When Manuel Zelaya was elected president in 2006, he seemed squarely within the mainstream of Honduras's elite-dominated two-party system.

In office, he moved to the left, in concert with much of what has been described as Latin America's "pink tide" and in a direct challenge to the neoliberal turn described above. Under his watch, Honduras drew closer to Hugo Chávez's Venezuela, joining the Venezuelan-sponsored, alternative Latin American trade bloc and petroleum alliance. Domestically, he raised the minimum wage, supported the rights of small farmers, and opposed the privatization of the country's ports, schools, and utilities. One author called Zelaya's minimum wage legislation "wildly popular among Hondurans" and "the first truly systematic piece of social legislation that had been implemented in decades." For that very reason, it "set in motion a series of events that led to a coup d'état on June 28, 2009."[42] For the United States and its allies among the Honduran military and business elites, Zelaya posed a clear threat to the economic model they supported and profited from.

In early 2009, Zelaya announced that a June referendum would determine whether a question calling for a constitutional assembly should be included in the November ballot. Several Latin American countries, from conservative Colombia to revolutionary Venezuela, had written new constitutions with substantial popular participation in the previous two decades. "Members of the country's poor majority . . . saw changing the constitution as beginning the kind of systemic change necessary to make Honduras more equitable."[43] The right and the military claimed that Zelaya's goal was to overturn the constitutional ban on reelection so he could serve a second term, and vowed to stop him.

THE 2009 COUP

On the eve of the June referendum, the military refused to distribute the ballots. As tensions rose, the Honduran Supreme Court and Congress supported the military, and on June 28 soldiers stormed Zelaya's house, arrested him, and put him on a plane to Costa Rica. Congress president Roberto Micheletti declared himself president.

As Hondurans protested in the streets, the military took over the country. The world—except for the United States—condemned the coup and called for a restoration of the elected president. A week later, Zelaya attempted to fly back to Honduras, accompanied by Nicaraguan Miguel D'Escoto, the president of the UN General Assembly. Military vehicles filled the airport's runways to prevent his plane from landing, while hundreds of thousands of Zelaya's supporters crowded the surrounding streets.

The United Nations and the European Union denounced the coup, as did the OAS, which suspended Honduras's membership.

The United States, in contrast, worked hard to legitimize the coup and eliminate Zelaya from the picture. "In the subsequent days [after Zelaya's departure] I spoke with my counterparts around the hemisphere . . . We strategized on a plan to restore order in Honduras and ensure that free and fair elections could be held quickly and legitimately, which would render the question of Zelaya moot," Hillary Clinton, then US secretary of state, wrote later.[44] By declining to acknowledge that Zelaya had in fact been ousted by the military, Clinton ensured that US aid would continue to flow.

Dana Frank summarized the evidence indicating the likelihood that the United States had actually authorized the coup beforehand—beyond the fact of its supportive response:

> The plane in which the Honduran military flew Zelaya out of the country stopped to refuel at Soto Cano Air Force Base, a joint US-Honduran base . . . Four of the six top generals who oversaw the coup were trained by the United States at the School of the Americas/Western Hemisphere Institute for Security Cooperation . . . The night before the coup, top Honduran military officials attended a party thrown by the US Embassy's defense attaché . . . The commander of US forces in Honduras left the party to meet with Gen. Romeo Vásquez Velásquez . . . The next morning, Vásquez led the coup.[45]

In September, Zelaya managed to finally enter Honduras covertly, and on the 21st appeared publicly in the Brazilian Embassy. There he remained for several months, as the new government cut off the embassy and declared another state of siege. On October 30, US-sponsored negotiations concluded with an agreement that, pending approval by the Honduran Congress, Zelaya would be restored to finish his term. Since the Congress did not approve, that never happened.

Meanwhile the Obama administration announced that the United States would honor the results of the new election regardless of whether Zelaya was restored. Zelaya, still in the embassy, called for a boycott of the election. Most of the world denied the legitimacy of the November election under military control, which was won by Porfirio "Pepe" Lobo of the country's conservative Nationalist Party. The United States stood alone in celebrating it. Zelaya finally left his refuge in the embassy for the Dominican Republic at the end of January 2010.

In February 2010, over the objections of Latin American countries that refused to recognize the new government and prohibited its reentry into the OAS, the United States pushed the three major international funding agencies—the World Bank, the Inter-American Development Bank, and the International Monetary Fund—to restore loans to Honduras. Clinton also announced that the $31 million in US aid that had been held in limbo since the coup would be restored.[46] For the world's powers, the coup, and the economic model it promised to restore, had been legitimized.

HONDURAS AFTER THE COUP

A frenzy of neoliberal reforms followed the coup, attempting to undo the protections implemented under Zelaya and turn Honduras into a true investor's paradise. A September 2010 employment law created new categories of part-time, temporary employment in which workers would not be covered by existing labor law or protections. A 2011 foreign investment law passed under the slogan "Honduras Is Open for Business" guaranteed immunity from tax increases or lawsuits, and sped up permitting processes. Another law gutted the country's teachers union and opened the door to privatizing the country's educational system.

Perhaps the most extravagant invitation to foreign investors was the model cities project, which designated areas of the country as Zones for Employment and Economic Development where private interests could build entire cities exempt from the Honduran legal system. The Honduran Supreme Court ruled that the project violated the constitution, only to reverse its ruling at the end of 2012 after a reshuffling of the court. Local resistance, corruption, and international skepticism prevented the cities from immediately coming to fruition.

Three years after the coup, poverty rates had reached 66 percent, with 46 percent of Hondurans living in extreme poverty. Unemployment had almost doubled to 14 percent, and almost half of those employed were earning less than the minimum wage.[47]

Protests were frequently met with violence. "Honduran security forces . . . mastered the art of using [tear] gas canisters as deadly weapons, not just against protesters but against journalists identified with the resistance . . . State repression of demonstrations . . . came on top of an unrelenting daily bombardment of death threats, harassment, and assaults by paramilitaries and other extralegal agents, directed against all sectors of the opposition."[48]

A series of new laws and concessions bombarded the rural and especially the Garifuna communities on the northern coast. The 2013 mining law overturned the Zelaya government's prohibition on new mining concessions. This was followed by a 2015 law that allowed large-scale commercial fishing to come closer to the coast, undermining small-scale fishing communities, and by a tourism law promoting cruise ship and hotel development. The coast became a site of intense conflict as foreign and domestic capital moved in and expropriated village lands for development, aiming to turn the entire coast into a "mega-resort." Palm oil plantations in the Bajo Aguán and the expansion of drug trafficking increasingly encroached on Garifuna lands. The coup "opened the opportunity for the state to start handing over natural resources and common goods of nature," explained a leader of the Black Fraternal Organization of Honduras (OFRANEH).[49]

In 2013, a contested and fraudulent election ended in what many called a "technical coup," and Juan Orlando Hernández (JOH) took office in January 2014. As JOH prepared to take office, Congress passed another spate of laws, privatizing the National Electrical Energy Company and the state telephone company and imposing a new *paquetazo* freezing government salaries and imposing additional sales taxes on basic goods.

The following year, JOH's reformed Supreme Court struck down the constitutional prohibition on reelection. After an even more blatantly fraudulent election in November 2017, JOH declared victory. The United States quickly recognized him. Meanwhile the country erupted in protest, and the OAS (unsuccessfully) called for a new election.

DRUG TRAFFICKING AND THE DRUG WARS

"Some commentators talked about Honduras as a 'failed state,'" wrote historian Dana Frank, "because the rule of law had so completely collapsed, and the judiciary, police, and prosecutors were so overwhelmingly corrupt. But it wasn't a failed state. The Honduran state worked great for those who controlled it—for the landowners and drug traffickers and oligarchs and transnational corporations and US-funded and trained military, and the corrupt public officials who served them."[50]

Militarization, drug trafficking, counterinsurgency, and export agriculture had all established a presence on Honduras's northern coast in the 1980s. When the CREM closed and the Facussé businesses moved in during the 1990s, violence spiraled as the drug traffic became a pretext for further militarization, which in turn protected and increased the traffic. The various public and private security forces generally worked *with* the traffickers (many of whom were also tied to the elites), and their targets were most often campesinos who were trying to defend their territories. "These public servants put the power, the uniform and the weapons the state gave them to protect the citizenry in the service of the darkest part of drug trafficking and organized crime, in many cases with the complicity and tolerance of the high command," the Honduran newspaper *El Heraldo* concluded.[51] In Dana Frank's words, "[T]hose gangs and drug traffickers took over a broad swath of daily life in Honduras in part because the elites who ran the government permitted and even profited from it."[52]

Frank's "elites who ran the government" received full US support for their efforts. Journalist Dawn Paley defined the US policy of "arming the state in its fight against drug cultivation and trafficking" in Honduras and elsewhere as "drug war capitalism." "Rather than stopping the flow of drugs, funding the drug war has bolstered a war strategy that ensures transnational corporations access to resources through dispossession and terror." The war on drugs allows "the expansion of the capitalist system into new or previously inaccessible territories and social spaces."[53] This expansion, and its accompanying land loss, in turn increased both campesino mobilization and the economic desperation that pushed youth into gangs and drugs. The drug wars justified US aid and militarization, which were used in large part to defend and implement dispossession in the interests of capital.

Honduras became the most violent country in the world by the early 2010s. Its still-high homicide rate actually fell from eighty-seven per hundred thousand in 2011 to forty per hundred thousand in 2018. Yet the number of Hondurans who felt insecure rose to 90 percent in 2018, and the number of massacres in which three or more people were killed rose sharply. The involvement of high government officials as well as gangs in large-scale drug trafficking and extortion, and continuing high levels of impunity especially for those at the top, contributed to the widespread sense of mistrust and insecurity.[54]

Poverty and violence are intimately related: violence imposes an economic development model that consigns much of the population to poverty, and without opportunity for work or education, gangs and the drug trade beckon many youth. Despite aggregate figures showing economic growth over the past decade, 60 percent of Hondurans live in poverty.[55]

REPRESSION IN THE BAJO AGUÁN

The contested region of the Bajo Aguán illustrates the connections between capitalism, dispossession, protest, militarization, and drugs. Peasant cooperatives had received land there in the 1970s, been surrounded by the military in the 1980s, and lost much of their land in the 1990s. In the late 1990s, peasants revived their traditions of militancy and organized the Campesino Movement of the Aguán (MCA) and the Unified Campesino Movement of the Aguán (MUCA) and began a land reform from below, carrying out "recuperations" on state or illegally claimed lands. President Zelaya started a negotiation with campesino organizations to review the issue of land loss and fraudulent sales. The coup overturned that, and the campesino organizations increasingly faced violence and repression. "The post-coup regime's answer to agrarian conflict in the Aguán was to militarise the Valley and give a free hand to the landowners to protect their property however they saw fit, concluded one study."[56] During the next decade, the Bajo Aguán became "the site of the most large scale death squad killings since the peace processes in Central America."[57]

One recuperation was the community of Guadalupe Carney, named after the US-born Jesuit priest who had worked with the land reform communities in the 1970s. About twelve hundred peasants organized to start farming former CREM lands claimed by Facussé in the fall of 2010. Some Guadalupe Carney residents had come to the Aguán decades earlier with the land reform; others were more recent refugees from Hurricane Mitch. As a group approached the contested plantation on November 15, 2010, heavily armed security guards and members of the military opened fire, killing five.[58]

Between 2010 and 2014, at least 150 campesinos in the Bajo Aguán would be killed as the communities struggled in the courts and through recuperations to obtain legal rights to farm their lands.[59] Some were killed in massacres like the one described above, some in targeted assassinations. In August 2011, the military occupied the valley permanently.

"Military, police, and private security forces are reported to exchange uniforms depending on the context, to mobilize jointly both in police patrol cars and automobiles that belong to private security companies employed by the African palm planters," concluded an exhaustive study of the repression there.[60]

As the security forces quadrupled in size between 2009 and 2010, social tensions inside the communities also deepened. As occurred so often in the 1980s, "guards and campesino movement members are neighbors, frequently even relatives."[61] Since 2013, the tensions have been further exacerbated by the development of an enormous open-pit iron mining project that has further militarized and contaminated the region.[62]

Meanwhile, reports emerged, through WikiLeaks and local newspapers, about Facussé's links with cocaine trafficking from Colombia. The struggles in the Aguán Valley and with the Garifuna along the coast were one of many in which the United States allied with forces controlling the drug trade in order to crush campesino organizing, even as the US used the drug wars as a rationale for pouring military aid into the region.[63]

BEYOND THE AGUÁN: THE LENCA INDIGENOUS PEOPLE, A HYDROELECTRIC DAM, AND THE MURDER OF BERTA CÁCERES

Berta Cáceres came from a family of activists among the Lenca Indigenous people of La Esperanza in southwestern Honduras. Her father served twice as mayor of the town; her mother worked with Salvadoran refugees in the 1970s and '80s. Berta was one of the founders of the Council of Popular and Indigenous Organizations of Honduras (COPINH). COPINH's fights for land rights brought it into confrontations with agribusiness, but also with mining and hydroelectric projects that increasingly displaced campesino and Indigenous communities, and poisoned the land and water that communities relied on. By 2020, some 30 percent of Honduras's territory was designated for mining concessions.[64]

In 2006, a new dam project, a joint venture between a Honduran and a Chinese company funded by the World Bank, threatened the Lenca village of Río Blanco. COPINH organized protests, first through the courts and then at the United Nations. In 2013, it began to carry out direct action, blocking the road to the construction site. Then the threats and assassinations began against anti-dam activists.

A union leader in the Aguán pointed out the similarities between the Indigenous land struggles and those in the Aguán. "It starts with a criminalization of organizations and people," she explained. "The same [happened] with Berta Cáceres. It was the same pattern: to criminalize them, wage attacks through social media, false profiles, invented news."[65] All of this creates a climate that then justifies militarization and repression in the interests of foreign investors and local elites.

The Lenca struggle was one of many in the twenty-first century that linked Indigenous rights with environmental rights, and environmental justice with anticolonialism. In the era of climate change, these struggles could capture the world's attention, and this one did. In 2015, Cáceres was awarded the Goldman Environmental Prize and met with celebrities from US Speaker of the House Nancy Pelosi to Pope Francis. But on March 2, 2016, she was gunned down in a home where she was staying in La Esperanza.

"Now everyone in Honduras knew that they really would kill anyone, no matter how famous," Frank wrote. "A shudder passed through the entire opposition. Whoever challenged the regime from then on was among the walking dead."[66] Other assassinations of COPINH members followed.

The US Congress considered HR 5474, the Berta Cáceres Human Rights in Honduras Act, directly modeled on the Boland Amendments of the 1980s, cutting military aid to Honduras and requiring the United States to vote against international loans. Unlike Boland, this bill did not pass and remained relatively unknown among the US public. It was not until Hondurans started fleeing en masse from the violent detritus of neoliberalism that people in the United States started to notice.

CHAPTER 8

CENTRAL AMERICA SOLIDARITY
IN THE UNITED STATES

Solidarity organizations in the United States proliferated, opposing US policy, especially under Ronald Reagan's presidency. Solidarity with revolutionary movements, sister cities, material aid, educational delegations, church-based movements, and sanctuary movements worked together and separately to support Central American rights and revolutionary processes and the rights of refugees from US-sponsored wars, or to oppose US intervention.

I traveled to Central America for the first time in 1987. I was ostensibly there to engage in research for my dissertation on workers' lives on the US-owned banana plantations on the Atlantic coasts of Costa Rica and Nicaragua. But I had a strong hidden agenda, which was to figure out what was really going on in Nicaragua and its revolution.

I was not alone. During the 1980s, many thousands of US citizens (and Europeans, Latin Americans, and others) took the same journey. We were skeptical of US policy and of what the US media told us about Central America; we were appalled by the stories of exploitation, inequality, and violence that we heard; and we were inspired to hear about ordinary people, poor people, organizing to overthrow oppressive governments and economic structures to build a different kind of society.

Historian Van Gosse wrote that "the waves of North American visitors, first to Nicaragua and [later] also to El Salvador, transformed and catalyzed the Central America movement as nothing else could."[1] By the end of the 1980s, hundreds of organizations were sponsoring solidarity and educational travel to Central America, and tens or hundreds of thousands of Americans had participated in this travel.[2]

The San Francisco Bay Area was steeped in Central America solidarity when I lived there in the early 1980s. I saw the San Francisco Mime Troupe perform "Last Tango in Huahuatenango."[3] I signed the Pledge of Resistance, promising to join a kind of nationwide general strike if the United States invaded Nicaragua. I used my Spanish skills to interpret for students from Nicaragua on tour to tell US audiences about their revolution, and to interpret for volunteer doctors at the Berkeley Free Clinic in their collaboration with the East Bay Sanctuary Covenant around the corner, to provide medical care for Central American refugees. I accompanied refugees to advocate and interpret for them at East Oakland's Highland Hospital. I attended talks on Berkeley's sister city San Antonio Los Ranchos in the FMLN-held zone of El Salvador and films on the Communities of Population in Resistance in Guatemala.

Berkeley was a historic hotbed of radicalism and a location close to San Francisco's Mission District and East Oakland, both magnets for Mexican and, increasingly, Central American migrants. But even in less likely towns and cities throughout the United States, Central America solidarity activities percolated. Expats and curious visitors in Nicaragua from all over the United States held weekly vigils in front of the US Embassy in Managua, protesting US support for the Contras.

During my own stay in Nicaragua, I spent many days in the archives of the Center for Research and Documentation of the Atlantic Coast (CIDCA), gathering fragments of documents and sources that ended up being not very useful for my dissertation. Instead, much more useful for my future career and political consciousness was my experience of daily life in Managua—in a country experiencing Third World poverty, revolution, and siege from its neighbor, the world's most powerful country. I became very familiar with some phrases that had somehow been left out of the textbooks I'd used when I studied Spanish in Barcelona and at UC Berkeley: "*se fue la luz*" (the electricity went off) and "*no hay agua*" (there's no water). I witnessed the hope and passion people had for changing their country.

One of the most moving experiences was a trip to Matagalpa to meet with the Mothers of Heroes and Martyrs. A group of us US Americans listened as the women talked about their commitment to the revolution, and the deaths of their children at the hands of the Guardia or the

US-sponsored Contra forces. After listening to their heart-wrenching stories, members of my group asked a question that I've been confronted with on a regular basis ever since, especially when I give talks about Latin America or lead delegations there: "What can we do to help you?"

Surely the mothers had heard the question before and had had plenty of time to hone their reply. But it seemed to come straight from the heart, and it certainly went straight to *my* heart. "We don't need your help," one explained firmly. "We need you to go back home and change your government's policy so that we can carry out our own revolution here, without your interference."

It was a lesson in humility, but also a lesson in power. Even the most politically conscious US Americans tend to subscribe to what Paul Farmer calls the myth of personal efficacy.[4] We think we have the knowledge, the resources, the technology, the capabilities, the drive necessary to solve the world's problems. It's an arrogance that has frequently had devastating results for the objects of our imperial dreams.

But the mothers' reply was also a challenge to rethink our understanding of power. In fact, we in the United States *do* wield incredible power. If we're willing or able to really recognize the power we possess, and the impact that our country has on distant, invisible, and forgotten (to us) peoples, we are the *only* ones who have the power to change that. Yet mostly unknowingly, unthinkingly, we use our power every day to tacitly enable or perpetuate US foreign policy.

I learned another lesson in humility while I was in Nicaragua. During part of my stay there I rented a room from a single mother of two daughters on a plain and unnumbered middle-class street in Managua. I'll call her Jessica. (It's quite common for Nicaraguans and other Central Americans to give their children unusual or English names.) She worked full-time as well as cooking and cleaning, and raising her daughters alone. Several days a week, a "little Indian friend" of hers came by to wash the laundry by hand in the backyard sink.

This arrangement didn't feel very revolutionary to me, and I was uncomfortable with having the "friend" launder my dirty clothes. I refused to give them to her, but when I was out, she found them in my room and returned them to me clean and neatly folded. I tried to hide them and, when that didn't work, began to ostentatiously wash them myself in the early morning before she arrived. Finally, Jessica confronted me. "Do you wash your clothes by hand at home?" she asked. "Of course not," I replied.

"There I have a washing machine." "And who," she continued, "made your washing machine?"

I don't know if Jessica remembers posing that question, but it made a big impression on me. I've heard it repeated, and repeated it myself, in numerous forms and forums over the years. My Oxfam mug asks, in Spanish, "*¿Adónde va el dinero que pagas por tu café?* [Where does the money that you pay for your coffee go?]" A documentary about Walmart is titled *The High Cost of a Low Price*. I myself edited a book titled *The People Behind Colombian Coal.*

Jessica's point, I think, was that we in the United States are part of a global system in which our comfort and privilege are based on the exploitation of people and nature. And part of our privilege is that we don't even have to know about it. We think we can use our privileged position to "help" people who are "less fortunate" than ourselves, but we are blind to the workings of the system that creates our fortune and their misfortune, and how the two are mutually dependent. In a way, it was the same argument that the Mothers of Matagalpa were making.

Paul Farmer offered his biographer Tracy Kidder another perspective on Jessica's point when he recounted the reaction of his Haitian wife the first time he took her to Paris. "Wasn't it the loveliest city in the world?" he had asked her. But her reaction to the joys of Paris was somewhat different. "This splendor came from the suffering of my ancestors," she commented, forever unsettling Farmer's view of the city.[5] Farmer, too, through his wife's words, was confronted with his own privilege of forgetting.

Ten years after I visited Nicaragua, I was working with Farmer and his team on a research project on structural adjustment and the health of the poor. We wanted to investigate the World Bank–sponsored structural adjustment programs requiring austerity policies and cutbacks in social services that were being imposed in Central America and other debt-ridden countries around the world in the 1990s. How did these policies play out in the daily lives and, in particular, in the health of the countries' poor majorities?

Meanwhile I was teaching in a well-regarded department in a small liberal arts college in New England. At one department meeting, the chair suggested that we go around the table and have each faculty member describe their current research project. When it came to me, I explained that I was researching structural adjustment and the health of the poor in Latin America. My intervention was followed by an awkward silence. Finally, a colleague asked, "Could you explain what you mean by 'structural adjustment'?" The rest nodded in agreement, so I explained. Structural adjustment referred to the economic program of austerity and government cutbacks—including in health care—that the United States and international financial institutions were imposing on poor, debt-ridden Third World countries.

I recounted this incident to a friend who was at the time a graduate student in anthropology, doing field research in a small village in Turkey. She rolled her eyes. "In the village where I work nobody knows how to read and write—but everybody there knows what structural adjustment is! How can US college professors not know!" Again, this is part of how invisibility and forgetting work. From the comfort of their suburban homes and the ivory tower, professors don't have to know how their country's policies prevent the planet's poor majorities from accessing basic health care.

But in the 1980s, the realities of Central America briefly came closer to the consciousness of the general population in the United States. Central Americans, both in their own countries and in the United States, worked hard to awaken the US public to their struggles and their revolutions, and to the violence, repression, death squads, disappearances, and torture that the United States was backing in their countries through its sponsorship of right-wing and military governments. Central American revolutionaries believed that the biggest obstacle to making progressive social change in some of the poorest and most unequal countries in the world was the US government, and that only by mobilizing the US public could they hope to counter its grim repression of their movements. The Catholic Church, which had become radicalized in part through its work with the poor in Central America, also became a victim of official violence, and this galvanized further attention, both inside and outside of religious communities.

The youthful radicalism and idealism of the revolutionary projects attracted widespread international support for their goals. In Europe and in the Third World, Central America's revolutions seemed to be a beacon of hope and attracted enormous sympathy, and US intervention there was widely denounced. In the United States, Reagan tried to mobilize anti-communism and a kind of knee-jerk patriotism that automatically assumed the benevolence of US foreign policy. But a large portion of the population didn't buy it. Domestic opposition to US policy spanned a spectrum from apolitical humanitarianism to horror at the US role in supporting death squads, torture, massacres, and repression to outright support for Central American revolutionary projects.

Opposition to US policy was nourished by the presence, activism, and testimonies of the tens of thousands of refugees from the violence in Guatemala and El Salvador who began to pour across the border, and by the tens of thousands of ordinary US citizens who traveled especially to revolutionary Nicaragua to witness for themselves the revolution and the impact of the US-sponsored Contra war. Books, music, and films also brought the wars home to the US public.

THE CATHOLIC CHURCH

The US Catholic Church developed connections to Central America through the Maryknoll and other religious orders. The US missionary presence there peaked in 1979 at over two thousand, and by the early 1980s, close to four thousand US religious had served in Central America.[6] Many of these lived in rural areas, understood and even participated in the struggles of the poor, and developed and imbibed Liberation Theology.

In 1977, Timothy S. Healy, then president of Georgetown University, a Catholic (Jesuit) school, traveled to El Salvador and came home describing "an agricultural people who starve to death on rich land while they farm it" and "distant and absentee landlords who suck the land dry, return nothing to it or the people, and live [at] a safe and protected distance."[7] Healy, along with the president of Notre Dame University and Massachusetts congressman Father Robert Drinan, were among the earliest prominent voices to challenge US Central America policy in the 1970s. The 1980 and 1981 murders of Archbishop Romero and the four US churchwomen in El Salvador further galvanized the church. In Chicago, the Religious Task Force on El Salvador formed in response to the murders and in 1982 expanded its name and scope to the Chicago Religious Task Force on Central America. This and other interfaith coalitions and individual congregations played a key role in coordinating nationwide grassroots movements like the Sanctuary Movement and the Pledge of Resistance.

INTERFAITH ORGANIZATIONS: SANCTUARY, WITNESS FOR PEACE, QUEST FOR PEACE, PLEDGE OF RESISTANCE, AND SHARE

Several major national-level organizations emerged from interfaith organizing, building on the politicization of religious faith that emerged during the Civil Rights and anti–Vietnam War movements. Churches and interfaith organizations provided important funding for these new organizations and their projects.

The Sanctuary Movement began among Quakers in Tucson, Arizona, and harkened directly back to the abolitionist struggle of the nineteenth century and the Underground Railroad.[8] It was civil disobedience at its finest: challenging the law of the land in the name of conscience. As the Immigration and Naturalization Service (INS) was deporting Salvadoran refugees who were fleeing terror and violence in their homeland, Tucson Quaker Jim Corbett teamed up with minister John Fife of the city's Southside Presbyterian Church to grant refuge—sanctuary—to the refugees. At first the project focused on raising bail money and providing legal aid, but as the scale and the nature of the problem became more obvious, it shifted into providing actual sanctuary in churches or in members' homes. In January 1982, under threat of prosecution by the INS, the church voted to go public with its civil disobedience and called on churches around the country that were already quietly engaging in sanctuary activities to join them.

Sanctuary mushroomed in size, with hundreds of congregations joining and offering their facilities or their members' homes, as well as in scope. Education and consciousness raising about the situations in Central America that were causing people to flee strengthened the political, as opposed to strictly humanitarian, nature of the movement. The refugees themselves became protagonists rather than victims, as their testimonies and activism pushed congregations and local communities to confront issues of US policy, revolution, and political economy. Over half the refugees coming through Tucson resettled in Los Angeles, where refugees including "students, labor leaders, religious representatives, and others who had been persecuted because of political involvement in their respective countries" turned the city into a center of refugee organizing.[9] Sanctuary congregations and coalitions like the East Bay Sanctuary Covenant organized to provide basic needs like health care as well as shelter.

Another faith-based group that creatively used nonviolent direct action was Witness for Peace. By taking US citizens to Nicaragua and putting their bodies on the line in areas under Contra attack, Witness hoped to at once save lives—because the Contras pulled back when they saw Americans among the villagers—demonstrate solidarity in action, and educate US citizens as to the impact of their country's policy so they could go home and actively work to change it. Reagan's Contra war relied on secrecy. The more the public learned about the brutality of the Contras and the popularity of the revolution, the harder it became to justify US policy. Between 1983 and 1990, Witness for Peace maintained a permanent presence in Nicaragua and brought thousands of volunteers to visit the war zone. After the war ended, Witness remained in Nicaragua and expanded its focus to accompanying threatened human rights activists and bringing delegations from the United States to other parts of Central America, Mexico, Colombia, Venezuela, and Cuba as well as Nicaragua. Its focus also broadened to emphasize US economic policies like structural adjustment, foreign investment, and megaprojects, but with the same interrelated goals: using a US presence to protect Latin American activists, bringing the US public face-to-face with the impacts of its country's harmful policies, and fostering protest within the United States against these policies.

The Quixote Center, founded in 1976 as a religious-based "multi-issue social justice organization," expanded in 1985 to form Quest for Peace in solidarity with the Nicaraguan revolution. Quest challenged US aid to the Contras by seeking to raise equivalent funds to support the victims of Contra violence, working with the John XXIII Institute for Social Justice at the Jesuit university in Managua. Like Witness, the Quixote Center evolved after the war ended and continued its partnerships with Nicaraguan organizations working on affordable housing and irrigation systems for small farmers.[10]

Nicaraguan religious leaders worked with their counterparts in the United States to respond to the US invasion of Grenada in 1983 and Nicaraguans' fears that their country would be next. The radical Protestant journal *Sojourners* convened religious leaders who came up with the idea of the Pledge of Resistance, and published the call in its August 1984 issue.[11] The organization asked US citizens to sign a pledge committing to massive civil disobedience in the event of any US invasion of Nicaragua. Witness for Peace networks and returnees formed a key component of the network. "I never saw anything explode the way the Pledge did," one organizer recalled. By the end of 1984, over forty thousand had signed, and many of them attended civil disobedience trainings and actions.[12] By the end of 1985, there were eighty thousand pledged.[13]

When Reagan announced the trade embargo against Nicaragua in 1985, over ten thousand took to the streets and over two thousand Pledge signers were arrested in protests in eighty cities around the United States.[14] Over the following years, the Pledge engaged in everything from sit-ins to guerrilla theater to creative forms of civil disobedience in ongoing protests against congressional approval of aid to the Contras and to El Salvador's military.

In late 1987, Pledge activist and Vietnam veteran Brian Willson was among a group of veterans holding a forty-day fast and human blockade of the train tracks leading out of the Concord Naval Weapons Station in northern California, to prevent arms-loaded trains from departing to the port en route to El Salvador. Instead of stopping, a train sped up and ran over Willson, severing both of his legs. I was among those who flooded the area in protest in the following days and watched in awe as a group of many dozens literally tore up the tracks with their bare hands. I still keep a rusted iron railroad spike from that day on the mantelpiece in my living room.

Another interfaith organization, the Salvadoran Humanitarian Aid, Relief, and Education (SHARE) Foundation, responded to refugees not only in the United States, but especially in camps inside El Salvador and in Honduras. Many of the refugees in Honduras came from politically mobilized communities and had been organized in Base Communities and/or popular organizations, some affiliated with the guerrillas. SHARE emphasized religious and humanitarian goals, but could not help being politicized when confronted with the repression in El Salvador. SHARE supported refugee organizations and also became active in the repopulation movement, accompanying refugees back to their communities in rebel-held zones at the end of the 1980s.[15]

Nicaraguan Foreign Minister (and Maryknoll priest) Miguel D'Escoto explained the importance of this type of faith-based organizing in the United States:

Reagan needs to create internal conditions in the US to launch an invasion . . . but he has not yet succeeded in convincing the US people . . . The people of the United States . . . are the ones who can and should stop Reagan. To achieve this, the most effective actions are those which they themselves are carrying out with courage, patience and constancy, those thousands of women and men who have made a "pledge of resistance" against the aggressiveness of US government leaders. They are "resisting" the policy of violence and terrorism with non-violent actions . . . Achieving peace will depend in large part on their non-violent actions and on the conviction that they are essential.[16]

CISPES: SOLIDARITY WITH THE SALVADORAN REVOLUTION

The Committee in Solidarity with the People of El Salvador (CISPES) had closer, and different, ties to El Salvador's revolutionary movement. Unlike in Nicaragua where many refugees went home after the 1979 Sandinista victory, Salvadoran exiles stayed in the United States, and their numbers grew rapidly in the 1980s. In El Salvador, the armed opposition—the FMLN—remained illegal and clandestine, though the different parties that made up the guerrilla organization also had strong ties with technically legal popular organizations and unions in El Salvador. Many exiles were also linked to these organizations.

Unlike some solidarity groups, CISPES was an explicitly leftist organization. When El Salvador's popular organizations united in the FDR in early 1980, they immediately reached out to Salvadoran exiles and US supporters. CISPES brought together established church groups and more left-wing and revolutionary grassroots organizations in the United States in support of El Salvador's revolution.[17]

For CISPES, working with the highly organized and politicized Salvadoran left, "solidarity was seen as directly committed to responding . . . to the immediate conjunctures and long-term dynamics of a revolutionary process . . . The solidarity group itself was defined ultimately as another actor in the war, and the United States as another front, no more and no less."[18] Salvadoran revolutionaries in El Salvador and in the United States needed US constituencies to press for changes in US policy. Well-oiled networks could quickly spread information about atrocities like the El Mozote massacre and mobilize networks to pressure Congress, public opinion, and the media in the fight against US military aid.[19] The Sandinistas engaged in similar activism regarding US aid to the Contras.

The FMLN, like the Sandinistas, welcomed US solidarity travelers to witness and support their revolution in progress, and to mobilize opposition to US military aid upon their return home. In the second half of the 1980s, US volunteers and visitors traveled to communities in FMLN-held zones as well as to revolutionary Nicaragua. Some, like Charles Clements (the doctor who worked in an FMLN zone in El Salvador) and Benjamin Linder (who was working on a water project in rural Nicaragua when he was killed by the Contras), stayed for the long term. Others, like poet Carolyn Forché, returned repeatedly to Central America to witness and document the situation.

The FMLN used church networks to reach out to US journalists after the massacre at El Mozote. Although the journalists were not motivated by political support for the revolution, their ability to document atrocities that the US government was deliberately covering up led the revolutionaries to welcome them. CISPES also brought Salvadoran revolutionary activists on speaking tours in the United States.

In the second half of the 1980s, the US–El Salvador Sister Cities Project worked with El Salvador's Christian Committee for the Displaced (CRIPDES) to support and accompany the return of refugee populations in the camps in Honduras to repopulate their villages, many of them in FMLN-held regions that had been subject to repeated army incursion and bombardment. For many Salvadorans, the repopulations were a highly politicized action to build the new revolutionary society on the ground. In the United States, the sister-city movement had long been an intentionally apolitical form of people-to-people diplomacy. In the context of El Salvador and Nicaragua in the 1980s, it became politicized as an explicit challenge to US policy opposing the revolutions.

REFUGEES ORGANIZE

In Los Angeles, refugee activists created social service organizations with a strong political orientation. El Rescate, the Central American Refugee Center (later changed to Central American Resource Center, keeping its acronym CARECEN), the Guatemala Information Center, the Casa Rutilio Grande, and the Clínica Óscar Romero (the latter two named after Salvadoran religious figures assassinated for their activism) provided services for immigrants. CARECEN later founded branches in Washington, DC; San Francisco; and other cities. In Oakland, California, refugees formed the Central American Refugee Committee (CRECE). Salvadorans formed the backbone of most of these organizations, and all infused their social service provision with a revolutionary outlook that asserted the rights of Central Americans to determine their own destinies in their home countries and denounced US policy there.

Inside the United States, Salvadorans and Guatemalans self-identified as refugees even as the US government continued to deny them that status. Their claims and testimonies inspired even those who did not necessarily identify with Central American revolutionary organizations to join the larger movement against US military involvement. The refugees offered living evidence that the governments' wars were primarily wars of repression against their own civilian populations.

SOLIDARITY WITH THE NICARAGUAN REVOLUTION

During the last years of the Somoza regime, revolutionary exiles in several US cities protested the repression in their country and US support for the Somoza dictatorship. Nicaraguan liberation theologian Ernesto Cardenal was a founder of the Mission Cultural Center for Latino Arts in San Francisco, which became an important organizing node. Nicaraguan exiles published the *Gaceta Sandinista* in support of the revolutionary movement.

Nicaraguan exiles helped to found the National Network in Solidarity with the Nicaraguan People (NicaNet) after the revolution's triumph in 1979 to support Nicaragua's literacy campaign and to coordinate speaking tours for Sandinista officials. Many exiles returned home after the revolutionary triumph in 1979 to help build the new Nicaragua. As Reagan's Contra war escalated, the Nicaraguan government called out for support and especially called upon US citizens to come to Nicaragua and see the revolution for themselves. The government collaborated closely with US-based supporters.

Sociologist Héctor Perla writes that "the Sandinistas believed that only the North Americans could stop their government's aggression and that they would do so if they were exposed to the real effects of U.S. policy on the average Nicaraguan." One Sandinista official explained that "the solidarity movement was an integral part of our multifaceted resistance strategy."[20] The Sandinistas translated their daily newspaper *Barricada* into a weekly international edition in English for distribution in the United States and elsewhere.

LIVING AND WORKING IN REVOLUTIONARY NICARAGUA

Beyond Witness for Peace, the Nicaraguan government welcomed solidarity tourism, and tens of thousands of Americans, Europeans, and others traveled there to work and learn.[21] Hundreds stayed on a long-term basis, for the experience of living in and contributing to a revolutionary society.

In the winter of 1983–1984, the first work brigade of six hundred Americans arrived to help pick coffee, many volunteering to work in regions where Contra attacks had undermined the harvest.[22] Beyond the coffee brigades, individuals and organizations offered specific professional skills to support the revolution's programs. TecNica was founded in 1983 to recruit technically skilled volunteers to work on short- and long-term projects providing expertise to Nicaraguan grassroots organizations. The organization "used highly skilled volunteers of conscience to train present and future agriculturalists, teachers, scientists, doctors, health care workers, engineers, lawyers, and administrators."[23]

One such volunteer was Ben Linder. A young mechanical engineer from Portland, Oregon, Linder was working building hydroelectric projects in the small towns of El Cuá and San José de Bocay in northern Nicaragua, in the heart of Contra territory. He had been working in El Cuá for almost two years when Congress approved new military funding for the Contras in late 1986, and Contra attacks from their Honduran bases increased. As Linder and members of a local farm cooperative traveled toward San José de Bocay one morning in April 1987, they were attacked by a group of Contras armed with rifles and grenades. Linder was killed instantly.

Some three hundred US volunteers were working in Nicaragua at the time, one hundred of them in war zones. The attack on Linder only heightened their disgust for the US war effort and their resolve. "Rather than being intimidated," one group wrote in a statement, "we reaffirm our decision to stand alongside the Nicaraguan people in their struggle for peace and justice." "Their life in the war zones," wrote the *Los Angeles Times*, "has led them to see ordinary Nicaraguans there, even those who resent the Sandinistas, as heroic people struggling to survive a conflict that they believe is kept going by U.S. funding of the contras."[24]

Under the auspices of Science for the People, a group of Boston-area scientists traveled to Nicaragua in 1986 to explore establishing "a program of collaboration in scientific education" with Nicaraguan universities.

"The energy and informality we felt at our first meeting are not unique to the [National Engineering University], and go a long way toward explaining why so many people from around the world have been drawn to work in Nicaragua and, in many cases, to relocate there more or less permanently," wrote one participant. At the medical university in León, another described student projects researching topics from epidemiology to graduation rates in the local area. "I left with the impression of a program and a way of doing science that truly strives to be a science for and by the people," he wrote. Science for the People established a Science for Nicaragua project to send teaching faculty and library materials to Nicaraguan universities. As the United States trained and funded "torturers and rapists [to] destroy the precious little Nicaragua has been able to build since 1979," Science for Nicaragua explained, "the role of progressive North Americans in promoting peaceful cooperation with Nicaragua has never been so important."[25]

GUATEMALA SOLIDARITY

The Guatemalans had a weaker revolutionary infrastructure and less organizational capacity to work with US support than did the Nicaraguans or Salvadorans. Guatemala's larger size and larger Indigenous population, though, had attracted more academic attention. Anthropologists who had worked for years in Guatemala's Indigenous regions were in a unique position to raise their voices in protest against the genocide in communities they knew well. Likewise, the Maryknolls in particular published, disseminated, and protested the violence against the communities where they had worked. The Maryknoll press Orbis Books published major works on Liberation Theology and its practitioners and martyrs in Central America.

In the San Francisco Bay Area, a group of scholars edited the volume *Guatemala: And So Victory Is Born Even in the Bitterest Hours* in 1974 about the growing revolutionary movement there and the suffering caused by US corporations and US policy. This was followed by the founding of the Guatemala News and Information Bureau (GNIB) shortly thereafter. GNIB published a regular news bulletin, *Report on Guatemala*. In 1981, the nascent solidarity committees and the Guatemala Scholars Network founded the Network in Solidarity with Guatemala (NISGUA) in Washington, DC, aimed at pressing Congress to end US support for the military regime and the unfolding genocide there.[26]

ORGANIZING IN THE BELTWAY: WOLA, COHA

The Washington Office on Latin America (WOLA) was established by several church groups in 1974 after the US-sponsored coup in Chile overthrew the elected socialist government of Salvador Allende and installed a reign of terror that would last for over a decade. "WOLA's unique mission," the organization wrote, "was to connect policy-makers in Washington to those with first-hand knowledge of the thousands of deaths, disappearances, cases of torture, and unjust imprisonment occurring under the dictatorships of that era."[27] WOLA's research helped it to become a major voice in Washington documenting human rights violations by the US-supported Guatemalan and Salvadoran governments and by the Nicaraguan Contras, pushing for reversals of US military aid and involvement, and supporting negotiated solutions in Central America.

The Council on Hemispheric Affairs (COHA), founded the following year and also supported by labor and religious groups, focused primarily on the news media. Its small staff regularly sent out "a blizzard of press releases" trying to provide alternative sources of information aimed at promoting more "rational and constructive U.S. policies toward Latin America."[28]

THE LABOR MOVEMENT

Cold War anti-communism, adherence to US foreign policy, and the purging of leftists within its own ranks characterized the US labor movement after World War II. During the Vietnam War, the main US labor federation, the AFL-CIO, staunchly supported the war, although individual unions and certainly workers opposed it. In Central America, the AFL-CIO was represented by AIFLD, which worked hand in hand with USAID and other government agencies to maintain the status quo and counter leftist and revolutionary movements there.

In the 1980s, AIFLD was funded through Ronald Reagan's new National Endowment for Democracy (NED). Although officially an independent nonprofit, the NED was fully financed by the federal government to "promote democracy" outside of the United States by funding organizations that were friendly to US political goals.[29] In Central America, its main goal was counterinsurgency: to undermine revolutionary governments and movements. AIFLD thus worked to promote anti-communist and antirevolutionary unions.

The federation's rationale was that US workers' interests were best served by allying with industry and government to promote capitalist economic growth. If companies and production grew, there would be more to spread around, and workers would benefit. Anything that threatened corporate profits would end up harming workers. Fighting to protect the system sometimes outweighed fighting for workers' rights within the system and almost always precluded trying to change the system.

In Central America, though, like almost everywhere in the Third World, the system was so rigged against the poor that many rural and urban workers, and their unions, did want to fundamentally change it. Their unions called for land reform, for radical redistribution of their countries' resources and political power. Some of them were communists, while others were socialists of different stripes or radical Christians. But instead of supporting them, the AFL-CIO closed ranks with the US government to brand them all as "communists" and to support the elites and governments that were determined to crush any threat to their domination.

Although the AFL-CIO campaigned against Reagan in 1980 and opposed many of his domestic policies, the federation wholeheartedly adopted his framing of Central American revolutions as communist threats to the security of the United States. AFL-CIO president Lane Kirkland sat on Reagan's bipartisan Kissinger Commission in 1983, and the federation and its officials generally supported US economic and military aid to the Nicaraguan Contras and to El Salvador. In Central America, it supported unions that opposed the Sandinista revolution and those that supported El Salvador's government, opposing leftists and nationalists in both countries.[30]

AIFLD training institutes for Latin Americans taught union leaders how to stay out of politics and avoid addressing big social issues, and instead to focus on bread-and-butter or shop-floor issues in the workplace. The organization offered money and resources to unions that agreed to follow its political orientation. It intervened in unions' internal politics, promoting candidates and positions that eschewed radicalism. It worked closely with the US Embassy, US multinationals operating in Latin America, and the CIA, earning the federation the nickname "AFL-CIA" among many critical Latin Americans.

One study called El Salvador in the 1980s "perhaps the most notorious recent case" with "a string of AIFLD attempts to split militant labor organizations, peel away more cooperative members, create U.S.-controlled alternatives, and then promote their creations as the true spokespersons for Salvadoran labor. The results—assassination, torture, arbitrary arrest, and other official harassment of non-AIFLD unionists—provide a tragic example of the effects of the AFL-CIO's strategy of promoting 'moderate' unionists in hopes of undercutting those the U.S. federation feels are vulnerable to communist influence."[31]

In Honduras, AIFLD helped to create the moderate Honduran National Association of Agricultural Workers (ANACH) in the early 1960s as a counter to existing radical and communist-affiliated rural unions. In Nicaragua, the institute supported the anti-Sandinista Confederation of Trade Union Unity (CUS). AIFLD brought anti-Sandinista unionists to the United States and to international gatherings, and published antirevolutionary reports. In 1983, the Sandinista government expelled AIFLD from the country.[32]

AFL-CIO leadership developed its foreign policy in secret, and most members were uninvolved and unaware. In 1981, a group of dissident AFL-CIO union presidents formed the National Labor Committee in Support of Democracy and Human Rights in El Salvador (NLC) to push for a different union voice in foreign policy, one more supportive of workers' and peasants' struggles in El Salvador. By 1985, NLC member unions represented over half of unionized workers. The NLC lobbied openly for an end to military aid to El Salvador and the Contras and nonintervention in Central America, as well as pushing within the AFL-CIO to change the federation's positions. The NLC concurred with the larger solidarity movement that Central America's wars had domestic causes and should not be seen through a Cold War lens.

Two types of unions tended to be most critical of the AFL-CIO's Cold War rigidity: manufacturing unions, which had begun to see that anti-communist labor repression in the Third World created ripe conditions for US plants to relocate there, and public-sector unions, which saw how military spending undercut the domestic programs that employed them.[33] As the peace treaties and austerity programs of the 1990s drew more US factories to Latin America and privatization and austerity further undermined unions at home, these concerns multiplied. In 1995, the AFL-CIO dismantled AIFLD and partially disavowed its goals. The new Solidarity Center formed in its place promised to take a more progressive stance in supporting Latin American unions across the political spectrum. Around the same time, the AFL-CIO renounced its long-standing anti-immigrant stance and vowed to organize low-wage immigrant workers. The Solidarity Center's continued reliance on US government funding, and the AFL-CIO's reluctance to open the archives on AIFLD's past activities, made some Latin Americans remain skeptical of the depth of the changes.

BOOKS, MUSIC, AND FILM

An outpouring in various media helped to raise the consciousness of the US public to the struggles of Central America's poor, their inspiring organizations and revolutions, and the bitterness of government and death squad violence and repression there. Eyewitness accounts, testimonies, academic analyses, photographs, documentary and feature films, and revolutionary music all brought different aspects of Central America's reality into the daily lives of people in the United States.

Readers of the *Washington Post* and the *New York Times* learned of the massacre at El Mozote through the intrepid eyewitness reporting of journalists Alma Guillermoprieto and Raymond Bonner. Bonner's 1985 *Weakness and Deceit: U.S. Policy and El Salvador* joined an outburst of books in the 1980s that brought the realities of Central America and US policy to the US public. Other notable publications included Rigoberta Menchu's *I, Rigoberta Menchu*; Walter LaFeber's *Inevitable Revolutions*; Mark Danner's *Massacre at El Mozote*; Noam Chomsky's *Turning the Tide*; Richard White's *The Morass*; Robert Armstrong and Janet Shenk's *El Salvador: The Face of Revolution*; Holly Sklar's *Washington's War on Nicaragua*; Margaret Randall and Lynda Yanz's *Sandino's Daughters*; Robert Pastor's *Condemned to Repetition*; and Reed Brody's *Contra Terror in Nicaragua*. A plethora of human rights reports by organizations like America's Watch and Amnesty International provided further documentation. The small publisher Curbstone Press, founded in 1975 to publish literature promoting "human rights, social justice, and intercultural understanding," emphasized Central American revolutionary authors. Its list included several volumes of Salvadoran poet Roque Dalton's poetry, as well as his testimony collaboration with revolutionary leader Miguel Mármol.[34]

Jean-Marie Simon's arresting photographs in *Guatemala: Eternal Spring, Eternal Tyranny* captured an astonishing spectrum of the war in Guatemala, from Indigenous villages occupied by the military, to dying children, to courageous protests. Susan Meiselas captured the faces of the dramatic last year of fighting leading up to the 1979 Sandinista victory in Nicaragua.[35]

Documentary films also brought Central America closer to US public consciousness. *El Salvador: Another Vietnam* (Glenn Silber and Teté Vasconcellos, 1981) detailed the growing US involvement in the country. *Roses in December* (1982) chronicled the lives and deaths of the four American churchwomen killed in El Salvador, while *Romero* (John Duigan, 1982) did the same for Archbishop Romero. *When the Mountains Tremble* (Newton Thomas Sigel and Pamela Yates, 1983) brought US audiences into the maelstrom of the Guatemalan army's scorched-earth attacks against Mayan villages in Guatemala. *The Houses Are Full of Smoke* (1987) amplified the voices of Central America's revolutionary actors in three parts focusing on Guatemala, El Salvador, and Nicaragua. *Maria's Story: A Documentary Portrait of Love and Survival in El Salvador's Civil War* (Monona Wali and Pamela Cohen, 1991) allowed FMLN leader María Serrano to speak directly to US audiences. One feature film in particular, *El Norte* (Gregory Nava, 1983), reached wide US audiences, following two young Indigenous Guatemalans who flee their highland village and struggle to survive undocumented in Los Angeles after death squads murder their father for union organizing.

CENTRAL AMERICA SOLIDARITY IN PERSPECTIVE

Central America solidarity was in some ways a unique historical phenomenon. For every foreign war the United States has fought, even the world wars, some people have opposed US involvement. Before Central America, huge numbers of people mobilized to try to end the US war in Vietnam. Afterward, smaller numbers have opposed wars in Iraq, Afghanistan, and elsewhere. But in the 1980s, the antiwar movement was embedded in deeper ties of solidarity and connection with the supposed US "enemies" in Central America. Héctor Perla challenges those who have identified the solidarity movement as just a US phenomenon, describing it instead as "a transnational social movement in which U.S. and Central American citizens acted together for a common purpose."[36] It was antiwar, but even more so, it was a movement in solidarity with Central Americans and their struggles for justice.

PART III

KILLING HOPE

CHAPTER 9

PEACE TREATIES
AND NEOLIBERALISM

The peace accords of the 1990s set the stage for Central America's integration in a rapidly globalizing economy as social services were decimated and new forms of export-oriented agriculture, industry, and extractive megaprojects flourished. This form of economic development strengthens international ties that encourage migration even as it contributes to desperation and instability that have the same result. The rise of gangs (due partly to the deportation of US gang members to Central America), drug trafficking, and violence contributed to the crisis even as investors applauded.

The 1980s were known as the "lost decade" in Latin America in terms of economic development. After accruing huge debts from banks and international lending agencies in the 1960s and '70s, Latin America was confronted with spiking interest rates, deteriorating exchange rates (which meant that local currencies lost value with respect to the dollars they needed to repay loans), and falling prices for their exports. After Mexico defaulted on its debt in 1982, international agencies took over whole economies, requiring countries to abide by IMF structural adjustment programs that prioritized debt repayment over social development. Governments were forced to cut back social spending and social safety nets, and prioritize inviting in foreign investors to promote economic growth.

The end of Central America's wars in the early 1990s signaled the defeat of projects of radical mobilization and redistribution. Guerrilla movements disarmed and entered the realm of organized politics, based on elections, compromise, and frequently, corruption. "New social movements" based on narrower identities and goals emerged.[1] Socialist and revolutionary solidarity gave way to more hierarchical relationships with international courts and institutions, and nongovernmental and private aid organizations. Reliance on these kinds of ties encouraged local organizations to frame their goals in ways that could garner attention and funding.

A related shift that began in the 1980s was the decline of the Catholic Church and the rise of evangelical Protestantism. The Catholic Church's association with Liberation Theology and revolution left its followers vulnerable to fierce repression in El Salvador and Guatemala. The evangelical church, linked with figures on the far right ranging from Oliver North to Efraín Ríos Montt, might provide a safer alternative. Evangelicals challenged local hierarchies and authorities in a different way than Liberation Theology had. By emphasizing the individual's relationship with God, and embodying at least a superficial egalitarianism, they offered an alternative to rural community institutions, hierarchies, and obligations. Their ban on alcohol was also a strong draw in communities plagued by alcoholism.

The election of the US-backed, anti-Sandinista candidate Violeta Chamorro in Nicaragua in 1990, and the signing of peace accords in El Salvador in 1992 and in Guatemala in 1996, brought about an end to one phase of Central America's wars. Some of the structural changes brought about by the Sandinista revolution survived, making Nicaragua's neoliberal experiment in the 1990s quite different from what ensued in Guatemala, El Salvador, and Honduras. In all but Honduras, formal democratic institutions, including regular and internationally observed elections, proved durable. But poverty, land struggles, and violence did not end with the signing of formal peace agreements.

Chapter 7 traced the events and issues in Honduras during the period covered in this chapter. So there is no separate section on Honduras here, though I'll draw connections where relevant.

NEOLIBERALISM IN CENTRAL AMERICA

Nicaragua, El Salvador, and Guatemala entered the 1990s with societies and economies devastated by war. Much of the damage had been caused by the United States and its military "aid" to the forces that destroyed infrastructure, services, and livelihoods. Instead of the massive reparations they needed for reconstruction, the countries got structural adjustment and neoliberalism.

The term *neoliberalism* refers to a political, economic, and social philosophy and set of policies that directly opposed the revolutionary goals of the 1980s. In the economic realm, neoliberalism called for privatization, deregulation, cutbacks in state spending and social services, austerity measures, and invitations to foreign capital. The goal of the state was to ensure optimal conditions for investors, not to provide for social welfare or social justice. Individuals competing in the marketplace, rather than social solidarity, was held up as the basis of social organization.

NGOs rushed in to fill the gaps left by the state with large- and small-scale economic development projects. NGO-led development became the go-to solution for governments that were impoverished, at the mercy of international economic forces and rules imposed by lending agencies and committed to austerity policies. But NGO projects could be deeply undemocratic, responding to the goals and needs of private donors rather than communities, and fostering competition and patronage.

In the political realm, neoliberalism promoted decentralization, local self-governance, and the promotion of formal democracy. Political activism was to be channeled into formal elections. Decentralization initiatives granted local governments and cultural and ethnic minorities greater recognition and autonomy. But it was an "autonomy without resources" that failed to address the larger structures that kept communities marginalized.[2]

New investment was to be the key to economic development. In order to attract this investment, Central American governments had to keep their wages and taxes low. The "favorable investment climate" they were supposed to create undermined environmental and other kinds of regulation of foreign companies. International loans were made conditional on these kinds of policy reforms. Popular organizations and protests against the economic model were frequently met with violence.

Central America's traditional agro-export crops, especially coffee, waned in importance. An International Coffee Agreement (ICA) in 1962 had created a quota system so coffee producers could avoid flooding the market and undermining prices. But the ICA contradicted the free-market fundamentalism that the United States was now pushing on Latin America. When the United States withdrew its support in 1989, the agreement collapsed, as did, predictably, coffee prices.

Some new sectors officially flourished under the neoliberal regime: maquiladoras, nontraditional agricultural exports, tourism, and mining and megaprojects. These were complemented by a growing participation in the international drug trade, remittances, and growth in the banking and financial sector. These legal, illegal, and semi-legal forms of economic development responded to, and contributed to, deep structural problems in Central American society. Together, they fostered inequality, corruption, violence, and the flood of out-migration that followed the end of the wars.

The ideology of free trade that reigned in the neoliberal era is famous for advocating the free movement of capital but restricting the movement of labor. Free-trade agreements transcend borders at the same time that new walls and laws ensure that people don't have the same rights that capital does. In a way it makes sense: the whole history of capitalism is one of removing, enslaving, transporting, and regulating workers. "Freedom" for capital requires un-freedom for workers.

What neoliberal free-trade advocates didn't expect, or at least didn't acknowledge, was that migration would play a key role in their economic model, even as the model illegalized it.

CAFTA and the Maquiladora Industry

After the North American Free Trade Agreement (NAFTA) went into effect in 1994, the Clinton administration (1992–2000) pushed further for a Free Trade Area of the Americas (FTAA). The term "free" was something of a misnomer. The agreements created "freedoms" for corporate investors, and imposed restrictions similar to those demanded by the World Bank and IMF on Central American workers and governments. With the FTAA derailed by the end of Clinton's presidency, George W. Bush switched to pursuing a series of regional agreements, including a Central America Free Trade Agreement (CAFTA, to which the Dominican Republic was later added), signed in 2004. The agreement went into effect as it was ratified by the different parties (with significant opposition, especially in Costa Rica) between 2006 and 2009.

During these years, the maquiladora industry grew rapidly, as US manufacturers took advantage of the peace, already-existing benefits, and CAFTA provisions to relocate their labor-intensive production to low-wage, low-regulation countries in Central America. As of 2005–2006, 442,000 Central Americans worked in the maquila sector, mostly in Guatemala and Honduras, but with 80,000 in El Salvador and 75,000 in Nicaragua.[3]

The maquiladora model of development contributed to a race to the bottom in which Central American countries competed with each other to attract companies by offering the lowest wages and the least regulation. Changes in the US trade quota system that allowed more Asian imports after 2005 exerted further downward pressure on wages. When Guatemala raised its minimum wage in 2006, thirty thousand maquila-sector jobs fled. To woo them back, the country passed new laws to allow companies to hire part-time workers with fewer protections. That, a US trade representative announced cheerily, "is expected to be a significant boon for the industry."[4]

In Honduras, people noted "a correlation between the growth of the maquiladora industry and rising levels of street violence and alcohol and drug consumption," writes Adrienne Pine of San Pedro Sula, where both types of social pathologies mushroomed.[5] In El Salvador, concluded another study, CAFTA proved a significant spur to migration. "Although supporters of CAFTA-DR promised that the legislation would create jobs, increase economic investment in Central America, and strengthen the relationship between Central American nations and the United States, so far it has only exacerbated inequality . . . increased inflation, decreased jobs, deteriorated labor rights, and allowed less investment in social welfare programs. Under these conditions, it should be of no surprise that people will continue to seek survival elsewhere."[6]

PEACE PROCESSES, TRUTH COMMISSIONS, AND TRANSITIONAL JUSTICE

Countries riven by war must find some way to understand and come to terms with what has happened, especially in cases like Guatemala and El Salvador where significant numbers of the country's population were killed by its armed forces and their paramilitary allies. After World War II, the Nuremberg trials aimed at punishing actors who were on the losing side of the war. They were removed from power and their crimes were widely acknowledged and repudiated. In contrast, truth, or truth and reconciliation, commissions often take place in contexts where there is no clear winner or social consensus repudiating particular actors or their organizations or governments. Instead, the actors who committed the crimes may remain in power.

Truth commissions aim not at punishment but at creating a new shared understanding of history. They may offer perpetrators light sentences or immunity in exchange for their participation in the process. Their investigations acknowledge the previously silenced voices and experiences of the victims of war crimes, crimes against humanity, and violence. The goal is healing and reconciliation.

The International Center for Transitional Justice explains,

> In the aftermath of a devastating conflict or a repressive regime, knowing the truth about the past is more than just an important step toward justice, it is a recognized human right to which all victims and survivors of armed conflict and repression are entitled . . . It is especially important to uphold this right given that repressive regimes often deliberately rewrite history and deny atrocities in order to legitimize themselves, fuel mistrust, and even instigate new cycles of violence. Truth seeking contributes to the creation of a historical record that prevents this kind of manipulation.[7]

Thus, transitional justice does not necessarily include punishment for the guilty.

Both El Salvador and Guatemala established truth commissions as part of a national reconciliation process inscribed in the peace treaties of 1992 (in El Salvador) and 1996 (in Guatemala). Local armed actors agreed to full, impartial investigations of wartime atrocities. But they also agreed to far-ranging amnesty for those who committed such crimes. In Nicaragua, President Chamorro also approved a general amnesty for crimes committed during the Contra war, and no truth commission was formed.

There were some glaring absences in the work of the truth commissions. Because they focused on the direct perpetrators of wartime crimes, they ignored the role of the countries' oligarchies in building and sustaining the militarized systems that fostered the atrocities. Furthermore, the role of the United States in promoting (and covering up) wartime abuses was completely excluded from the commissions' purview. The historical record the commissions created could be used to challenge US attempts to "deny atrocities" as it had during the 1980s. But the new record still allowed it to "deliberately rewrite history" to whitewash its own role in the crimes, and thus "even instigate new cycles of violence."

NICARAGUA

In Nicaragua, the economic project of the revolution began to crumble long before the Sandinistas were voted out of office in 1990. Pressed by the opposition and by unremitting economic and actual war, the Sandinistas pulled back on their revolutionary economic goals in hopes of mollifying the United States, keeping capital at home, and wooing international lenders. The diversion of resources to the war effort meant that resources for social programs like schools and hospitals simply were not available. Even though the Contras lost on the battlefield, in some ways they won the battle to derail the gains of the revolution.

Much more dramatically, some Sandinista leaders themselves blatantly abused their power in the months before they left office to skim as much as they could off of the public sector and into their own hands. The presidency of Violeta Chamorro pulled the country thoroughly into the IMF/World Bank embrace, imposing austerity measures, cutting back public services, selling off almost the entire public sector, and reversing the land reform. She also pleased her US supporters by withdrawing Nicaragua's legal case against the United States before the International Court of Justice. Her successor, former far-right Managua mayor Arnoldo Alemán, was even more draconian in his social and economic policies.

New divisions emerged in the Sandinista party once it was in the opposition. The party was deeply identified and intertwined with the revolution and the state and its institutions, from the Sandinista army to the official *Barricada* newspaper to the schools and public health system. How would it operate in the new context?

The *ortodoxos* closed ranks around Daniel Ortega and the top-down party structure and mindset forged during the decades of war. The *renovadores* were critical of Daniel Ortega, and what they saw as the centralized and top-down rigidity of the party and argued that the party needed more internal democracy to renew itself. At the party's 1994 Special Congress, the *ortodoxos* prevailed. A year later, the *renovadores* split from the FSLN to form the Sandinista Renovation Movement (MRS).

For many of the rural and urban workers who made up the Sandinista base, loyalty to the revolution meant loyalty to the Sandinistas. One analyst pointed out that the progressive defection of the FSLN's middle-class and intellectual supporters eerily fulfilled Sandino's 1930 prediction that "only the workers and peasants will fight to the finish."

Another explained that the MRS "could not penetrate the wall of solidarity that they had helped to build during the 1970s and 1980s: any attack on the FSLN was an attack on the revolution and all that was sacred to the Nicaraguan people."[8]

In 2006, Daniel Ortega ran for the presidency again, on a platform some termed "neo-Sandinismo." Through Supreme Court manipulation, he managed to be reelected twice more, in 2011 and 2016, gaining in both number of votes and percentage in each of the latter two elections. His small-scale but still meaningful poverty-alleviation programs that replaced the idea of major social transformation were extremely popular. Some criticized these as replicating the top-down patron-client relationships of the Somozas. One-man rule, corruption, and economic inequality were nothing new to Nicaraguans. His stepdaughter's 1998 accusation that Ortega had sexually abused her for years, and the appearance of his wife, Rosario Murillo, as his running mate in 2016, added to the criticism of his personalist ruling style. Yet Ortega won in 2016 with over 70 percent of the vote.

Nicaragua benefited from an influx of aid from oil-rich Venezuela under Hugo Chávez, as part of Chávez's attempt to create a twenty-first-century socialism in Latin America. Yet the private sector and foreign investment also flourished, due to a combination of Nicaragua's poverty and low wages, austerity measures and economic incentives, and the country's safety and low levels of crime and violence compared to its neighbors. For over a decade, Nicaragua under neo-Sandinismo appeared to be a social and economic "success story."[9]

Venezuela's collapse in the middle of the 2010s undermined one source of neo-Sandinismo's economic stability. In April 2018, Ortega announced a new round of austerity measures mandated by the IMF, reforming the social security system to cut benefits and increase employee and employer contributions. When small-scale protests were met with disproportionate violence by the Sandinista police, the protests exploded into mass rebellion. Violence against protesters by government forces and armed Sandinista supporters escalated, and hundreds were killed. But protests only increased. Some targeted historic revolutionary monuments and symbols; some proclaimed "Ortega y Somoza, son la misma cosa [Ortega and Somoza are the same thing]."[10]

Some have pointed to different moments as indicating the defeat of the Nicaraguan revolution: the 1990 Sandinista electoral loss, the split of the Sandinista party, Daniel Ortega's neo-Sandinismo, or the violent response to the 2018 protests. Yet despite post-1990 efforts to dismantle some of the revolution's key achievements, despite the literal whitewashing of revolutionary murals and art, and despite Nicaragua's welcoming of maquiladoras and megaprojects in recent decades, it's clear that the legacy of the revolution still profoundly shapes Nicaraguan history. Perhaps, some recent studies suggest, the revolution's most enduring legacy has been "a sense of agency," "a commitment to active participation," and a "belief in [citizens'] capacity to affect the forces that shape their lives and society."[11]

EL SALVADOR

In El Salvador, the FMLN entered peace negotiations with the government from a strong position. The guerrillas held a good portion of the country's territory and had established state-like institutions including health-care and education systems, and even a radio station that had become the country's most trusted source of information. And the FMLN enjoyed strong international political and material support through solidarity organizations, volunteers, sister-city relationships, and material aid.

The accords signed in 1992 provided for the FMLN's demobilization and its legalization as a political party. Deep democratization and electoral reform would allow for full participation on the local and national levels. The army was reduced and placed under civilian authority, and the judicial system was strengthened. Politically, the accords seemed to promise far-reaching change.

Truth Commission

The accords called for a truth commission, sponsored by the United Nations, to investigate war crimes and human rights abuses. The commission investigated twenty-two thousand cases, and its 1993 report concluded that state- and state-sponsored security forces were responsible for 85 percent of violations, including the assassination of Archbishop Romero and the El Mozote massacre.[12] Only five days later, the ARENA-dominated legislature clarified the limits of transitional justice when it passed a sweeping amnesty law that precluded any prosecution for crimes committed during the war and any judicial investigation of victims' claims.

The FMLN, torn among its commitment to the victims, the need to compromise in delicate negotiations, and its self-interest in protecting its own members from prosecution, reneged on its calls for accountability and supported the amnesty. Amnesty meant that survivors of torture, massacres, disappearance, and other crimes received no reparations, and had no recourse against those responsible. While some popular organizations and victims clamored for justice as well as truth, they were not part of the negotiations.

Another glaring absence in the work of the truth commission was that it erased the role of the United States, which had spurred, trained, and armed the perpetrators in El Salvador. This too contributed to a climate of impunity. According to an American lawyer who worked with El Salvador's postwar judicial reform, legislated impunity and the failure to remake the country's judicial system have been major factors in the explosion of street and organized crime that have plagued El Salvador since the 1990s.[13]

Land and the Economy

One thing El Salvador's accords did not do was transform the economy. In fact, peace, coming as it did at the beginning of Latin America's neoliberal era, set the stage for exacerbating, rather than dismantling, the country's profound structural inequalities. The far-right ARENA party that took power in 1989 won every subsequent election until 2009, so was able to oversee two decades of neoliberal policy implementation.

Rapid economic transformation in the form of austerity, investment in export-oriented industrialization, market-based reforms, out-migration, and dependence on remittances came to characterize the postwar period. The country's poor who were displaced, excluded, and exploited by the modernization projects of the mid-twentieth century, and who constituted one of the pillars of support for revolutionary change, turned out to be just as marginalized by the new market-based modernization at the end of the century.

At the end of the war, 83 percent of the agricultural population did not have enough land to survive on, and 52 percent had no land at all.[14] The peace agreement created a program to transfer land to demobilized government soldiers and FMLN guerrillas and some noncombatants in the conflict zones—a total of forty thousand families. But much of the land was of poor quality, and recipients had little access to infrastructure or credit. Land concentration actually increased overall in the 1990s.[15]

In some significant ways, the situation of the rural poor was even worse than it had been before the war. Villages and farms had been abandoned and destroyed. Able-bodied young men and, to a lesser extent, women had been killed or returned home disabled. Families were broken and traumatized. Old patronage relationships may have been unjust or exploitative, but they also provided a kind of safety net in terms of access to land, jobs, or loans. These too crumbled during the war and postwar years.

In urban areas, neoliberalism was felt in massive public-sector layoffs and cuts in basic government services. In the mid-1990s, small housefront stores proliferated as laid-off state-sector workers entered the informal economy. "Everywhere, people were selling *chocobananos* (frozen chocolate-covered bananas) out of new freezers. Or they were flipping *pupusas* (the national dish, fat tortillas stuffed with meat, beans, and/or cheese) on new grills in garages converted to picnic-table-furnished eateries. Or they were importing used car parts from North American junkyards. Or they had managed to nab some kind of job with one of the many new nongovernmental organizations unevenly carrying out some of the functions of a recalibrated state."[16]

El Salvador's economy became ever more tied to the United States. In 2001, the country adopted the US dollar as its official currency, meaning that the government gave up control over its monetary policy. It can't print money or adjust interest rates. Policies set by the US Federal Reserve respond to conditions in the United States, with little regard for their impact in El Salvador.

By the end of the war in 1992, some 25 percent of El Salvador's population had fled to the United States. Although migration declined in the 1990s, tens of thousands continued to make the trek north every year, with the Salvadoran population in the United States reaching 2.3 million by 2017.[17] They remitted over a billion dollars a year, accounting for 10 percent of the gross national income, twice that brought in by coffee exports.[18] Remittances grew to fill the holes left by declining government services, as two sides of the neoliberal coin that urged individual over collective responsibility.[19]

El Salvador also led the hemisphere in homicides and violent crime (until it was overtaken by Honduras in the 2010s). The six thousand to seven thousand murders every year exceeded the number killed during most of the war years.[20]

The impunity that began with the amnesty was compounded by underfunded and ineffective policing and justice throughout the society. Neoliberal thinking came to pervade the concept of security. By 1996, 45 percent of Salvadorans surveyed reported that they believed people had the right to take justice into their own hands because the state was unable to provide security, and supported organizations of armed vigilantes and death squads to carry out "social cleansing." A year later, it was over 50 percent.[21]

Politics and the FMLN

In many municipalities, the demobilized FMLN won local elections in the 1990s. But with the national government in the hands of the ARENA party and under fiscal austerity, local governments had little ability to bring about social change or better the conditions of the poor. Two historians argue the FMLN's "acceptance of the social economic status quo in order to presumably gain national legitimacy and organizational stability led directly to the squandering of political capital."[22] Researcher Ralph Sprenkels pointed to "postinsurgent disillusionment" with party leaders, many of whom made out well in the demobilization, and with the hopes and solidarity inspired by the revolution, which seemed to crumble in the new order.[23] "Revolutionary armed struggle created strong expectations among participants, and what remained of the revolutionary movement in the postwar period had a hard time coming to grips with these expectations," he argued.[24]

The "political culture of revolutionary militancy" itself created new forms of clientelism as the FMLN transitioned to a political party. Clientelism drew on deep roots in Latin American political culture, with particular postrevolutionary twists. As with the Sandinistas in Nicaragua, "inherited militant practices and imaginaries, including sectarianism and conspiracy thinking, actually contributed to shaping clientelist networks . . . Key elements of armed struggle's political repertoire may have hybridized into contemporary leftwing politics."[25]

Many FMLN cadres moved out of party politics altogether and into the left-wing NGOs that proliferated in the 1990s and 2000s. There too they navigated the challenges of the struggle for resources and the lures of clientelism.[26]

The FMLN in Power

Despite all of the obstacles it faced, the FMLN won El Salvador's national elections in 2009, seventeen years after it demobilized as an armed guerrilla force. It was the first time that a Latin American guerrilla group came to power through an election.[27]

Like the FSLN in Nicaragua, the FMLN drew on its historical revolutionary legitimacy and identity and its new clientelist networks to gain electoral support. But also as in Nicaragua, "the scarcity of state resources available for distribution . . . rendered these postwar clientelist relations relatively unstable and precarious. Considering these political developments in the mirror of the aspirations and sacrifices of revolutionary armed struggle, many former Salvadoran insurgents lamented what they saw as the postwar scramble for public resources, but few could afford not to participate in it."[28]

Still, the FMLN government succeeded in pushing through some important policy reforms and maintained enough popular support to win the presidency a second time in 2014. Under the FMLN, El Salvador cut fees and greatly expanded access to health care and education, promoted small-scale agriculture, passed legislation guaranteeing women's and Indigenous rights, and became the only country in Latin America to ban metallic mining. FMLN projects were limited by its lack of a majority in the legislature, pressures from the United States, and ongoing high levels of violence. In 2019, the FMLN lost to maverick candidate Nayib Bukele, who ran on a platform one analyst called a "messianic, post-ideological populism."[29]

Repopulations and Neoliberalism

The repatriations into the guerrilla-held zones that took place in the 1980s and 1990s created a space in which revolutionaries tried to enact their dream of a new El Salvador and confronted multiple obstacles. Neither the government nor the international NGOs that had supported the refugees were enthusiastic about making long-term commitments to the kind of infrastructure that could overcome the poverty and isolation that had plagued northern El Salvador for decades. One Inter-American Development Bank official explained that he "wasn't sure whether the [bank] or any other institution should be investing in programs that encourage people to stay in Morazán."[30]

A decade after the repopulation of Ciudad Segundo Montes in Morazán, the community's dreams of the new society struggled against neoliberal realities and grinding poverty. Many of the residents felt that things were getting worse, not better. "Over two-thirds of residents do not earn enough to purchase the minimal goods considered sufficient for meeting basic needs. With no regional economy in which to integrate, permanent employment in Ciudad Segundo Montes workshops has collapsed . . . Factories sit idle, donated equipment has been sold, and people have returned to prewar survival strategies in subsistence agriculture or employment in the informal sector," one study found. Almost half of the population had abandoned the repopulation. Morazán province had the highest rate of emigration in the country.[31]

The solidarity organization Voices on the Border, which had supported the repopulation for decades, gave a more uplifting picture of life in the community fifteen years later. "After 24 years of hard work, the advances in the development of the community are visible . . . They have the best library in all of the eastern region, the best high school in Morazán, and 20% of all youth have finished or are in the process of finishing their university degrees. There is no gang presence in the region and youth dedicate their free time to practice sports, or learn dance, theatre, painting or music. There are childcare facilities as well as community centers where older residents receive meals and other services."[32] The communities' intimate relations with—and dependence on—international solidarity organizations may encourage residents to present an overly rosy view, but the two descriptions are not necessarily contradictory. Segundo Montes, much like Nicaragua, could both be better off than its neighbors and struggling to survive against insurmountable odds.[33]

In another highly politicized resettlement in Chalatenango, named for Jesuit martyr Ignacio Ellacuría, a study in 2012 found most of the radical collective experiments of the 1990s in shambles, including the women's center, the shoe factory, and the egg farm. The school still stood, but the popular education teachers had been replaced as the school was incorporated into the government system. Lack of jobs had pushed large numbers to seek opportunity in the United States. Improvements in individual houses showed a startling contrast to the decay of the collective projects. "Purely on remittances," a local youth explained.[34] FMLN leaders, many villagers felt, had done well for themselves in the transition from guerrilla organization to political party, but campesinos had been left behind to fend for themselves.[35] Another researcher found that the revolutionary consciousness of the war years had "lost [its]meaning for many residents struggling under close to a decade of neoliberal, privatizing, and structural adjustment policies."[36]

GUATEMALA

In Guatemala peace seemed more elusive, and any hope for an agreement that would address the deep structural inequalities that lay behind the revolution was crushed. The URNG's position was much weaker than that of the FMLN, and Guatemala's popular organizations more disarticulated and terrorized. Guatemala's peace accords were the last to be finalized, in 1996.

The accords provided for demobilization and reintegration of the guerrilla URNG along with the civil patrols and military police, amnesty for war crimes, restitution for victims, human rights guarantees, an end to impunity, recognition of Indigenous rights, guarantees for the return of refugees and displaced people, creation of a civilian police force to replace the army in domestic law enforcement, and establishment of democratic institutions. The United Nations would maintain a presence in Guatemala to oversee the implementation.

Conspicuously evaded, once again, was land reform. The accords "reaffirmed the absolute right of private property" and rejected any concept of the "social use" of land. A new land survey promised to "delineate ownership of all existing properties." This meant that Indigenous communities that had lost their lands before the accords were signed could not use the law to regain them: the existing property regime would be the new baseline.[37]

Truth Commissions and Transitional Justice

The United Nations Commission for Historical Clarification (CEH) that investigated wartime crimes and human rights abuses was predicated on anonymity and immunity for those implicated except in cases of crimes against humanity including genocide. The Catholic Church carried out its own Recovery of Historical Memory (REMHI) project. Unlike the UN Commission, the church report challenged impunity by naming names.

The two reports documented the appalling viciousness and impact of the war and made it clear that it was in large part a war by the country's army and other institutions against its Mayan population. The military and paramilitary forces were responsible for 93 percent of the atrocities committed, and 83 percent of those killed were Mayan Indigenous people. At least two hundred thousand were killed, and over six hundred villages destroyed. When the UN Commission concluded that the attacks on Indigenous communities constituted genocide, it opened the door to prosecution.

As if to undermine the REMHI report's title, *Guatemala: Never Again*, the bishop who coordinated its work, Juan Gerardi, was brutally murdered two days after the report's release in 1998. "As his death sadly showed, memory is a dangerous political tool in Guatemala; this brutal killing was also a symbolic one, an attempt to obliterate the possibility of revisiting past truths."[38]

Well before the truth commissions, in 1992 the Guatemalan Forensic Anthropology Foundation (FAFG) had formed to uncover and identify massacre victims. In 2004, the foundation expanded its work to join with organizations like GAM and FAMDEGUA in their search for the disappeared. Together they have exhumed clandestine mass graves on military property and in villages, slowly piecing together a record of the dead and disappeared.

An anthropologist who accompanied the process explained that "these clandestine cemeteries were hidden in that they were silenced, but survivors, witnesses, and most community members know the locations of these graves. Thus, they are truly clandestine only in the official negation of their existence and the silence imposed on communities." The purpose of the exhumation is to create "a community space for local healing and a site for the reconstruction of larger social relations. A space for the physical exhumation of bones and artifacts, as well as the excavation of individual and collective memory." Exhumations constitute "the process of excavation of memory and retaking of public space."[39] But the problem of impunity remained.

In 2007, the UN and the Guatemalan government formed an International Commission against Impunity in Guatemala (CICIG). Especially after the appointment of Claudia Paz y Paz as attorney general, the CICIG was able to strengthen judicial independence and enabled the prosecution of several high-level officials. The work of these organizations and agencies, and pressure from international legal bodies, helped to bring about Guatemala's first convictions. In 2013, former president Ríos Montt himself was convicted of genocide for his campaign against the villages of the Ixil triangle, although sentencing was delayed and he died before he could serve time for his crimes. In 2016, fourteen former military officers were arrested in connection with a mass grave discovered on one military base. This and other cases have continued to wend their way through the courts.[40]

At the end of 2019, though, CICIG was dismantled, dealing a blow to those seeking justice. Meanwhile, a new bill was proposed to expand the amnesty to cover all crimes committed during the war, including the crimes against humanity that had been explicitly left open to prosecution.[41]

Complexities

While applauding the courageous work of those who participated in the truth commission projects, some scholars who have studied the process in Guatemala found that it often failed to bring the promised healing. "Uncovering history and reclaiming the past," explained one researcher, "is an ambiguous process that may often have effects that are more unsettling than cohesive."[42]

Because much of the political and social structure of the society remained unchanged, and most of the guilty could never be punished, the documentation of atrocities alone did not necessarily signal a true repudiation. The Guatemalan government brushed off most of the commission's recommendations, and they were further rejected in a 1999 referendum. Since the institutions and individuals responsible for the genocide were still in place, "in many highland areas people remain too terrorized" to come forward publicly.[43] Can memory be enough, researchers wondered, if perpetrators remained in power and the structures of fear and oppression remained solid?

Moreover, the truth commissions' presuppositions may have promoted their own form of erasure. Anthropologist Patricia Foxen argued that the commissions' "official memory project" assumed that the guilty and the innocent could be clearly distinguished.[44] But these categories could do violence to people's actual experiences and individual or collective memories. Commissioners' national and international perspectives sometimes blinded them to local realities.

Guilt and innocence were not always clearly separable on the ground. In the struggle to survive the fog of war, many peasants collaborated or were forced to collaborate with the army or with the guerrillas. For some, the memory of their own betrayals and violence continues to torment them. Many peasants saw themselves "as both guilty participants as well as pawns in the violence." The commissions' questions and categories "could not encompass the messiness of such memories or the understandable desire to forget or deny their shame or guilt."[45]

The "messiness of such memories" was precisely a consequence of the nature of the violence in Guatemala. As the army sought to divide and fragment communities, its strategies included the "use of forced complicity (which compelled people to witness or execute acts of brutality against their own) and the criminalization of victims (which turned anyone who acknowledged or questioned the army's brutality into 'legitimate' targets of repression)." "In many communities, the line between forced and willing complicity, between actual participation in violence and necessary allegiance with killers, and between who was 'right' and who was 'wrong' remains extremely confusing and fuzzy . . . Moreover, the broader terror often became intimately intertwined with preexisting local power dynamics, land feuds, and interpersonal or familial *envidias*."[46]

Grassroots understandings based in local and personal conflicts compete with "an often internalized official army/PAC discourse, which claims that those missing or dead (or those associated with them) were 'subversives' and therefore guilty" and "a counter-memory reinforced by the UN and the Catholic Church (both of which, in the eyes of most Guatemalans, are far from politically neutral), which argues, conversely, that the army (and those who carried out its evil deeds) are primarily to blame . . . These contradictory moral frames lead people to depict an ambiguous scenario where all community members, including the *conocidos* (acquaintances) who carried out violence as well as their dead victims and surviving relatives, are both guilty *and* guiltless, to varying degrees."[47] The truth commission "seemed to represent one more foreign body that had parachuted in, urging them to join a cause that could help them."[48]

Neoliberal Economics, Politics, and Security

As elsewhere in Central America, neoliberalism came before peace to Guatemala. By the late 1980s, the government was promoting new export initiatives in the maquiladora industry and a new wave of nontraditional export agriculture.[49] And as in the rest of Central America, the end of the war enabled an influx of investment in these areas, as well as tourism and extractive industries.

The peace accords promoted Indigenous demands for local democratization and cultural rights, while burying the revolutionary movement's socioeconomic demands. "Democratization" in the form of decentralization and local self-governance complemented the defunding and dismantling of the state's regulatory and social welfare capacities. In many highland Mayan communities, Ladino power brokers were replaced by elected Indigenous mayors. But "autonomy without resources" undermined their ability to address the overwhelming poverty and destruction in their communities.[50]

Politics turned into a competitive struggle for access to resources.[51] Elected officials became brokers competing for NGO funding, promoting market-based development and cultural projects, and creating new clientelist networks. Electoral politics hinged on patronage and corruption, with candidates promising voters individual rewards rather than social change.

Just as the war had forced Mayans into collaboration in their own repression, so did the postwar.[52] Mayan politicians and officials became collaborators in the very system that perpetuated long-standing poverty and exclusion. Their actions fomented further competition, mistrust, division, and disillusionment, which further contributed to "repressing memories of past struggles."[53]

As in El Salvador, crime and insecurity spiked in the postwar. State security forces encouraged individuals and communities to take the law into their own hands. The civil patrols reemerged as Comités de Seguridad, as the new neoliberal order tasked communities with policing themselves.[54]

A 2000 study found that only 6 percent of the population had faith in the judicial system to protect their rights, which in turn "encouraged preferences for unofficial, punitive, and authoritarian mechanisms to provide security and resolve conflicts."[55] Vigilante justice and lynching flourished. As in the economic and political sphere, the new localized security regime brought more division and violence to already traumatized communities.

Over 50 percent of Guatemala's population lives below the poverty line; among the Maya population, 76 percent live in poverty and 38 percent in extreme poverty. Forty-three percent of children under the age of five are malnourished.[56] "As long as we're still poor, peace hasn't arrived for us," a Mayan villager told Jennifer Burrell. Or, in the words someone left on a wall in Huehuetenango, "*No hay paz sin trabajo* [There is no peace if there is no work]."[57]

Indigenous Peoples and Identities

The 1990s saw a surprising resurgence of Indigenous rights movements in Central America. Throughout the continent, Indigenous peoples worked to contest the celebration of the Colombian quincentenary in 1992. The International Labor Organization (ILO) Convention 169 (1989) on Indigenous peoples proclaimed their fundamental rights to self-determination, land, and cultural rights. The convention emphasized both *equal* rights and *special* rights of Indigenous peoples.

For centuries, the two had been posited as contradictory, and the contradiction used to keep Indigenous peoples marginalized. "Equal" rights translated into forced assimilation and loss of land, languages, culture, and autonomy; "special" rights brought exploitation, marginalization, and abandonment. ILO 169 insisted that states must guarantee both full access to the rights of all citizens *and* "full realisation of the social, economic and cultural rights of these peoples with respect for their social and cultural identity, their customs and traditions and their institutions."[58] The even stronger UN Declaration on the Rights of Indigenous Peoples (UNDRIP) of 2007 provided added guarantees for this spectrum of rights. (Notably, only four of the world's countries voted against the UNDRIP, all of them settler colonial nations: the United States, Canada, Australia, and New Zealand.)

A postwar resurgence of organizing based on Indigenous identity provoked debates in Central America, both within and outside Indigenous communities. In Guatemala during the 1970s and '80s, "culturalists" had focused on reviving and promoting Mayan languages and spiritual and cultural traditions, while "popular" movements like the CUC sought to unite Mayans and Ladinos for socioeconomic goals (although there was significant overlap, as we've seen). With the crushing of the popular organizations, culturalists took center stage. Through the 1990s, culturalists encouraged a new, collective "pan-Mayan" identity based on continuity with pre-Columbian Mayan cultures.

Urban, educated Mayans spearheaded pan-Mayanism. Many of the rural poor identified more with their local language and community than with the larger category "Maya." For most, the idea of "Mayan" religion had little meaning: many were Catholic, followed local *costumbre* that combined Catholic and Mayan elements, or belonged to newer evangelical churches. Some rural people rejected culturalists' promotion of education in Mayan languages as something that would hinder their children's access to the dominant Spanish-speaking society and institutions.

Some intellectuals critiqued what they called "neoliberal multiculturalism": governments promoting the idea of cultural rights that add folkloric color to national identity without threatening socioeconomic structures. Some on the left saw the culturalist approach as a poor, albeit safer, substitute for the claims for land, social, and economic rights. Indigenous rights could harmonize with neoliberal governments' drive for decentralization and local governance. Cost-conscious governments could give up on actually governing—or providing services to—Indigenous areas, touting their withdrawal as an acknowledgment of Indigenous rights, while enabling drug trafficking, multinationals, and violence to proliferate in the ungoverned space.[59]

Despite their differences, the culturalist and leftist approaches often overlapped and complemented each other as they had in the 1970s and '80s. Indigenous resistance emerged at the forefront of land and environmental struggles in many parts of rural Central America, even where explicitly Indigenous movements had not existed before. The postwar boom in agricultural, mining, energy, and infrastructure projects threatened communities across the region. Resistance to megaprojects and in defense of the right to land, water, and survival put Indigenous organizations at the center of global movements against neoliberal capitalism and for food sovereignty that Naomi Klein termed "blockadia."[60]

MINING, ENERGY, AND THE NEW EXTRACTIVISM

Extractivism—an economy based on the extraction of natural resources—has played a role in Latin America's history since the arrival of the Spanish seeking gold at the end of the 1400s. It has been associated with wanton deforestation; destruction of farmland, subsistence resources, and communities; contamination of air, water, and land; and enslavement, labor exploitation, and impoverishment as foreigners drained the region of its resources for their own benefit. Uruguayan author Eduardo Galeano famously titled his classic history *Open Veins of Latin America: Five Centuries of the Pillage of a Continent.*

The twenty-first century saw an upsurge of extractivism in Latin America, as well as new forms of resistance. The global economy became ever more resource dependent as populations grew rapidly and the global rich and middle class increased their consumption levels. Postwar Central America played an important role in both the new extractivism and resistance.

Opening their economies to foreign investment in resource extraction meant doing things like reducing companies' royalty and tax obligations, easing the licensing process, and promising relative freedom from labor and environmental regulations. In El Salvador, a 1999 foreign investment law allowed foreign corporations to sue in business-friendly international tribunals like the World Bank's International Centre for Settlement of Investment Disputes (ICSID) in disputes with the government. CAFTA contained similar provisions allowing foreign investors to sue if government policies threaten the value of their investments.[61]

The end of the wars in itself opened up new territories for mining. In El Salvador, significant gold deposits lie in the north of the country in areas that had been under FMLN control. In Guatemala much of the new extractivism is going on in Indigenous territories that also bore the brunt of the counterinsurgency.

Even as national laws welcomed mining, international law created some restrictions. ILO Convention 169 (1989) stipulated that any development project in Indigenous territories required "prior consultation" with the communities that would be affected. (All of the Central American countries except El Salvador signed ILO 169, although Nicaragua didn't sign until 2010.) The 2007 UNDRIP created even stronger protections: projects must obtain "free, prior, and informed consent" from Indigenous communities that would be affected. This meant that the consultation wasn't just a formality—in theory, communities have the right to reject such projects.

Extractivism has had devastating impacts on communities. Industrial and chemical processes suck up and contaminate scarce water resources. The few jobs these projects provide often don't go to local people, who may lose their lands. Their operations pour toxic waste into the air, land, and water. Those who protest find themselves facing the same kinds of private and public repression they faced during the war years. The profits go into the hands of the multinationals that own the mines and a few domestic elites and collaborators, while the resources are enjoyed by foreign or urban consumers. When the mines close, communities are left to deal with the devastation.

The upsurge of resistance to mining and megaprojects that swept Latin America had a decidedly Indigenous cast. It's been framed as the defense of territory, land, and water, and intersects with environmental justice movements and resistance to neoliberalism worldwide. These movements challenge the basic principles of neoliberal, market-based development and call for a completely different model that prioritizes the rights of mother earth, food sovereignty, radical democracy, and *buen vivir*: living well in harmony with nature rather than privatizing nature as a commercial resource. Battles against particular megaprojects are conceived as part of a larger struggle against colonialism, exploitation, and exclusion and for the rights of the global poor.

Over half of the hundreds of environmental activists killed in the past decade lived in Latin America. Guatemala has the highest per capita rate in the world of killings of environmental defenders. In 2018, a record sixteen environmental activists were killed there.[62]

Extractivism and Resistance in Guatemala

The end of the war led to an explosion of mining licenses granted to foreign companies in Guatemala as elsewhere in the region. Guatemalan president Óscar Berger (2004–2008) "placed intense direct pressure on all limbs of the state to conform to his mining-led development approach."[63]

Exploration in the Indigenous western highlands of San Marcos province began in 1997, under the auspices of the US-based Glamis Gold Company, later acquired by the Canadian multinational Goldcorp. Their Marlin Mine there went into production in 2005. One affected community, Sipakapa, argued that it had never been consulted as required under ILO 169, and organized its own popular community consultation in 2005. Ninety-eight percent voted against the mine. The slogan "*Sipakapa no se vende!*" ["Sipakapa is not for sale/does not sell out"] reflected the revolutionary language of the 1970s and '80s.[64]

In neighboring Huehuetenango, several municipal mayors (some from the URNG) received notice the same year that large new concessions in their municipalities had been granted to Canadian mining companies. They too organized community consultations to protest the decisions that had been made about their territories without their participation.

By 2019, over a hundred communities throughout Guatemala had organized community consultations, and all of them rejected mining.

Mining and oil interests also surged into Guatemala's long-conflictive regions of the Petén and the Northern Strip. In the Petén, local peasants saw the new Maya Biosphere Reserve as yet another project that took their lands for the benefit of outsiders.

Local movements articulated with national and global Indigenous and environmental organizations and NGOs to bring their protest to national courts and to international human and Indigenous rights tribunals. In 2017, Guatemala's Constitutional Court suspended operations at a US-owned silver mine, one of the world's largest, for failing to properly consult with Indigenous Xinca communities.[65]

Extractivism and Resistance in El Salvador

El Salvador's gold deposits and mining region overlapped significantly with the northern territories that were the heartland of FMLN control and had suffered greatly during the war. The region was environmentally and economically devastated (as was, in fact, much of the small and densely populated country), but also highly politicized.[66]

El Salvador's Catholic Church, still strongly influenced by the legacy of Liberation Theology, issued a proclamation against mining in 2007. A national poll the same year found that over 60 percent of the population opposed mining.[67] In 2005, the National Roundtable against Metallic Mining formed and, in 2006, pressed FMLN lawmakers to promote a ban on new mining permits. When the FMLN won the presidency in 2009, the new government announced that no new permits would be granted during its five-year term.[68]

In response to the ban, two international mining companies sued the government of El Salvador before the ICSID for causing loss in their profits, based on provisions in the 1999 investment law and CAFTA. In 2016, after seven years of closed-door deliberations, the ICSID ruled in favor of El Salvador.[69]

Heartened by the victory, in 2017 El Salvador became the first country in the world to ban metallic mining permanently, an extraordinary accomplishment by Indigenous and popular organizations and their allies in the FMLN government. Even members of the ARENA party signed on. But the country was still left with the toxic legacy of the thirty-one mining concessions that had occupied over 5 percent of the small country's territory, and of the Cerro Blanco mine over the Guatemalan border in the west of the country, whose runoff contaminated the Lempa River that supplies drinking and irrigation water for over half of the country.[70]

Honduras

Chapter 7 examined the mining development and resistance in Honduras, which had eliminated royalties entirely in 1998 and welcomed mining even more warmly after the 2009 coup.[71] By the end of the next decade, close to 30 percent of the country's territory had been granted to foreign companies in mining concessions. The explosion in mining led to a concomitant expansion in hydropower projects, in part to provide electricity to the industry. Despite the international outcry over the murder of Berta Cáceres in 2016, repression against environmental activists continues unabated in Honduras.

VIOLENCE AND GANGS: CONNECTING THE DOTS

How can it be that violence *increased* in Guatemala and El Salvador (though not in Nicaragua) after the peace treaties were signed, guerrillas were demobilized, and militaries reformed?

In the first five years after the signing of Guatemala's peace accord, there were 415 lynchings there, mostly in Indigenous communities, with 215 people killed.[72] Gangs proliferated, and Central America became a transit point for the international drug trade. Street crime also spiked. El Salvador, Honduras, and Guatemala consistently rank among the ten most violent countries in the world (measured by homicide rates).[73] In El Salvador, a decade after the peace treaty was signed, people lamented that the situation was "worse than the war."[74]

Recent scholarship has demanded that we expand the definition of "violence." Concepts like "slow violence" and "structural violence" remind us that physical harm, suffering, and death don't always happen as a discrete event at a single point in time. Poverty, lack of land, dangerous working conditions, exposure to toxins, unemployment, lack of health care: all of these human-caused phenomena cause physical suffering that accrues over time and can cause permanent damage or death. The perpetrators may not be as immediate and visible as the soldier or paramilitary who shoots a gun. They may sit in Oval Offices or corporate boardrooms. Direct violence is just the tip of the iceberg in Central America.

The legacy of the wars of the 1980s underlies today's violence in multiple ways. Several studies of Guatemala emphasize how people raised in and surrounded by violence and trauma may absorb and reenact such violence themselves.[75] In Honduras, "death cars" roam the streets in a frenzy of social cleansing, reincarnating the government's violent social control tactics of the 1980s.[76] The neoliberal order that arose from the ashes of the revolutionary projects relies on the continued suppression of social movements that threaten it. The war on drugs (described in chapter 7) has kept US military aid flowing. A culture of impunity and mistrust encourages local actors to take the law into their own hands. Perhaps nothing illustrates the tangled and intimate ties between Central America and the United States, and among official, interpersonal, and structural violence, than the rise and violence of Central America's gangs.

"Transnational" Gangs

In the United States, Central American violence is often automatically associated with the proliferation of gangs in the region. US president Donald Trump described Central American gangs as a foreign threat to US national security, declaring that "deadly loopholes" in US immigration law "have allowed MS-13, and other criminals, to break into our country." "The violent animals of MS-13 have committed heinous, violent attacks in communities across America," he insisted.[77] "The savage gang, MS-13, now operates in at least 20 different American states, and they almost all come through our southern border," he reiterated in 2019.[78]

Trump could have been channeling Thomas Jefferson, who, in enumerating King George's crimes in the US Declaration of Independence, explained that he had "endeavored to bring on the inhabitants of our frontiers, the merciless Indian savages, whose warfare is an undistinguished destruction of all ages, sexes, and conditions." Then, like now, US actions inside and outside its "frontier" played a big role in creating the very violence its leaders decried.

Countering Trump's narrative, many journalists and academics have pointed out that Central America's gangs are transnational in one important way: their roots are in Los Angeles, where Salvadoran youth fleeing the civil war began to arrive in significant numbers during the 1980s. Confronted with other ethnic gangs in schools and in their neighborhoods, they formed the MS-13 in self-protection. Their arrival coincided with the domestic wars on drugs and crime that sent a generation of petty offenders, mainly youth of color, into the US prison system. California's "three strikes" law and its shift to charging minor gang members as adults compounded the effects of President Clinton's 1996 immigration reform, which turned criminal charges into grounds for deportation. "By the turn of the 21st century, gang members were an American export," journalist Dara Lind concludes.[79] Between 2001 and 2010, the United States deported over a hundred thousand people who had been convicted of crimes to Central America, over forty thousand of them to Honduras.[80]

But that's only part of the story. The vast majority of Central American gang members have never been to the United States. Most of Central America's gangs are rooted in local communities and realities. And unlike other transnational gang or criminal organizations, Central America's MS-13 and its rival Calle 18 are not really organizations. They have no central leadership or coordination, and they operate at a local, not a transnational, level.[81]

But in Central America, as this book has argued, the local is inseparable from the transnational. US culture has permeated many aspects of Central American reality, and gangs are no exception. The small number of gang members who did spend time in the United States and were deported or returned to El Salvador brought new "gang styles" to existing Salvadoran gangs: "the use of tattoos, hand signs and the observance of street rules. Dazzled, homegrown gangsters took those new identities from the U.S."[82]

A look at how Guatemala City's youth gangs changed over time reflects deeper aspects of the US–Central America connection. In the 1970s and '80s, Guatemala City's population grew with refugees fleeing from rural war zones. Youth gangs or *maras* grew in the context of the popular organizing and leftist politics of the time. The maras first came to the public's attention in 1985, when they turned out to join a student-led protest against an increase in bus fares.

With the vicious counterinsurgency and the defeat of the urban working class and the left, the gangs absorbed the violence and hopelessness that surrounded them. Their exaggerated and horrific violence in later decades "was the product of what [the] military victory and its consequences have spawned . . . : a Guatemala wherein practices and mentalities of solidarity, trust, and mutual concern have been ripped apart."

The youth of the 1990s and beyond "came of age in a Guatemala City largely remade and reassembled by violence. They remember the stories of cadavers and not of the struggles for social justice."[83] To the extent that the United States played a decisive role in Guatemala's war and postwar, it shaped the context that produced the country's gangs.

Neoliberalism fostered lawlessness and violence as the state withdrew from governance and social welfare. The collapse of decent employment left poor youth with few alternatives. In Honduras, a study emphasizes the loss of male employment and the growth of female maquiladora employment as another factor influencing the growth of gangs. Unable to find work in the formal economy, "many men have begun to participate in alternate economies to earn the money and respect that is denied them." Gangs offered men "networking and economic opportunities, as well as protection against the emasculation resulting from economic dependence on women."[84]

Central America's response to gangs drew directly on the US experience as countries imported anti-crime tactics from the United States. They "zeroed [in] on youth gangs and embraced draconian anti-crime policies" based on those developed in Los Angeles. In Central America, these were termed *mano dura*. Many youths deported from the United States were incarcerated immediately upon arrival, and "prisons became schools for gang recruitment."[85] High incarceration levels in Central America only strengthened the gangs and linked them more tightly to organized crime. Violence and murder rates skyrocketed in all three countries.[86]

The local realities shaping gangs have become transnationalized in one more important way. As the drug trade moved into Central America, powerful drug cartels drew in local gangs to carry out their low-level footwork. Replicating long-standing patterns in Central America's history, the region's gangs became transnationalized and exploited at the same time.

By 2000, up to 80 percent of the cocaine entering the United States was shipped through Guatemala. Global organized crime took advantage of local societal breakdowns to "incorporate mareros [members of the maras or gangs] as cheap labor within a system of networks that employs down-and-out youth everywhere in the world."[87]

Gangs were also a fact of life in Nicaragua, but they were quite different from the gangs elsewhere in the region, in large part because of differences in Nicaragua's history. In Nicaragua, the revolution succeeded in taking power, and the militarized state characterized by torture, massacre, and death squads was defeated. Even after the Sandinistas were voted out of office in 1990 and the neoliberal right was in control until 2007, and even though corruption and political disenchantment flourished, the state and its institutions were not imbued with the horrors that characterized the other three countries.

The Nicaraguan government eschewed the *mano dura* policies followed by its neighbors. "Nicaragua is less homicidal than its neighbors in no small part because of the ways in which the revolution enabled the then youthful revolutionary leaders and subsequent non-Sandinista governments to experiment with and then institutionalize things like gun control, alternative policing models, and other policies and social programs, especially ones focused on altering Nicaraguan masculinity in ways first pushed by revolutionary Sandinista women," concludes one study.[88]

POST-NEOLIBERAL CENTRAL AMERICA

In the first decade of the new century, doubts about market reforms came to the fore again. Central America followed the continent's "pink tide" that brought the left back into power in country after country in the 2000s. In Nicaragua, Daniel Ortega was elected president again in 2006, after sixteen years of right-wing governance. In Honduras, Manuel Zelaya moved to the left after his election in 2006, only to be overthrown in a coup in 2009. In El Salvador, the FMLN's Mauricio Funes in 2009 replaced the right-wing ARENA party that had governed for twenty years. Guatemala proved the exception, with the right firmly in control of national politics.

But progressive and redistributive politics have been constrained as the collapse of the socialist bloc, and then of Venezuela, left small, poor countries adrift in the unfavorable seas of global capitalism. While in the United States, the fall of the USSR led a lot of people to conclude that "socialism doesn't work," in poor Latin American countries, it's also abundantly clear that capitalism doesn't work.

Latin American revolutionary socialists of the twentieth century faced unremitting hostility and sabotage when they tried to challenge oligarchies and foreign investors. Twenty-first-century socialists and nonsocialist leaders on the left sought to create hybrids that bolstered redistributive, antipoverty, and social safety programs while welcoming foreign investment, tourism, and mining and energy exports to keep capital flowing in. It was a difficult balance that often put them on a collision course with peasant, Indigenous, and environmental organizations that felt that their interests were being sacrificed.

In contrast to the FMLN in El Salvador, which banned metallic mining, the twenty-first-century Sandinista government pinned its development hopes on a major megaproject. Ortega dreamed of a canal that would rival Panama's and bring untold shipping and transport riches into the country. The Nicaraguan canal became "the centerpiece of Sandinista development policy" after the government signed a contract with a Chinese company to move forward in 2013. "One of the world's largest infrastructure projects to date, the canal comes with a $50 billion price tag and a host of environmental and social costs that have provoked wide ranging opposition," wrote one anthropologist. The concession included the right to build tourist resorts, a free-trade zone, an international airport, and a petroleum pipeline.[89] Environmentalists point to the loss of forest and wetlands and the contamination the project itself and the arrival of the shipping industry will bring. Local communities, many of them Indigenous and Afro-descended, fear they will be displaced or lose the territories they rely on for farming and fishing.

Central America's countries continue to be devastated by decades of war and violence and a global economic system that extracts its resources and enriches the few while impoverishing the many. The always drought-prone region is on the front lines of the climate catastrophe. By 2020, five consecutive years of drought had left small farmers desperate for food. Increasing numbers of Central Americans came to see migration as their only hope for survival.

CHAPTER 10

MIGRATION

Few predicted that the peace accords and neoliberal reforms of the 1990s would lead to a flood of out-migration in the following decades, as flight would increasingly become the last resort of people desperate to survive, and ties to the United States made it the obvious destination.

Migration has been an inherent aspect of all human history, including Central American history. Pretty much every individual on the planet is located where they are because either they or multiple ancestors migrated voluntarily or by force over time. In the twentieth century, Central American migration was primarily internal, as the rural population lost lands and moved to colonize frontiers or to work in plantation agriculture or in the capital cities. During the wars of the 1980s, many more were displaced within their own countries, to other Central American countries, to Mexico, and increasingly, to the United States.

This chapter will examine how and why they came, and how their migration changed their lives and their communities in sometimes complex and unexpected ways.

FLEEING HOME

The Central American wars of the 1980s caused millions to flee their homes. Some became internal refugees, relocating with relatives, hiding in the mountains, or moving to the anonymity of the capital city or hastily established refugee camps. Others crossed borders to find refuge in camps or on their own in Costa Rica, Honduras, and Mexico. Some two hundred thousand Nicaraguans fled their country during the 1978–1979 insurrection, though many of these returned after the 1979 revolutionary victory. By the end of the 1980s, around 3 million Central Americans had fled from their countries of origin. Seven hundred and fifty thousand remained in Mexico, while a million crossed through Mexico into the United States. Some continued on to Canada.[1]

Working with the United Nations High Commissioner for Refugees (UNHCR), Mexico built camps along its southern border for forty-six thousand mostly Mayan Indigenous refugees from Guatemala. Another two hundred thousand Guatemalans, along with half a million Salvadorans, found their own way to seek a living, informally and unrecognized, in Mexico.[2]

In 1970, the US census counted 114,000 Central Americans. By 1980, this had risen to 350,000; by 1990, over a million. Instead of slowing as the wars ended, migration increased: in 2000, the census counted over 2 million Central American–born. In 2010, there were over 3 million, and in 2017, close to 3.5 million. (These numbers do not include the growing population of US-born children of Central American migrants who are not tallied among the "foreign-born" but reached about 1.2 million in 2015.)[3]

Using self-identification rather than birthplace, the Pew Research Center calculated a population of 2.3 million Salvadorans (57 percent foreign-born), 1.4 million Guatemalans (60 percent foreign-born), 940,000 Hondurans (62 percent foreign-born), and 464,000 Nicaraguans (55 percent foreign-born) in the United States as of 2017. The foreign-born percentage is of interest because it shows the recent nature of the immigration: Central Americans have a much higher proportion of foreign-born than do Hispanics as a whole, for whom 33 percent were foreign-born in 2017.[4] Sixty percent of immigrants born in Honduras were undocumented, along with 56 percent of those from Guatemala and 51 percent of those from El Salvador.[5] The real figures are likely higher than what's recorded in the census, because immigrants, especially those who are undocumented, are notoriously undercounted.

A much larger Mexican migration to the United States also grew rapidly during the same decades, with the Mexican-born population growing from well under a million in 1970 to close to 12 million in 2010. But Mexico's migration slowed considerably after that, reaching "net zero" in

2011 and then reversing, so that the Mexican-born population shrank by some five hundred thousand by 2017. Mexicans continued to arrive—but even more were leaving.[6]

A smaller number of Central Americans—some eight hundred thousand—relocated elsewhere in Central America during the decade of the 1980s. About 10 percent of them received benefits as recognized refugees. Some others received aid from religious and humanitarian NGOs; most struggled to reconstruct their lives without organized aid.[7] Many of those who had relocated inside Central America, whether in refugee camps or at the margins of the mainstream, returned home after the various peace accords of the 1990s.

THE LEGAL LANDSCAPE IN THE UNITED STATES

Contrary to the oft-repeated phrase that, in then president Barack Obama's words, the United States has a "tradition of welcoming immigrants from around the world," this is far from the case.[8] It's more accurate to say that, as a settler colonial nation, the United States has a tradition of welcoming *white* immigrants. This tradition began in its Declaration of Independence, which decried the British Crown's restrictions on migration from Britain, and was reinforced with the new country's first naturalization law in 1790 that offered entry and citizenship to "any Alien being a free white person," and the post–Civil War naturalization law revision that extended its provisions to "Aliens of African nativity and to persons of African descent" (virtually none of whom at the time had the slightest desire or ability to migrate to the United States, a voyage that for Africans had historically meant enslavement, not freedom). The 1870 law explicitly excluded from welcome or naturalization those nonwhite immigrants who were actually arriving at that time: Chinese and Mexicans. Indeed, most of the world's peoples, who were neither "white" nor "persons of African nativity," were systematically refused entry to the United States on racial grounds until the mid-twentieth century.

A special set of laws applied to Mexicans, whom Secretary of State James Buchanan termed "an inferior, indolent, mongrel race."[9] While they were racially "ineligible to citizenship," Mexican workers were essential for the railroad, mining, and agricultural development of the western United States. So rather than exclude Mexicans physically, Congress left entry open, but designed a plethora of systems to ensure that Mexicans entered the country as temporary laborers, rather than potential settlers or citizens. Exploitative guest worker programs and spectacular mass deportations in the 1930s and 1950s confirmed that Mexicans were not among those immigrants who were "welcomed."

The 1965 immigration overhaul known as the Immigration and Nationality or Hart-Celler Act (INA) is generally hailed for removing, once and for all, racial quotas and restrictions on immigration. That perspective has some validity if we look at how the law affected Europeans, Africans, and Asians. But for Mexicans, the 1965 law just created a new kind of restriction: the first-ever immigration quota that turned many Mexican migrant workers into "illegal" immigrants. By 1980, there were some 1.5 million undocumented Mexicans in the United States; by 1986, this had grown to 3.2 million, due to a combination of Mexico's debt crisis and a booming US labor market. "Illegality" was a new way to criminalize Mexicans and justify continued exploitation and exclusion. Meanwhile "wars" on drugs and crime did the same to other populations of color.[10]

Most Central Americans fleeing persecution or violence in the 1980s had no path to legal entry into the United States. Like so many Mexicans, they simply crossed the border "without inspection," evading official crossing stations, and entered the underground world of undocumentedness.

Popular and congressional concern about the growing undocumented population grew in the early 1980s, and in 1986 Congress passed the Immigration Reform and Control Act (IRCA). IRCA had three main components: employer sanctions, which penalized employers for hiring workers who were undocumented; increased border control, to prevent people from entering without documents; and legalization, which allowed a significant number of people without documents to regularize their status. IRCA sweetened its terms for agricultural employers who relied on Mexican workers, adding special provisions for their legalization and a new guest worker program.

The first two components of IRCA—employer sanctions and increased border control—have been permanent and ongoing, and laid the basis for increasingly punitive anti-immigrant law and practice from the 1990s on. The third, legalization, was a onetime olive branch to immigrants themselves. Two of its parameters made it clear that it was Mexican migrant workers, rather than Central American refugees, that were its target.

First, legalization was offered only to migrants who could prove that they had been in the United States continuously since January 1, 1982.

That automatically excluded large numbers of Central Americans, whose numbers only started to grow significantly after 1980. Second, IRCA offered residency status to seasonal farmworkers, most of whom were Mexican. In the end, IRCA enabled 2.7 million immigrants to legalize their status, 70 percent of them Mexican.[11]

Still, almost three hundred thousand Central Americans were able to gain legal status through IRCA. Most (60 percent) were Salvadorans, followed by Guatemalans (25.4 percent) and Nicaraguans (6 percent). Smaller numbers from other Central American countries made up the difference.[12]

Asylum

Since the vast majority of Central Americans who reached the United States in the 1980s were fleeing violence and persecution, one might imagine that US refugee law, newly updated under President Carter in 1980, would enable them to obtain legal status. The old law had applied primarily to refugees from communist countries. The new one adopted the United Nations definition that anyone with a "well-founded fear of persecution" based on membership in one of several defined categories (race, ethnicity, religion, etc.) should be eligible.

Yet during the 1980s, immigration authorities approved only 1.8 percent of Guatemalans' applications and 2.6 percent of Salvadorans.'[13] Nicaraguans fared somewhat better, with 25 percent of applications being approved. Denial of asylum to Guatemalans and Salvadorans was mostly a foreign policy decision. In order to keep US military aid flowing, the government needed to deny that those countries' governments were committing atrocities, war crimes, and massacres. Granting asylum would have acknowledged that these human rights violations were, in fact, rampant.

Canada, in contrast, accepted 80 percent of its much smaller number of Central American applicants. By 1996, there were forty thousand Salvadorans, thirteen thousand Guatemalans, and over eight thousand Nicaraguans in Canada. After the Central American wars ended, Canada's policies turned against Central Americans, and migration there slowed considerably.[14]

It's worth noting the difference between refugee status and asylum. Candidates must apply for refugee status from outside the United States. After what's usually a lengthy screening process, a person who is approved is eligible for a host of benefits to aid their resettlement in the United States. Asylum is a different process, through which individuals arriving at the border, or already inside the country, can appeal for the right to stay based on criteria similar to those used for refugees—but without the walfare benefits. While there is an annual quota on the number of people granted refugee status, there is no limit on how many asylum applications can be approved.

Both processes were stacked against Central Americans, though. There was no infrastructure in place for in-country processing for Central Americans. For those that applied from inside the United States, officials interpreted Carter's new law narrowly, despite protests from international agencies, including the UNHCR, arguing that those fleeing violence should be granted refuge even if they fell outside the parameter of persecution based upon membership in a particular group.

Many thousands of Central Americans never even got the chance to apply for asylum. Apprehended at the border, they were placed in detention centers, where mistreatment was rampant. "Women and children were sexually abused; private correspondence was photocopied for government prosecutors; money and property were stolen; phone calls were taped; refugees were denied access to translated legal forms and documents; and many were denied access to legal counsel."[15]

The goal was to coerce or trick refugees into signing "voluntary departure" papers so they could be quickly deported without ever applying for asylum.

> One common tactic was to separate family members and tell one spouse that the other had already signed a request for "voluntary departure." Investigators found evidence that some refugees were drugged with tranquilizers and then coerced into signing the I-274A form that waived their right to counsel and a deportation hearing, and then immediately scheduled for voluntary departure. And in particularly tragic cases, information about the deportees was sent to security forces in the homeland, leading to the detention, torture, and murder of some of them.[16]

The ACLU and Amnesty International documented dozens of cases in which Salvadorans deported back to their country were captured, tortured, or killed after their return.[17]

In 1985, the American Baptist Church (ABC), representing a coalition of eighty religious and refugee rights organizations, brought a class action lawsuit against the US government, claiming that given the dire situations in their countries, the extraordinarily low rate of application approvals for Salvadorans and Guatemalans constituted discrimination. A 1990 settlement rescinded over 150,000 negative asylum decisions and required the government to grant relief from deportation, work authorization, and a new or reopened asylum hearing for all Guatemalans and Salvadorans in the country as of that year.

Also in 1990, Congress created Temporary Protected Status (TPS), a two-year program that allowed Salvadorans (but not Guatemalans) to apply for a new temporary legal status based on the dangerous conditions in their home country. TPS was only available to those in the United States at the time the designation was made; later arrivals were not eligible.

Some two hundred thousand undocumented Salvadorans took advantage of TPS. Others who had been living under the radar of US immigration authorities worried that by applying and making themselves known to immigration authorities, they would be quickly deported when TPS expired: "practically signing your own deportation orders." For others, the time, paperwork, and costs involved were a disincentive.[18] Cecilia Menjívar termed the status a kind of "liminal legality" because recipients were consigned to limited rights and ongoing uncertainty.[19]

In 1992 when TPS ended, Salvadorans were granted one more two-year respite with Deferred Enforced Departure. More recently, Hondurans and Nicaraguans became eligible for TPS in 1999 after their countries suffered the devastating effects of Hurricane Mitch, and Salvadorans in 2001 after major earthquakes in their country. Despite Trump's objections, TPS for Salvadorans, Nicaraguans, and Hondurans was extended through 2021.

Congress created another path to legalization in 1997 with the Nicaraguan Adjustment and Central American Relief Act (NACARA). As its name suggests, NACARA granted Nicaraguans the right to "adjust" their status—that is, to become legal permanent residents (i.e., obtain a "green card"). Some Salvadorans and Guatemalans were also eligible, but the criteria were narrower: they had to prove that they had been in the United States continuously since 1990; had applied for asylum, ABC benefits, or TPS; and that their deportation "would result in extreme hardship."[20]

At the end of 2014, in the context of growing numbers of unaccompanied youth crossing the border, President Obama created the Central American Minors Refugee/Parole program, allowing a small number of youth to apply for asylum within their own countries instead of making the dangerous trip to the border. The program's narrow parameters excluded many: the minor must have parents with legal status in the United States and meet the legal qualifications for refugee status. Six months into the program, just over 3,000 applications had been submitted, from 2,859 Salvadoran, 426 Honduran, and 59 Guatemalan minors.[21]

For many vulnerable youth, the program seemed inherently contradictory. If their lives were in danger, how could they begin a months- or years-long legal process that might or might not end in permission to enter the United States? They needed to escape urgently, and without drawing attention to their plans. In any case, Trump ended the program shortly after taking office.

The Trump administration also implemented new policies making it harder for anyone to win an asylum case. In fiscal year 2018, immigration courts' asylum approval rates dropped to 23.5 percent of Salvadorans, 21.2 percent of Hondurans, and 18.8 percent of Guatemalans who applied. One reason was the US attorney general's June 2018 ruling that victims of gang violence or domestic violence were no longer eligible. The proportions dropped even lower in fiscal year 2019.[22]

"Enforcement" After 1990

Other changes to immigration law and policy in the 1990s expanded the harsh aspects of IRCA, increasing what was called "enforcement"—militarization of the border and criminalization and deportation of undocumented immigrants inside the country. President Bill Clinton's 1996 Illegal Immigration Reform and Immigrant Responsibility Act epitomized the neoliberal approach in its very title: immigrants had to take individual "responsibility" for their actions. The creation of Immigration and Customs Enforcement (ICE) under the new Department of Homeland Security, in 2003, meant that now an entire agency was dedicated to treating immigrants as criminals.

The "enforcement" drive hardened with ongoing militarization of the border and growing attention to "interior enforcement" under presidents Bush and Obama, and President Trump's radical anti-immigrant thrust after 2016. The border patrol grew from around 4,000 in 1992 to a peak of 21,444 in 2011. Since then, it's hovered around 20,000, despite Trump's frequent promises and designated funding to increase the numbers by many thousands.[23] The agency has simply been unable to recruit sufficient candidates to make up for its high attrition rates, much less grow.[24]

Criminals and Innocents

Presidents Obama and Trump both criminalized immigrants with their rhetoric, in different ways. Obama and his policies tried to draw a clear, bright line between "criminal" immigrants and innocent, deserving immigrants. His agenda called for helping immigrants he deemed "innocent" while punishing the rest. Deportations of "criminals" rose under Obama, even though many of those categorized as criminals had committed long-ago, minor infractions. During his first years in office, Obama pressed Congress to pass a "comprehensive" immigration reform that would combine enforcement with some sort of amnesty, while alienating his allies on the left by implementing only the enforcement side of the agenda.

In 2012, Obama finally took some steps toward addressing the demands of an increasingly active youth immigrant movement. His signature program, Deferred Action for Childhood Arrivals (DACA), was a pared-down version of the Dream Act, which Congress had debated and failed to pass numerous times. The Dream Act would have created a path to citizenship for young immigrants who had grown up in the United States—"Dreamers"—the ultimate "innocents," since they were brought by their parents "through no fault of their own." DACA was a stopgap that did much less—it granted Dreamers relief from deportation and permission to work for two years.[25]

Like TPS, DACA required that people who were undocumented come out of the shadows and provide the government with reams of information. Many DACA-eligible youth lived in mixed-status families and feared potential consequences for their parents or siblings. The costs were also prohibitive for some, though many organizations mobilized to raise funds to help people apply.

Like IRCA, DACA favored Mexicans over Central Americans by excluding recent arrivals—only those in the country as of 2007 were eligible. Notably, 2007 is just when Mexican migration began to drop, and Central American to rise again. Almost 80 percent of DACA recipients were Mexican—some 550,000. Still, as of 2017, 60,000 Central Americans had obtained DACA status, including 26,000 from El Salvador, 18,000 from Guatemala, and 16,000 from Honduras.[26]

For Trump, almost all immigrants were potential criminals, especially those from what he termed "shit-hole countries." He vowed to end DACA, proclaiming that "many of the people in DACA [are] . . . very tough, hardened criminals." He created a special office for Victims of Immigrant Crime and gloried in parading "angel families," the "victims of illegal immigration."[27]

THE 1980S: REVOLUTION, WAR, AND MIGRATION

The immediate roots of today's Central American migration to the United States lie in the wars of the 1980s. Not surprisingly, the three countries at war—Nicaragua, El Salvador, and Guatemala—sent the most migrants, while Honduras and Costa Rica sent almost none.

Nicaragua

Although tens of thousands of Nicaraguans fled their country during the 1978–1979 war, many of them returned after the Sandinista victory. The first Nicaraguans to flee the revolution were those associated with the old (Somoza) regime, and many of them joined the ranks of the new counterrevolutionary force that the CIA was building in Miami.

Those who came from the upper classes were more likely to have established ties in the United States, especially in Miami, which became the prime destination for Nicaraguan migrants. As the reach of the revolution and the Contra war expanded over the decade of the 1980s, so did the socioeconomic and political composition of those who left Nicaragua. While some opposed the revolution, others wanted to escape the war or the draft or simply find economic opportunity.

About 40 percent of Nicaraguans (two hundred thousand) settled in "Little Managua" in Miami, though they also went to other centers of Central American population like Los Angeles, San Francisco, Houston, New York, and New Jersey.[28]

Because the United States supported the counterrevolution and wanted to portray the Sandinistas as a repressive government, it was more willing to grant asylum to Nicaraguan refugees than to other Central Americans. Nicaraguans were also eligible for several different short-term relief programs. Still, the majority of Nicaraguans, like their Salvadoran and Guatemalan counterparts, remained undocumented.

Honduras allowed 13,500 Miskitu Indians from Nicaragua to resettle across the border. Other Nicaraguans, many headed for US-funded Contra camps, poured into the border region. Another twenty thousand sought official refuge in Costa Rica; tens or hundreds of thousands more entered unofficially, some working with opposition groups there. Refugees even found homes in other war-torn countries; over a hundred thousand Nicaraguans were estimated to reside in Guatemala by the end of the decade.[29]

El Salvador

The number of Salvadorans fleeing the war and the death squads increased rapidly after late 1979. Some half a million abandoned the country between 1979 and 1982. By the end of the 1980s, another half million had left, and half a million were internally displaced. In 1983, eighteen thousand Salvadorans were housed in UNHCR-run refugee camps across the Honduran border. The Honduran government estimated that another two hundred thirty thousand refugees, mostly Nicaraguans and Salvadorans, were living illegally in Honduras by the end of the 1980s.[30] The Honduran army implemented its own immigration policy, frequently attacking Salvadorans to prevent their entry, as in the Río Sumpul and Río Lempa massacres. The army even attacked Salvadorans inside UN-run refugee camps.[31]

Another twenty thousand Salvadorans obtained official refuge in Costa Rica; tens of thousands more resettled there informally. Perhaps seventy thousand relocated in Guatemala; seven thousand were granted refugee status in Nicaragua and another twenty thousand settled there on their own. In 1992, Costa Rica permitted Central American refugees who had remained in the country to legalize their status.[32]

A careful study of the geography of migration in and from El Salvador found that the war zones held by the FMLN and under continuing army attack had the highest death rates and produced the most internal migrants and refugees in Honduras. The government-held zones that experienced the war more in the form of economic sabotage by the FMLN—attacks on infrastructure like roads, bridges, dams, and power stations—and political mobilization like strikes were the source of most migration to the United States. Those who came to the United States, then, tended to be better off and more urban. Many were student, union, and other activists who were the target of urban repression.[33]

By 1987, Salvadorans in the United States were sending 350 to 600 million dollars a year in remittances to El Salvador, and President Duarte appealed to US president Reagan to halt deportations, saying El Salvador's economic stability depended on their remittances.[34]

Something similar happened after the 2001 earthquakes that left a quarter of El Salvador's population homeless. Then President Francisco Flores pressed US president Bush to extend TPS to Salvadorans in the United States, explaining that their remittances would be crucial to the country's recovery. The 1.8 million Salvadorans living in the United States at the time were sending home 1.5 billion dollars a year. President Bush agreed: "This will allow them to continue to work here and to remit some of their wages back home to support El Salvador's recovery efforts." Any Salvadoran in the United States as of February 13, 2001 (the date of the second earthquake) was eligible.[35]

Guatemala

Guatemala created a million internal refugees during the height of the counterinsurgency campaign between 1982 and 1984.[36] Smaller numbers were able to find refuge in UN camps across the border in Mexico, while some continued on to the United States. As the counterinsurgency ground on, the very issues that had motivated poor people to fight for change motivated them to flee.

By the late 1980s, people in the highlands of Huehuetenango began to "speak of men . . . who have returned from work in the United States with 'bags full of money' to start bus and truck lines into northern Huehuetenango. In absolute contrast to ten years ago, [villagers] now almost invariably ask about work and wages in the United States and about the journey there and back," reported US anthropologist John Watanabe, who carried out research in one village there from 1978 to 1980 and again in 1988.[37]

From another highland town, Todos Santos, many fled to the Ixcán and to refugee camps in Mexico in the early 1980s. When they returned later in the decade they confronted not only the same land and resource scarcity but heightened local divisions and suspicion. "Intracommunal and even intrafamilial distrust, the omnipresent threat of denunciation by parties to a conflict, financial pressures, lack of democratic alternatives,

continuing impunity, rumors of *orejas* (literally 'ears' but used colloqui-
ally to refer to spies), and the accompanying economic crisis all contributed to the earliest wave of men migrating to the United States." It was
hard to separate economic from political reasons for migration: "Early
wage-labor migrants to the United States almost always identified the
ongoing war and uneasy political situation as a major contributing factor
to why they left." By the mid-2000s, a third of the village had migrated
temporarily or permanently to the United States.[38]

In the Ixil triangle, site of some of the most horrific repression in
the 1980s, the war uprooted villagers from their homes into flight in the
mountains, or imprisonment in military-run model villages. As hopes for
a better future in Guatemala were crushed, the north beckoned.

In one colonization project in the Ixcán, migration to the United
States began in the mid-1980s, and about fifty people had left by 2004.
"The money they have sent has been important to the village and has created new divides." "There were some similarities," one villager who now
lives in East Oakland told an anthropologist, "between his trek down
from the mountains to the rain forest in Guatemala and his crossing the
border into Arizona: in both cases he was hoping for a better life, did not
know the way, and was opening the path with his hands."[39]

One migrant reported that "all in all, the situation never changes fundamentally for Guatemalans; for him the rain forest and what he calls
the 'cement forest' or the 'gold cage' have unfortunate similarities." Many
rural Guatemalan migrants to the United States found themselves con-
fined to "the most depressed areas where violent crime, racial hostility,
and drug use are common. The poverty and social decay of the inner city
often places new arrivals side by side with the poorest, most neglected
and discriminated against Americans."[40]

POST-1990S MIGRATIONS

Instead of decreasing after Central America's wars ended, migration to
the United States increased significantly, especially from the three countries sometimes called the "Northern Triangle": Guatemala, El Salvador,
and Honduras. Nicaragua, notably, was an exception, sending few migrants northward. Flight from Honduras, much lower in earlier decades,
spiked after the 2009 coup.

As described in the previous chapter, "peace" in Central America
failed to solve the structural problems that had caused the revolutions.

Inequality, poverty, landlessness, un- and underemployment, and lack of access to basic social services like health care and education were long-term problems, exacerbated by war and by postwar neoliberal policies. The wars uprooted and destroyed traditional safety nets, exploitative and unjust as they were. And the neoliberal era brought new social problems into the mix, including growing violence and insecurity, the drug trade, and the threats posed by increasingly powerful gangs.

Add to these the impact of climate change, which has particularly affected the always drought-prone Northern Triangle countries. Subsistence agriculture has been devastated by drought. Warming temperatures also contributed to an outbreak of coffee rust from 2012 to 2014, undermining the livelihoods of small farmers and workers. Over half of recent migrants are agricultural workers, and the most common reason they give for migrating is "no food."[41]

The establishment of Central American refugee communities in the United States laid some groundwork for subsequent migrations. Migrants sent home news, photographs, and remittances that often gave an exaggerated view of the kind of opportunity that awaited new arrivals. Having incurred debts and embodying a family's investment toward a better future, migrants could be ashamed to confess the loneliness and poor conditions they confronted in the United States. The remittances they sent could also be used to fund new trips north by family members, and for conspicuous consumption in the home country like new houses and cars that motivated others to try their luck. The presence of relatives or even acquaintances in cities and towns around the United States encouraged Central Americans to follow, assuming that they would receive a helping hand upon arrival.

In many cases, one or both parents came to the United States as a last resort to secure the family's survival, pay off debts, provide for basic needs, or pay for children's education, leaving the children in the care of relatives. A decade later, many of these youth contributed to what came to be called a "surge" of unaccompanied minors seeking to reunite with their parents: twenty-four thousand in fiscal year 2012, thirty-nine thousand in 2013, and sixty-nine thousand in 2014, when the media first noticed. Between March and July of 2014, the surge "overwhelmed government capacity, sparking a political crisis for the Obama administration and a firestorm of public attention." A survey by the UNHCR found that 41 percent of migrant youth had at least one parent living in the

United States. Another study concluded that "child migration is strongly tied to parents' migration histories and is virtually nonexistent when parents have no U.S. experience."[42] Despite slight drops in 2015 and 2017, the trajectory was upward, reaching 69,488 in fiscal year 2019.[43]

The second decade of the century also saw more parents bringing their children on the dangerous journey north. The year 2019 saw a big rise in those arrested in family units—475,000, up from just over 100,000 in fiscal year 2018, which, in turn, was the highest ever.[44]

The Changing Face of Migration

The rise in Central American migration in the twenty-first century was accompanied by a startling drop in Mexican migration. The changing face of migration was reflected in border apprehension statistics. Until 2012, the vast majority of those apprehended were Mexicans. As the Mexican numbers continued to drop after 2007, Central American numbers rose, as a whole surpassing Mexicans in 2014 and accounting for nearly all of a 2019 spike in apprehensions. The year 2019 saw 264,168 Guatemalans and 253,795 Hondurans detained on the southern border, followed by 166,458 Mexicans and 89,811 Salvadorans. That year was the first time in history that any individual country—and in this case, two of them—surpassed Mexico in numbers apprehended.[45]

The militarization of the border that coincided with the rise in Central American migration had little effect in deterring refugees from trying to flee to safety. What it did accomplish was to push migrants out of physically safer crossing areas in California and into the Arizona desert, where death from exposure and dehydration became a tragic addition to the perils faced by migrants. The border patrol estimated that over seven thousand migrants died trying to cross the desert between 1997 and 2017, but a USA Today Network investigation found that the real numbers were up to 300 percent higher, because many or most deaths went unrecorded and uncounted.[46]

Migration and Neoliberalism

Neoliberalism created the structural and material situation that caused so many to abandon their countries. Some fled the gang, drug, and official violence, while others fled the grinding poverty and lack of opportunity.

Migration sustained the neoliberal order by serving as a safety valve to siphon off unemployed and impoverished youth. Migrants' remittances helped to resign the poor to low wages and the dismantling of social services.

Remittances can also drive migration, as recipients flaunt their new-found wealth. US-acquired individualism and competitive values align comfortably with the neoliberal culture overtaking Central American countries.

Remittances played a role in the rise of crime, interpersonal violence, and gangs. Sudden influxes of dollars created new inequalities, jealousies, and opportunities. Local gangs targeted families receiving remittances or known to have relatives in the United States. Larger organized crime rings kidnapped migrants en route to the United States or even after arrival, holding them for ransom they were confident US-based relatives could muster.

National and international aid programs aimed at reducing the need for migration could have a similarly contradictory impact. In the war-devastated Ixil triangle town of Nebaj, an influx of microcredit opportunities came to be invested where villagers saw the greatest potential profit: traveling to the United States where higher-wage jobs awaited them. Or they invested in land, pushing prices up and further spurring migration. When the US job market began to tighten after 2006, and then the economy contracted massively in 2008, the impoverished village-level system of incurring debts to finance migration in the hopes of big returns collapsed just as dramatically as it did for college students, home-owners, or Wall Street bankers in the United States. When the bubble burst the pyramid scheme collapsed.[47]

"Migration," one study concludes, "is a process that runs on debt, with migrants indebting themselves and their relatives to the migration stream in ways that many are unable to repay. The debts not only enable migration but pressure more people to go north, in a chain of exploitation that can suck more value from the sending population than it returns."[48]

One study of Honduras adds that the upsurge of migration after 2009 also reflects neoliberalism's culture of individualism. Revolutionary and even reformist dreams of the twentieth century, whether through state-led modernization, the social welfare state, the Catholic Church, or revolutionary socialism, were crushed by the 1990s. As "participation in collective political movements puts people at risk of imprisonment, torture, or death," revolutionary dreams gave way to "politically resigned pragmatism." Migration was a quintessentially individual path to a better life.[49]

Migration became a link in the chain of neoliberal land grabs for megaprojects, tourism, and new plantations. "Poverty is created as a breeding ground to kill hope," said Garifuna doctor and activist Luther Castillo. "They make us more miserable so that our youth don't see hope in the communities and migrate. And when they migrate, others come to grab the land. It's a systemic process of displacement."[50]

COMING FULL CIRCLE

Central American migrants brought the realities of US policies into the living rooms of ordinary US Americans in the 1980s. Decades later, the legacies of those wars were still playing out in Central America, but also in cities and suburbs around the United States as perpetrators and victims of war crimes escaped ongoing violence and painfully protracted and limited justice. Many of them settled quietly on the margins of US society and economy.

Just as Central America's gangs had multinational roots that are impossibly entangled, so did its death squads. The United States trained and funded them, and some of them first organized among exiles inside the United States. After El Salvador's reformist 1979 coup, right-wing Salvadorans in Miami formed the "Miami Six" organization that later became the ARENA party. The US Embassy in El Salvador reported that the Miami Six "organize, fund, and direct death squads, through their agent Roberto D'Aubuisson." The exiles "often summoned Salvadoran businessmen to Miami, sat them at a long table, and then threatened them with death or kidnapping if they continued to collaborate" with the reformist government.[51]

El Salvador's death squads came "home to roost" in the United States in 1987, when Yanira Correa in Los Angeles and her father and brother in El Salvador began receiving letters threatening them for their activism with leftist organizations. A few months later, Correa was abducted outside of the CISPES office in downtown Los Angeles. Three men tortured her using methods characteristic of El Salvador's death squads while questioning her about her brother's activities in El Salvador. Activists documented over two hundred separate threats inside the United States, including fourteen against Salvadorans who had been leaders in popular organizations in El Salvador before fleeing.[52]

Meanwhile, the FBI had hired a Salvadoran immigrant to infiltrate CISPES and report on Salvadoran activists and visitors to the United

States—information that was then shared with Salvadoran security forces, as was information on Salvadorans who were slated for deportation.[53] The circle was most definitely being squared.

Many of the actors in Central America's conflicts chose anonymity in the United States or remained visible only inside their immigrant communities. "One of the most feared and ruthless" civil patrol leaders from a Guatemalan K'iche' village fled to Providence, Rhode Island, in 1984, "having heard that there was work and money there and also fearing revenge on the part of [his] victims' families." As an early arrival, the former patroller replicated his status and control in his new home, lending money and providing shelter while controlling and abusing villagers who followed him into exile. "So persistent are his mistreatments that stories abound in both Xinxuc [a pseudonym] and Providence regarding his evil deeds. He has strived to maintain power through various forms of intimidation, including creating financial and other forms of debt, threatening to turn people in to *la migra*, attempting to sexually coerce indigenous women, and pressuring other Mayans to convert to [his] evangelical sect." As one of the few Mayans in Providence with legal status, he can travel back and forth and "circulate and capitalize on information and rumors in both communities, reinforcing his power."[54]

Meanwhile in Guatemala, the Ladino military commissioner from the same region, Juan Alecio Samayoa Cabrera, was charged in 1992 with torture, rape, and extrajudicial killings. While one of his collaborators was convicted and served time in prison, Samayoa disappeared, entered the United States undetected across the Mexican border, and also settled in Providence, "where he had resided in plain sight alongside a number of his victims and fellow perpetrators for 25 years, working as a landscape gardener and living a quiet life with his family."[55] While the governments remained clueless, among Indigenous Guatemalans in Providence "for over two decades it has been an open secret—and an open wound—that Samayoa was living in plain sight, and amongst his victims." In late 2019, he was deported to Guatemala, where he finally faced trial and was quickly acquitted.[56] In a curious twist, investigators from ICE—an agency usually deplored by immigrant and human rights advocates—played a key role in bringing the case for Samayoa's deportation to Guatemala.[57]

"Sadly," wrote Patricia Foxen, "most of the patrol leader's victims, all K'iche' Maya living in either Providence, New Bedford or El Quiché, were too terrified to present themselves as witnesses, almost 40 years after the crimes of which he was accused; many of Xinxuc's Ladinos, however, hailed him as a hero, praising God for his release."[58]

The events in Providence echoed Héctor Tobar's novel *The Tattooed Soldier*, set in Los Angeles in 1992. Tobar, the child of Guatemalan immigrants, told the story of a migrant who fled to LA after his wife and child were murdered by a death squad, only to find their killer was also there.[59]

Samayoa was far from the only protagonist in the dramas of Central America's wars who lived an unremarkable life as an immigrant in the United States in the decades that followed. Many high officials were drawn to Florida, where the "diverse population, year-round sunshine, low cost of living and endless shopping opportunities—not to mention 1,500 golf courses—has long offered an attractive destination for war criminals seeking to evade justice," the *Guardian* reported.[60]

Honduras's General Gustavo Álvarez Martínez, who oversaw the dirty war in that country from 1982 to 1984, was joined there by Salvadoran generals José Guillermo García and Carlos Eugenio Vides Casanova, who led the Defense Ministry and the National Guard that oversaw the murders of the four US churchwomen and Archbishop Romero, the El Mozote and Sumpul River massacres, as well as the disappearance, torture, and death of tens of thousands of Salvadorans. Vides Casanova obtained a coveted immigrant visa (green card) under a special program for CIA collaborators, and García received political asylum.[61]

The Center for Justice and Accountability filed several lawsuits against the generals in the names of the families of the four churchwomen and a group of Salvadoran migrants who had been tortured by the National Guard. In his defense, Vides Casanova argued that his actions during the war were simply carrying out official US policy.[62] In 2015 and 2016, the two were deported to El Salvador, where under the 1993 Amnesty Law, they would remain exempt from prosecution.

The case of former Salvadoran colonel Inocente Orlando Montano Morales followed a different route, avoiding El Salvador's frail judicial system altogether. Montano oversaw a radio station that issued threats against the Jesuit rectors of the UCA, and he stood accused of participating in a meeting in which the orders were given to carry out the brutal 1989 attack that assassinated the six.

Because five of the murdered Jesuits were Spanish citizens, in 2011 a Spanish judge indicted Montano and nineteen others, including two former defense ministers, and demanded their extradition. The Center for Justice and Accountability tracked Montano down living "a quiet life in a modest apartment building in Everett," Massachusetts. Before he could be extradited to Spain, he was charged and convicted with immigration fraud and perjury for lying in his TPS application. After he served two years in federal prison, US authorities began proceedings for his extradition, which finally occurred in 2017.[63]

The film *Finding Oscar* followed the trail of another case. One of the hundreds of villages destroyed by the Guatemalan army in its counterinsurgency drive of the early 1980s was Dos Erres. Unlike most of the villages targeted by the army, Dos Erres was mainly Ladino, not Indigenous, founded in the late 1970s during the government colonization project in the Petén. When villagers resisted recruitment into the army's civil patrol, Dos Erres was stormed by the army's feared Kaibil commandos.

Recounting the horrors of the massacre becomes almost mind-numbing, knowing that such scenes were repeated hundreds of times around Guatemala's remote countryside over the course of years. Young girls were raped in front of their families. A group led by commando Gilberto Jordán began throwing babies and children live into a well; then the adults were flung on top of them as the pile of living and dead bodies grew, until the well "overflowed with corpses." When the carnage ended, the soldiers discovered that five children remained alive. They raped and strangled the teenage girls but took the two small boys with them. The deputy commander of the unit, Óscar Ramírez Ramos, decided to take the youngest toddler home, naming the boy after himself. Two hundred fifty corpses were all that remained as silent witnesses to the carnage.

Three decades later, Gilberto Jordán, at least three other Kaibiles involved in the massacre, and the kidnapped boy, Óscar Ramírez, were all living in the United States. Jordán crossed the border shortly after the massacre. He settled in Boca Raton, Florida, where he worked as a cook. Taking advantage of IRCA, he was able to obtain legal status in 1986, and ten years later, he applied for and obtained US citizenship, falsely claiming that he had never served in the Guatemalan military or committed any crimes. The three others settled in California and Houston.

Óscar, who was only three years old when he witnessed the massacre of his village and his family and was adopted by Ramírez's family, had no recollection of these events. In late 1998, he too headed for the United

States, entering without documents and settling in a town west of Boston. He married, had children, and worked in a supermarket and then at a local fast-food franchise. Until he was contacted by Guatemalan prosecutors investigating the Dos Erres case in 2011, he had little reason to question his identity, but DNA tests confirmed that he was indeed the child kidnapped in 1982. All four Kaibiles were eventually deported to Guatemala to face charges.[64]

INTERNATIONAL ADOPTION

Not generally thought of as "migration," international adoption was another way that Central Americans came to the United States through complicated links woven especially with Guatemala and El Salvador in the late twentieth century. In precisely the countries where US policies oversaw massacre, displacement, and the destruction of family and community ties, US civilians were then invited to demonstrate US generosity by saving some of the children left behind.

As in the case of Óscar described above, Dominga Sic was a child survivor of a 1982 Guatemalan army massacre, this one in the Mayan village of Río Negro in the central highlands. Río Negro had no apparent guerrilla presence, but it stood in the way of a major World Bank–funded development project, the Chixoy hydroelectric dam. When villagers protested being forcibly removed, the army stepped in to eliminate them. Over thirty-five hundred were forcibly displaced, and hundreds were killed in a series of massacres that followed the grisly pattern described above in Dos Erres. Dominga was nine when the army and civil patrol attacked Río Negro in March 1982. By the end of the evening, 177 were dead, including Dominga's family.

When the girl was found, she was sent to an orphanage. Two years later, she was adopted by an Iowa Baptist minister and his wife. Unlike Óscar, Dominga was old enough to have clear memories of the horror, despite her later conventional Midwestern upbringing. As an adult, she returned to Río Negro and, like Óscar, became an actor and a witness in Guatemalan genocide victims' ongoing attempts to seek justice. Also like Óscar's, her story became the subject of a searing documentary.[65]

Dominga was one of thousands of children from Guatemala and El Salvador who "disappeared" during the war, went through a maze of legitimate and corrupt systems, and ended up being adopted by generally white, well-meaning families in the United States. Even the notorious

US ambassador to Honduras, John Negroponte, adopted five Honduran children, two during and three after his ambassadorship there in the early 1980s.[66]

Many of these supposed orphans had surviving family members or even parents from whom they had been forcibly separated. All were "somebody's children."[67] If their families were killed and communities destroyed, or if women were coerced by violence or hunger into relinquishing their children, the chain of responsibility for the crimes could be traced all the way back to the White House. Sentimentalizing "orphans" can be another way of erasing the histories that destroyed so many families.

The country hardest hit by violence, death, and disappearance in the 1980s became the largest source for transnational adoption for over two decades. Adoption became an unregulated big business in Guatemala during the chaos of the war years, and studies estimate that some five thousand children were abducted and sold on the international market during the 1980s.[68] The infrastructure only grew after the war ended, with tens of thousands of children exported between 1996 and 2008.

By the mid-1990s, rumors circulated in the press and elsewhere that Guatemalan children were being stolen for sale abroad. In despair at high-level complicity, in some villages mobs took justice into their own hands and attacked foreigners they suspected of searching for children to steal. The *robachicos* (child-stealers) scares and the resort to informal "justice" mirrored the despair and the privatization of justice in remote villages throughout the country. And the theft of Indigenous children mirrored the global order. As a colleague of mine—who is also the parent of a child adopted internationally—put it wryly, "[I]t's the neoliberal phase of imperialism. First we take their land, then we take their resources, then we take their workers, and then we take their children."

By 2007, one out of every hundred babies born in Guatemala was adopted by Americans. In 2008, the Guatemalan government finally acknowledged the abuses built into the system and banned international adoption.[69]

The Guatemalan Mental Health League attempts to provide a clearinghouse for parents who have lost children and children searching for their birth parents, and has managed to reunite nearly five hundred.[70] In El Salvador, Jon Cortina, the sole survivor of the 1989 UCA Jesuit massacre (because he was away at the time), founded the organization

Pro-Búsqueda to help parents or relatives of young children who had been abducted or disappeared during the war there. By 2020, Pro-Búsqueda had collected information on over nine hundred disappeared children, though the organization believed that was just the tip of the iceberg. Close to four hundred had been reconnected with their birth families. Sixty-one of these had been adopted in the United States. Yet the US Department of State had granted over twenty-three hundred visas for Salvadoran adoptees during the war years. Every one of these was somebody's child and had a history.[71]

MIGRATION AND CULTURAL CHANGE

Migrants frequently follow people who they know, recreating local communities in cities and towns in the United States. As we saw with the community of Xinxuc in Providence, these new nodes can reproduce the very violence and inequalities that people were fleeing. Migration, divided families, and remittances can also create new forms of inequality and suffering, as well as new opportunities.

Anthropologists found that migration could contribute to unsettling racial hierarchies in Guatemala. There, Indigenous people ranked at the very bottom of the social hierarchy. In the context of the United States, Indigenous identity could become irrelevant, or even valued. Indigenous migrants and their families back home can leapfrog class status. Some Indigenous migrants and their families gained money and social status, and overturned romanticized stereotypes of Indigenous purity and discriminatory stereotypes of Indigenous backwardness.[72]

Age hierarchies were also challenged when youth returned with money and social capital—like knowledge of English—that is valuable in the new rural economy where tourists and NGOs had become important sources of power. These tensions could lead to violence. Elders sometimes automatically assumed that rebellious youth were gang members and revived civil patrol-like "security" patrols.[73] Conversely, those who were injured, died, or were deported back to Central America before they had a chance to earn enough to repay the costs of their trip sank their families into debt.

Parents' migration could have complicated impacts on the children left behind. Among divided families from El Salvador, Leisy Abrego found that while there are always emotional and psychological costs to the long-term separation of children from their parents, a lot depended on the parents' experience in the United States. If a parent was able to obtain decent work and provide real material and educational benefits for the child left at home, the child could grow to appreciate the parent's sacrifice. If parents were able to gain legal status, they could visit or even bring their children to the United States. But in many cases, parents failed to achieve the stability that would make their sacrifice worth it. Their children endured not only the loss of parental presence, but also ongoing material deprivation and resentment at being abandoned.[74] In some areas of El Salvador, as many as 40 percent of children have one or both parents in the United States.[75]

Even when migrants resettled with relatives or in recreated communities, the new context could transform cultural expectations. In El Salvador, community ties and reciprocity were fundamental to survival. But Salvadorans arrived in the United States laden with debt and obligations. Their first priority was to repay those back home who sacrificed to fund their travel and risked losing their homes and land if funds didn't flow back. Draconian immigration laws and lack of social capital consigned migrants to a low-wage, unstable labor market. Salvadoran migrants faced "too many demands on their meager resources" and little capacity for generosity to their compatriots.[76] Competitive individualism and finding ways to make money from other migrants was often the only way to survive. Mourning the reciprocity of their home communities, many migrants in the United States described their compatriots as "jealous," "competitive," and "egotistical."[77]

CONCLUSION

TRUMP'S BORDER WAR

Most of us know that Central American migrants are fleeing poor and violent countries for the wealth and safety of the United States. But that's only part of the story, as this book has tried to show.

Liberals argue that basic decency as well as international law require that migrants be treated humanely. They rightly decry President Trump's exaggerated anti-immigrant rhetoric and ostentatiously cruel policies. The fact that so many recent migrants are youth and families strengthens the humanitarian objections to Trump's policies. But a solely humanitarian position may fail to address the historical roots of today's migration. More humanitarian immigration policies alone will not alter its causes.

FAMILIES AND CHILD MIGRANTS

As far back as 1997, the United States began to implement special treatment for youths detained alone at the border. Acknowledging the vulnerability of such children, policies ensured that they would not be detained in adult prisons, that they would have the right to be quickly reunited with parents in the United States, and that they would be able to pursue claims to asylum.

Even before Central American youth began crossing unaccompanied in large numbers later in the decade of the 2000s, most youth placed in detention by immigration authorities had been Central American. Mexican youth caught crossing the border were simply returned to Mexico. After the 1997 reforms, Central American youth were released to the Office of Refugee Resettlement (ORR), which contracted with various agencies to house the children until they could be released to relatives or, in a small number of cases, to foster families, while their cases were adjudicated.

Under the new Trump administration, the situation deteriorated rapidly for unaccompanied children. A slew of new regulations relentlessly dismantled the protections that had been established for these young migrants. Conditions in facilities designed for minors were downgraded, and the legal protections that allowed youth a fair chance at applying for asylum were dismantled. As the director of the child advocacy organization Kids in Need of Defense put it in 2018, "[I]t's a coordinated effort across agencies that's wanting to hinder kids' abilities to go through the immigration system."[1]

The steps against unaccompanied minors were incremental and didn't attract much public attention. The same thing happened at first with another visible Trump target: families with small children who crossed the border together and turned themselves in to the border patrol asking for asylum. During previous administrations, most of these families would be sent temporarily to special family-detention facilities. Because of restrictions on how long children could be held, families would be quickly processed, given a court date to have their claim adjudicated, and released.

Trump derided this "catch and release" policy and vowed to replace it with what he called "zero tolerance." Now, more and more of those caught after crossing the border without inspection would be criminally prosecuted, even if they turned themselves in voluntarily and even if they had a valid claim to asylum. That meant that they were moved out of the immigration detention system and into the criminal justice system. Since children could not be held in adult jails, they would be separated from their parents and sent alone to the ORR centers that had been established for unaccompanied minors.

The centers had been set up to house teenagers who crossed the border alone, seeking to reunite with their parents. In almost all cases, they were quickly released to parents or guardians. Children who were taken from their parents at the border tended to be much younger—some were infants—and they couldn't be released to their parents because their parents were in jail. Many of these children ended up spending long periods in inadequate facilities or being released into foster care. Parents were sometimes deported while their children remained caught in the system.

In April 2018, the *New York Times* broke the story that "Hundreds of Immigrant Children Have Been Taken from Parents at U.S. Border."

Since the previous October, the *Times* reported, seven hundred children had been taken from their parents and turned over to the ORR, including a hundred children under four years old. "Operators of [ORR] facilities say they are often unable to locate the parents of separated children because the children arrive without proper records," the *Times* reported. "Once a child has entered the shelter system, there is no firm process to determine whether they have been separated from someone who was legitimately their parent, or for reuniting parents and children who had been mistakenly separated."[2]

But the Trump administration forged on, even as public and media ire grew. In the month that followed the *Times* story, almost two thousand more children were taken from their parents.[3] In early May, Trump took the final step that made family separation obligatory in all cases. Zero tolerance became official national policy; now every adult apprehended at the border would be criminally prosecuted for illegal entry. "If you are smuggling a child," stated then attorney general Jeff Sessions, conflating parents with smugglers, "then we will prosecute you and that child will be separated from you as required by law."[4] After six weeks and growing public outcry, a federal court ordered that the policy halt and that parents be reunited with their children. A year later, however, the ACLU found that over nine hundred more children had been separated from their parents at the border since the prohibition had been put in place.[5]

Then, in January 2019, Trump took the most dramatic step yet: the "remain in Mexico" policy mandating that anyone who presented at the border *legally* seeking asylum (as opposed to crossing without inspection and then turning oneself in to, or being caught by, the border patrol and being detained) would be barred from entry while they waited weeks or months for their cases to be adjudicated. Along the border, tent cities sprang up, as hundreds, then thousands, then tens of thousands of migrants were relegated to conditions a US congressional delegation in early 2020 termed "horrific" and "inhumane."[6] Human Rights Watch stated bluntly that the program "exposes children, as well as their parents, seeking asylum to serious risk of assault, mistreatment, and trauma."[7] In some cases, despairing parents sent their young children across the border alone, as unaccompanied minors, to escape the dreadful conditions in the camps.[8] By mid-2020, there were sixty thousand immigrants trapped in the camps.

Children also faced increasing risk as large numbers were forced to spend time in Customs and Border Patrol (CBP) facilities before being transferred to the ORR. Although the law required that they be transferred within seventy-two hours, it was increasingly ignored. As the numbers of families and unaccompanied children grew relentlessly, by mid-2019 there were about fourteen thousand people, two thousand of them children, in CBP custody at any given moment. By the end of the year, government figures showed that close to seventy thousand children had been held in CBP custody over the course of the year, with four thousand remaining and more arriving every day.[9] Between September 2018 and May 2019, seven children died while in, or shortly after being released or transferred from, CBP custody.[10]

The deaths, and the news photographs of children "in cages" that Representative Alexandria Ocasio-Cortez likened to "concentration camps," led to a public and media outcry.[11] Ocasio-Cortez's phrasing was perhaps unfortunate, given that in the United States, the term has become so closely associated with the Nazi death camps. But literally and historically, the phrase was accurate: a concentration camp is a place where populations are rounded up, concentrated, and imprisoned against their will, just because of who and/or where they are.

Other Trump initiatives sought to prevent migrants from reaching the border at all, enlisting Mexican security forces to his cause (and threatening Mexico's government with tariff increases if it did not comply), and requiring migrants to first request asylum in Honduras, Guatemala, or El Salvador if they have passed through those countries en route to the United States. As the *Christian Science Monitor* evocatively put it, "Mexico became Trump's wall" as it vastly increased militarization and deportation from its own southern border, while the country also struggled to deal with the tens of thousands stranded on the Mexican side of the US border.[12] After being coerced into signing "safe third country" agreements with the United States, the very countries that were sending refugees to the United States—Guatemala, Honduras, and El Salvador—were faced with influxes not only of their own citizens who were deported, but of asylum seekers from neighboring countries who the United States insisted must seek refuge there rather than in their actual destination, the United States. But these countries were plagued with the same problems the refugees had initially fled: violence, impunity, poverty, gangs, drought, unemployment, and organized crime. They had little infrastructure or capacity to care for newly arrived refugees.[13]

With the explosion of COVID-19 in early 2020, the very conditions that kept immigrants poor and marginalized put them at disproportionate risk for illness and death. Immigrant detention centers inside the United States and camps on the Mexican side of the border became dangerous vectors for contagion. Deportations continued, and some deportees carried the virus back to their home countries. Immigrants were concentrated in high-risk, low-paid "essential" jobs, working in meat and poultry processing, agriculture, warehouses, nursing homes, and supermarkets. Others worked in sectors where jobs vanished, like restaurants. They tended to live in high-density homes and neighborhoods where social distancing was virtually impossible. If they were undocumented, they were not eligible for unemployment or other relief measures. Not surprisingly, migrants suffered disproportionately from the virus and from the economic collapse that accompanied it.

MIGRATION AND SOLIDARITY: IMMIGRANT RIGHTS

Central Americans had played essential roles in the solidarity movements of the 1980s. Many of those who arrived in the 1990s and subsequent decades simply hoped to work and make a better life for themselves and their families, but many joined or led fights for immigrant rights and labor rights.

Unlike some solidarity organizations that faded after the 1980s, many refugee and immigrant organizations continued their work steadily. Organizations like CARECEN were leaders in the immigrant rights movements in the first decade of the twenty-first century, mobilizing the major immigrant rights May 1 marches in 2005 and 2006, and for local issues affecting immigrant communities.

Central American immigrants also helped to revitalize the US labor movement, which had long avoided organizing low-wage and immigrant workers and seen poor immigrants mostly as a threat to "American" jobs. Like the Mexican migrants who brought farmworker rights into the public eye in the 1960s, Central Americans brought organizing experience, and radical visions about social transformation and rights. They began their own campaigns and, by the mid-1990s, had inspired mainstream unions to pay more attention to Los Angeles janitors, Florida farmworkers, and North Carolina poultry workers.[14]

As the US immigration debate heated up in the early 2000s, twenty-first-century congregations revived the Sanctuary Movement of the 1980s and created a national network to offer sanctuary to refugees targeted by ICE or at risk of deportation. ICE under Obama had generally followed guidelines discouraging agents from entering and making arrests in "sensitive locations," including schools and churches. Around the country, migrants evaded ICE's reach by literally moving into church buildings, for months or for years.

After Trump's election and the ramping up of anti-immigrant rhetoric, more at-risk migrants sought this kind of sanctuary. By the end of 2018, some fifty migrants facing deportation had found sanctuary in churches around the country. But ICE agents also felt more emboldened to disregard the injunction. "Any foreign national who's in the United States illegally is subject to arrest and removal," ICE informed CNN after detaining (and then deporting) a migrant who had been granted sanctuary by a North Carolina church, "no matter how long they've been living in a so-called sensitive location."[15]

Beyond religious communities, cities, counties, states, and universities around the country responded to Trump's election by declaring themselves "sanctuaries." There was no single definition of the concept, but in general such resolutions sought to prevent local employees and law enforcement from providing information or help to ICE agents. When Trump threatened to cut federal aid and grants to locales implementing sanctuary policies, many decided to avoid the term, or weaken their provisions.

COLONIALISM, SETTLER COLONIALISM, AND REPARATIONS

This book has argued that Trump's policies are only the most recent iteration of over a century of US domination and exploitation of Central Americans. The violence and poverty that afflicts Central America today is a direct result of colonial and neocolonial development policies and the cultures of violence and forgetting needed to implement and justify them. If we want to create a more just world, we need to acknowledge the many layers of complicity and forgetting that underlie today's inequalities. We also need to remember and be inspired by Central Americans' valiant struggles for social and economic justice. The United States owes a huge moral and material debt to Central America. Remembering this debt is the first step toward trying to repay it.

Reparations means much more than mere cash transfers. Reparations means repairing the damage caused by centuries of domination, extraction, and exploitation. Today's palm oil plantations, drug wars, gangs, maquiladoras, displacement, and violence are the direct result of a history that not only Trump but almost all of our political leaders, mainstream media, and educational system would prefer to forget.[16] I hope that this book can inspire readers to remember and to work toward changing the structures and institutions that have brought so much harm.

ACKNOWLEDGMENTS

This book has been long in the making, and I could justifiably thank almost everyone who has been in my life since I first became involved with Central America in the early 1980s. Some of the people who taught and influenced me I've long lost touch with; others I still count among my closest friends. They are so many that I'd rather just send out a general heartfelt thank-you than try to list them all.

I do have to single out a few people though, for their specific contributions to this book. Guillermo Fernández Ampié read the entire manuscript and gave me detailed feedback on several of the chapters, helping me refine my arguments and fix mistakes. My editors at Beacon Press, especially Gayatri Patnaik and Maya Fernández, were, as always, a joy to work with. Thanks also to everyone at Beacon Press who worked on the book, including Marcy Barnes and Susan Lumenello. Alexandra Piñeros Shields helped me talk through knotty issues as I was revising the text. And Justin Wolfe's pandemic early-morning writing group and all its participants kept me on track day after day through the strange spring and summer of 2020.

GLOSSARY

AIFLD	American Institute for Free Labor Development
ARENA	Nationalist Republican Alliance (far-right party, El Salvador)
CAFTA	Central America Free Trade Agreement
campesino	peasant farmer or rural worker, categories that often overlap in Central America
CBC	Christian Base Community
cofradía	village-level religious brotherhood and governing body often led by traditional elders
compañero	comrade, partner
costumbre	traditional religion based on local Catholic/Mayan fusions (Guatemala)
CPR	Communities of Population in Resistance (Guatemala)
CUC	Committee for Campesino Unity (Guatemala)
DACA	Deferred Action for Childhood Arrivals
EGP	Guerrilla Army of the Poor (Guatemala)
Esquipulas agreement	Peace agreement signed by Central American presidents in Esquipulas, Guatemala, in 1987
FAR	Revolutionary Armed Forces (Guatemala)
FDR	Revolutionary Democratic Front (El Salvador)
FECCAS	Salvadoran Christian Peasants Federation
FMLN	Farabundo Martí National Liberation Front (El Salvador)

FSLN	Sandinista National Liberation Front (Nicaragua)
Guardia	Nicaraguan National Guard
guinda	Short-term flight to the mountains to escape army incursions (El Salvador)
ICE	Immigration and Customs Enforcement (United States)
ICSID	International Centre for Settlement of Investment Disputes (World Bank)
IMF	International Monetary Fund
IRCA	Immigration Reform and Control Act (United States, 1986)
ladino	Non-European or racially mixed people in the Americas who do not identify as Indigenous. During the colonial period, the Spanish used it to refer to Indigenous people who had learned Spanish and lived within the colonizers' world, as opposed to "Indians" who lived in legally defined Indian communities. Depending on the context, it can have negative, neutral, or positive connotations.
maquiladora	duty-free assembly and manufacturing plants located in low-wage countries
mara/marero	gang/gang member
mestizo	person of mixed European and Indigenous ancestry
NGO	nongovernmental organization
NSC	National Security Council (United States)
PAC	Civil Defense Patrol (Guatemala)
principales	Indigenous village-level elders and authorities
TPS	Temporary Protected Status
UCA	Jesuit university (Managua and San Salvador)
UNHCR	United Nations High Commissioner for Refugees
URNG	Guatemalan National Revolutionary Unity
USAID	US Agency for International Development
UTC	Union of Rural Workers (El Salvador)

NOTES

CHAPTER 1: INVISIBILITY AND FORGETTING

1. Elisabeth Burgos-Debray, ed., *I, Rigoberta Menchú: An Indian Woman in Guatemala*, trans. Ann Wright (New York: Verso, 1984), 1.

2. *I, Rigoberta Menchú*, 7, 9, 13, 14, 22. Menchu's testimony was recorded, edited, and published by a Venezuelan anthropologist and widely translated. In the original Spanish, Menchu uses *indígena* [Indigenous] rather than *indio* [Indian], because the latter is commonly understood as a racial slur in Guatemala. The quotes here follow the translator's choice to use "Indian" in English. In this text, I use "Indigenous" unless I am quoting or referring to the colonial period or a context in which people define themselves as "indio."

3. *I, Rigoberta Menchú*, 147–48, 199, 200.

4. See Ibram X. Kendi, "The Day *Shithole* Entered the Presidential Lexicon," *Atlantic*, January 13, 2019, https://www.theatlantic.com/politics/archive/2019/01/shithole -countries/580054; Dara Lind, "The Migrant Caravan That's Spurring Trump's Latest Temper Tantrum, Explained," *Vox*, October 18, 2018, https://www.vox.com/policy-and -politics/2018/10/17/17983362/caravan-honduras-trump-border-illegal.

5. Jordan Fabian, "Trump: Migrant Caravan 'Is an Invasion,'" *Hill*, October 29, 2018, https://thehill.com/homenews/administration/413624-trump-calls-migrant-caravan-an -invasion.

6. See Matthew Restall and Florine Asselbergs, *Invading Guatemala: Spanish, Nahua, and Maya Accounts of the Conquest Wars* (University Park: Pennsylvania State University Press, 2007), 100; Laura E. Matthew, *Memories of Conquest: Becoming Mexicano in Colonial Guatemala* (Chapel Hill: University of North Carolina Press, 2012), 101.

7. Alfred W. Crosby, *Ecological Imperialism: The Biological Expansion of Europe, 900–1900*, orig. 2004 (New York: Cambridge University Press, 2013).

8. W. George Lovell and Christopher H. Lutz, "The Historical Demography of Colonial Central America," in *Yearbook (Conference of Latin Americanist Geographers)* 17/18 (1991/1992): 127–38.

9. Adriaan Van Oss, *Catholic Colonialism: A Parish History of Guatemala, 1524–1821* (New York: Cambridge University Press, 1986), 17, 18, 77.

10. David McCreery, *Rural Guatemala, 1760–1940* (Palo Alto, CA: Stanford University Press, 1994), 3.

11. Greg Grandin, *The Blood of Guatemala: A History of Race and Nation* (Durham, NC: Duke University Press, 2000), 134.

12. Murdo J. MacLeod, *Spanish Central America: A Socioeconomic History*, orig. 1973 (Austin: University of Texas Press, 2007), 52, 56.

13. Under Spanish colonial rule, the term "creole" referred to persons of Spanish descent born in the Americas. In the British and French Caribbean, it referred primarily to persons of African descent or mixed race born in the colonies. It expanded to define new languages (like Haitian Kreyòl) and ethnicities that emerged in the colonial world.

14. MacLeod, *Spanish Central America*, 63.

15. Daniel Wilkinson, *Silence on the Mountain: Stories of Terror, Betrayal, and Forgetting in Guatemala* (Durham, NC: Duke University Press, 2004), 7.

16. Wilkinson, *Silence on the Mountain*, 213–15.

17. Otto René Castillo, "Apolitical Intellectuals," https://www.marxists.org/subject /art/literature/castillo/works/apolitical.htm.

18. Carolyn Forché, "The Colonel," from *The Country Between Us* (New York: Harper Collins, 1981), https://www.poetryfoundation.org/poems/49862/the-colonel.

19. Janet Shenk, "El Salvador," *NACLA Report on the Americas* (May-June 1985), https://nacla.org/article/el-salvador-new-and-old-war.

20. Wilkinson, *Silence on the Mountain*, 332.

21. Ronald Reagan, "Question and Answer Session with Reporters," December 4, 1982, Reagan Library, https://www.reaganlibrary.gov/research/speeches/120482g.

CHAPTER 2: MAKING THE UNITED STATES, MAKING CENTRAL AMERICA

1. Colin G. Galloway, *Indian World of George Washington* (New York: Oxford University Press, 2018), 6, 9.

2. Vine Deloria, Jr., and Clifford M. Lytle, *The Nations Within: The Past and Future of American Indian Sovereignty* (New York: Pantheon Books, 1984), chap. 2.

3. John Grenier, *The First Way of War: American War Making on the Frontier, 1607–1815* (New York: Cambridge University Press, 2005).

4. Van Oss, *Catholic Colonialism*, 187.

5. David McCreery, "State Power, Indigenous Communities, and Land in Nineteenth-Century Guatemala, 1820–1920," in *Guatemalan Indians and the State, 1540–1988*, ed. Carol A. Smith (Austin: University of Texas Press, 1990), 101.

6. Grandin, *Blood of Guatemala*, 104.

7. McCreery, "State Power, Indigenous Communities, and Land in Nineteenth-Century Guatemala," 102.

8. Erik Ching, *Authoritarian El Salvador: Politics and the Origins of the Military Regimes, 1880–1940* (Notre Dame, IN: University of Notre Dame Press, 2014), chap. 2.

9. Jeffrey L. Gould, *To Die in This Way: Nicaraguan Indians and the Myth of Mestizaje, 1880–1955* (Durham, NC: Duke University Press, 1998), 180. For the larger picture, see Steven C. Topik and Allen Wells, eds., *The Second Conquest of Latin America: Coffee, Henequen, and Oil During the Export Boom, 1850–1930* (Austin: University of Texas Press, 1998).

10. Grandin, *Blood of Guatemala*, 127.

11. Grandin, *Blood of Guatemala*, 126.

12. Grandin, *Blood of Guatemala*, 128–29.

13. Grandin, *Blood of Guatemala*, 135–36.

14. Grandin, *Blood of Guatemala*, 141.

15. Jeffrey L. Gould and Aldo A. Lauria-Santiago, *To Rise in Darkness: Revolution, Repression, and Memory in El Salvador, 1920–1932* (Durham, NC: Duke University Press, 2008), xvii–viii; Aldo A. Lauria-Santiago, *An Agrarian Republic: Commercial Agriculture and the Politics of Peasant Communities in El Salvador, 1823–1914* (Pittsburgh: University of Pittsburgh Press, 1999), 6, 3.

16. Héctor Lindo-Fuentes, Erik Ching, and Rafael A. Lara-Martínez, *Remembering a Massacre in El Salvador* (Albuquerque: University of New Mexico Press, 2007), 27.

17. Lindo-Fuentes et al., *Remembering a Massacre*, 26–27.

18. Virginia Q. Tilley, *Seeing Indians: A Study of Race, Nation, and Power in El Salvador* (Albuquerque: University of New Mexico Press, 2005), 135.

19. Quoted in Robert Armstrong and Janet Shenk, *El Salvador: The Face of Revolution* (Boston: South End Press, 1982), 27.

20. Tilley, *Seeing Indians*, 140, 154.

21. Tilley, *Seeing Indians*, 156, 164.

22. Lindo-Fuentes et al., *Remembering a Massacre*, 66–67.

23. Lindo-Fuentes et al., *Remembering a Massacre*, 5.

24. Tilley, *Seeing Indians*, 20.

25. Tilley, *Seeing Indians*, 9–10, 26.

26. Gould and Lauria-Santiago, *To Rise in Darkness*, xii, xxii, 287.

27. "Transcript of Monroe Doctrine," https://www.ourdocuments.gov/doc.php?.

28. Simón Bolívar, letter to Patrick Campbell, British Chargé d'Affaires, August 5, 1829. Reprinted in *El Libertador: Writings of Simón Bolívar*, ed. David Bushnell (New York: Oxford University Press, 2003), 173.

29. See Pekka Hämäläinen, *The Comanche Empire* (New Haven, CT: Yale University Press, 2008).

30. Michel Gobat, *Confronting the American Dream: Nicaragua Under U.S. Imperial Rule* (Durham, NC: Duke University Press, 2005), 2.

31. Michel Gobat, *Empire by Invitation: William Walker and Manifest Destiny in Central America* (Cambridge, MA: Harvard University Press, 2018), 5.

32. Walter LaFeber, *Inevitable Revolutions: The United States in Central America*, orig. 1983 (New York: W. W. Norton & Company, 1993), 31.

33. "Theodore Roosevelt's Annual Message to Congress, December 6, 1904," https://www.ourdocuments.gov/doc.php?flash=true&doc=56&page=transcript.

34. LaFeber, *Inevitable Revolutions*, 52–53, 60–61.

35. Major General Smedley Butler, USMC, excerpts from a speech in 1933, https://fas.org/man/smedley.htm.

36. In addition to LaFeber's *Inevitable Revolutions*, see Lester D. Langley, *The Banana Wars: United States Intervention in the Caribbean, 1898–1934*, orig. 1983 (Wilmington, DE: Scholarly Resources, 2002), chaps. 5–6 and 14–16.

37. Thomas W. Walker and Christine J. Wade, *Nicaragua: Living in the Shadow of the Eagle*, 5th ed. (Boulder, CO: Westview Press, 2011), 18.

38. Michel Gobat, "La construcción de un estado neo-colonial: El encuentro nicaragüense con la diplomacia del dólar," *Íconos: Revista de Ciencias Sociales* (Quito) (May 2009): 53–64, 55.

39. Quoted in Gould, *To Die in This Way*, 190.

40. Gould, *To Die in This Way*, 55.

41. Gould, *To Die in This Way*, 224, 230.

42. David C. Brooks and Michael J. Schroeder, "*Caudillismo* Masked and Modernized: The Remaking of the Nicaraguan State Via the National Guard, 1925–1936," *Middle American Review of Latin American Studies* 2, no. 2 (2018): 1–32, 9, 31.

43. Walker and Wade, *Nicaragua*, 21–22.

44. Joseph O. Baylen, "Sandino: Patriot or Bandit?," *Hispanic American Historical Review* 31, no. 3 (August 1951): 394–419, 404.

45. Brooks and Schroeder, "*Caudillismo*," 20.

46. Walker and Wade, *Nicaragua*, 22–23.

47. Alison Acker, *Honduras: The Making of a Banana Republic* (Boston: South End Press, 1989), 58.

48. LaFeber, *Inevitable Revolutions*, 42.

49. Acker, *Honduras*, 69.

50. Moody Manual Company, *Moody's Manual of Railroad and Corporation Securities*, vol. 2, 16th annual number (New York: Moody Manual Company, 2015), 3469.

51. LaFeber, *Inevitable Revolutions*, 63.

52. John Vandermeer and Ivette Perfecto, *Breakfast of Biodiversity: The Political Ecology of Rainforest Destruction*, orig. 1995 (Oakland, CA: Food First Books, 2013), 55.

53. Acker, *Honduras*, 62.

54. LaFeber, *Inevitable Revolutions*, 43.

55. Pablo Neruda, "The United Fruit Company," 1950, https://genius.com/Pablo-neruda-the-united-fruit-company-annotated.

56. Matthew Frye Jacobson, "Annexing the Other," in *Race, Nation, and Empire in American History*, ed. James T. Campbell, Matthew Pratt Guterl, and Robert G. Lee (Chapel Hill: University of North Carolina Press, 2007), 103–29, 113.

57. Gobat, *Confronting the American Dream*, 5, 22.

58. See Brian W. Dippie, *The Vanishing American: White Attitudes & U.S. Indian Policy* (Lawrence: University Press of Kansas, 1982).

59. Captain Richard H. Pratt on the Education of Native Americans, 1892, http://historymatters.gmu.edu/d/4929.

60. Wilkinson, *Silence on the Mountain*, 46.

61. Gould, "¡Vana Ilusión!': The Highland Indians and the Myth of Nicaragua Mestiza, 1880–1925," *Hispanic American Historical Review* 73, no. 3 (August 1993): 393–429, 416.

62. Stephen M. Streeter, *Managing the Counterrevolution: The United States and Guatemala, 1954–1961* (Athens: Ohio University Center for International Studies, 2000), 155.

63. Wilkinson, *Silence on the Mountain*, 38.

64. Gould, "Vana Ilusión!," 393, 416; Carol A. Smith, "Origins of the National Question in Guatemala: A Hypothesis," in Smith, ed., *Guatemalan Indians and the State*, 91.

65. Smith, "Origins of the National Question," 91.

66. Gould, *To Die in This Way*, 155–61.

67. Gould, *To Die in This Way*, 20.

CHAPTER 3: THE COLD WAR, TEN YEARS OF SPRING,
AND THE CUBAN REVOLUTION

1. Blanche Weisen Cooke, *Eleanor Roosevelt: The War Years and After, 1939–1962*, vol. 3 (New York: Penguin Books, 2016), p. 61.

2. Paul Dosal, *Doing Business with the Dictators: A Political History of United Fruit in Guatemala, 1899–1944* (Wilmington, DE: Scholarly Resources, 1993), 3.

3. LaFeber, *Inevitable Revolutions*, 83–85.

4. Greg Grandin, *Empire's Workshop: Latin America, the United States, and the Rise of the New Imperialism* (New York: Henry Holt and Company, 2006), 4.

5. Streeter, *Managing the Counterrevolution*, 12.

6. Streeter, *Managing the Counterrevolution*, 191.

7. Grandin, *Empire's Workshop*, 42.

8. Streeter, *Managing the Counterrevolution*, 19.

9. Streeter, *Managing the Counterrevolution*, 20.

10. Jim Handy, "The Corporate Community, Campesino Organizations and Agrarian Reform: 1950–1954," in Smith, ed., *Guatemalan Indians and the State*, 163–82, 169, 178.

11. Handy, "Corporate Community," 165.

12. Handy, "Corporate Community," 179.

13. Streeter, *Managing the Counterrevolution*, 22–23.

14. Piero Gleijeses, *Shattered Hope: The Guatemalan Revolution and the United States, 1944–1954* (Princeton, NJ: Princeton University Press, 1991), 243.

15. Gleijeses, *Shattered Hope*, 300.

16. Gleijeses, *Shattered Hope*, 338.

17. Betsy Konefal, *For Every Indio Who Falls: A History of Maya Activism in Guatemala, 1960–1990* (Albuquerque: University of New Mexico Press, 2010), 29.

18. Wilkinson, *Silence on the Mountain*, 183.

19. Armstrong and Shenk, *El Salvador*, 42.

20. Remarks of Senator John F. Kennedy at Democratic Dinner, Cincinnati, Ohio, October 6, 1960, https://www.jfklibrary.org/archives/other-resources/john-f-kennedy-speeches/cincinnati-oh-19601006-democratic-dinner.

21. John F. Kennedy, "Address on the First Anniversary of the Alliance for Progress," March 13, 1962, https://www.presidency.ucsb.edu/documents/address-the-first-anniversary-the-alliance-for-progress.

22. Armstrong and Shenk, *El Salvador*, 43.

23. LaFeber, *Inevitable Revolutions*, 153, 158.

24. Charles D. Brockett, *Land, Power, and Poverty: Agrarian Transformation and Political Conflict in Central America* (Boston: Unwin Hyman, 1988), 86.

25. See Donald Lee Fixico, *Termination and Relocation: Federal Indian Policy 1945–1960* (Albuquerque: University of New Mexico Press, 1990).

26. Brockett, *Land, Power, and Poverty*, 47.

27. Robert G. Williams, *Export Agriculture and the Crisis in Central America* (Chapel Hill: University of North Carolina Press, 1986), 52.

28. Williams, *Export Agriculture*, 65.

29. Brockett, *Land, Power, and Poverty*, 87.

30. *I, Rigoberta Menchú*, 22.

31. Williams, *Export Agriculture*, 113.

32. Williams, *Export Agriculture*, 114.

33. T. Lynn Smith, "Current Population Trends in Latin America," *American Journal of Sociology* 62, no. 4 (January 1957): 399–406.

34. Lovell and Lutz, "Historical Demography"; Worldometers, "Central America Population," https://www.worldometers.info/world-population/central-america-population; "Mexico Population," https://www.worldometers.info/world-population/mexico-population.

35. Brockett, *Land, Power, and Poverty*, 84–85.

36. Brockett, *Land, Power, and Poverty*, 62–63.

37. Bonar L. Hernández-Sandoval, *Guatemala's Catholic Revolution: A History of Religious and Social Reform, 1920–1968* (Notre Dame, IN: University of Notre Dame Press, 2019), introduction.

38. Susan Fitzpatrick-Behrens, "The Maya Catholic Cooperative Spirit of Capitalism in Guatemala: Civil-Religious Collaborations, 1943–1966," in *Local Church, Global Church: Catholic Activism in Latin America from Rerum Novarum to Vatican II*, ed. Stephen J. C. Andes and Julia G. Young (Washington, DC: Catholic University of America Press, 2016), 287.

39. Fitzpatrick-Behrens, "Maya Catholic Cooperative Spirit," 291, 294.

40. See Philip J. Williams, *The Catholic Church and Politics in Nicaragua and Costa Rica* (Pittsburgh: University of Pittsburgh Press, 1989), 21–22.

41. Gould, *To Die in This Way,* 183, 208–11.

42. Molly Todd, *Beyond Displacement: Campesinos, Refugees, and Collective Action in the Salvadoran Civil War* (Madison: University of Wisconsin Press, 2010), 44.

43. Frances Moore Lappé and Joseph Collins, *Now We Can Speak: A Journey Through the New Nicaragua* (Oakland, CA: Food First Books, 1982), 8, 107, 24.

44. LaFeber, *Inevitable Revolutions,* 210.

45. See, for example, Cheryl Rubenberg, "Israel and Guatemala: Arms, Advice, and Counterinsurgency," *MERIP Reports* 140 (May–June 1986), https://merip.org/1986/05/israel-and-guatemala; Cheryl Rubenberg, "Israeli Foreign Policy in Central America," *Third World Quarterly* 8, no. 3 (July 1986): 896–915.

46. LaFeber, *Inevitable Revolutions,* 275.

47. Grandin, *Empire's Workshop,* 67, 71.

48. Jeane Kirkpatrick, "Dictatorships and Double Standards," *Commentary,* November 1979.

49. Grandin, *Empire's Workshop,* 71.

50. Ronald Reagan, "Peace: Restoring the Margin of Safety," Veterans of Foreign Wars Convention, Chicago, August 18, 1980, https://www.reaganlibrary.gov/8–18–80.

51. All quoted in Peter Kornbluh, *Nicaragua: The Price of Intervention* (Washington, DC: Institute for Policy Studies, 1987), 159.

52. LaFeber, *Inevitable Revolutions,* 291.

53. LaFeber, *Inevitable Revolutions,* 292.

54. LaFeber, *Inevitable Revolutions,* 291.

55. Julia Preston and Joe Pichirallo, "Cuban Americans Fight for Contras," *Washington Post,* October 25, 1986.

56. John Brecher, Russell Watson, David C. Martin, and Beth Nissen, "A Secret War for Nicaragua," *Newsweek,* November 8, 1982.

57. Brecher et al., "A Secret War for Nicaragua."

58. The documents are available at "The Negroponte File," National Security Archive Electronic Briefing Book, ed. Peter Kornbluh, April 12, 2005. Part I, https://nsarchive2.gwu.edu//NSAEBB/NSAEBB151/index.htm; Part II, https://nsarchive2.gwu.edu//NSAEBB/NSAEBB151/index2.htm.

59. See *Report of the Congressional Committees Investigating the Iran-Contra Affair,* 100th Congress, 1st Session (Washington, DC, 1987), 395–407, for discussion of the various Boland Amendments and the Reagan administration's perpetual violation of their provisions.

60. "Psychological Operations in Guerrilla Warfare," 10. The CIA declassified a "sanitized" version in 2005, https://www.cia.gov/library/readingroom/docs/CIA-RDP86M00886R001300010029–9.pdf.

61. "The CIA's Murder Manual," editorial, *Washington Post,* October 21, 1984.

62. Ronald Reagan, "Executive Order 12513," https://www.archives.gov/federal-register/codification/executive-order/12513.html.

63. Lawrence E. Walsh, "Final Report of the Independent Counsel for Iran-Contra Matters," August 4, 1993. https://fas.org/irp/offdocs/walsh.

64. Walsh, "Final Report."

65. Raymond Bonner, "The Diplomat and the Killer," *Atlantic,* February 11, 2016.

66. Ellen Moodie, *El Salvador in the Aftermath of Peace: Crime, Uncertainty, and the Transition to Democracy* (Philadelphia: University of Pennsylvania Press, 2010), 34.

67. Mark Danner, *The Massacre at El Mozote: A Parable of the Cold War* (New York: Vintage Books, 1994), 132.

68. LaFeber, *Inevitable Revolutions,* 331.

69. Nathanial Sheppard Jr., "'USS Honduras' Adrift as America Loses Interest," *Chicago Tribune,* June 15, 1993.

70. National Security Decision Directive 225, May 20, 1986, https://www.reagan library.gov/digital-library/nsdds.

71. LaFeber, *Inevitable Revolutions,* 308.

72. LaFeber, *Inevitable Revolutions,* 289.

73. Jeffrey L. Gould, *Solidarity Under Siege: The Salvadoran Labor Movement, 1970–1990* (New York: Cambridge University Press, 2019), 233.

CHAPTER 4: GUATEMALA

1. Streeter, *Managing the Counterrevolution,* 39, 40.

2. Streeter, *Managing the Counterrevolution,* 38; Stokes Newbold, "Receptivity to Communist Fomented Agitation in Rural Guatemala," *Economic Development and Cultural Change* 5, no. 4 (July 1967): 338–61, 361.

3. Streeter, *Managing the Counterrevolution,* 43–45.

4. Streeter, *Managing the Counterrevolution,* 164, 199.

5. Streeter, *Managing the Counterrevolution,* 202, 204; Luis Solano, *Contextualización histórica de la Franja Transversal del Norte (FTN),* Centro de Estudios y Documentación de la Frontera Occidental de Guatemala (CEDFOG), February 2012.

6. Streeter, *Managing the Counterrevolution,* 205.

7. Streeter, *Managing the Counterrevolution,* 111, 108–9, 149, 139–40; Brockett, *Land, Power, and Poverty,* 105.

8. George Lovell, "Maya Survival in Ixil Country, Guatemala," *Cultural Survival Quarterly* (December 1990); Shelton H. Davis, "Introduction: Sowing the Seeds of Violence," in *Harvest of Violence: The Maya Indians and the Guatemalan Crisis,* ed. Robert M. Carmack (Norman: University of Oklahoma Press, 1988), 3–36, 14–15.

9. David Carey, "Guatemala's Green Revolution: Synthetic Fertilizer, Public Health, and Economic Autonomy in the Guatemalan Highland," *Agricultural History* 83, no. 3 (Summer 2009): 283–322, 304; John M. Watanabe, "Enduring Yet Ineffable Community in the Western Periphery of Guatemala," in Smith ed., *Guatemalan Indians and the State,* 183, 204, 188.

10. Arturo Arias, "Changing Indian Identity: Guatemala's Violent Transition to Modernity," in Smith, ed., *Guatemalan Indians and the State,* 230–57, 237.

11. Streeter, *Managing the Counterrevolution,* 153.

12. Brockett, *Land, Power, and Poverty,* 70.

13. Williams, *Export Agriculture,* 145, 143.

14. Ricardo Falla, *Massacres in the Jungle: Ixcán, Guatemala, 1975–1982* (Boulder, CO: Westview Press, 1994), 19.

15. Fitzpatrick-Behrens, "Maya Catholic Cooperative Spirit," 294–96.

16. Beatriz Manz, *Paradise in Ashes: A Guatemalan Journey of Courage, Terror, and Hope* (Berkeley: University of California Press, 2004), 77.

17. Alan Riding, "Guatemala Opening New Lands, but Best Goes to the Rich," *New York Times,* April 5, 1979.

18. Liza Grandia, *Enclosed: Conservation, Cattle, and Commerce among the Q'eqchi' Maya Lowlanders* (Seattle: University of Washington Press, 2012), 56.

19. Williams, *Export Agriculture,* 142; Solano, *Franja Transversal del Norte,* 28.

20. Norman B. Schwartz, "Colonization of Northern Guatemala: The Petén," *Journal of Anthropological Research* 43, no. 2 (1987): 163–83; Grandia, *Enclosed.*

21. Solano, *Franja Transversal del Norte*, 28.

22. Brockett, *Land, Power, and Poverty*, 105.

23. Riding, "Guatemala Opening New Lands."

24. David Stoll, *Between Two Armies in the Ixil Towns of Guatemala* (New York: Columbia University Press, 1993), 55.

25. Arias, "Changing Indian Identity," 233.

26. Stoll, *Between Two Armies*, chap. 2.

27. Konefal, *For Every Indio Who Falls*, 49.

28. Konefal, *For Every Indio Who Falls*, 36.

29. Arias, "Changing Indian Identity," 233.

30. Arias, "Changing Indian Identity," 248.

31. Megan Ybarra, *Green Wars: Conservation and Decolonization in the Maya Forest* (Berkeley: University of California Press, 2018), 41–42.

32. Carey, "Guatemala's Green Revolution," 305.

33. Carey, "Guatemala's Green Revolution," 306.

34. Arias, "Changing Indian Identity," 243–244.

35. Deborah Levenson-Estrada, *Trade Unionists Against Terror: Guatemala City, 1954–1985* (Chapel Hill: University of North Carolina Press, 1994), 124.

36. Levenson-Estrada, *Trade Unionists Against Terror*, 52.

37. Levenson-Estrada, *Trade Unionists Against Terror*, 85, 106.

38. Levenson-Estrada, *Trade Unionists Against Terror*, 147.

39. Konefal, *For Every Indio Who Falls*, 26.

40. Brockett, *Land, Power, and Poverty*, 108, citing Douglas E. Brintnall, *Revolt Against the Dead: The Modernization of a Mayan Community in the Highlands of Guatemala* (New York, London, Paris: Gordon and Breach, 1979), 141.

41. Arias, "Changing Indian Identity," 248–49.

42. Konefal, *For Every Indio Who Falls*, 70.

43. Arias, "Changing Indian Identity," 250.

44. Konefal, *For Every Indio Who Falls*, 71.

45. Victoria Sanford, *Buried Secrets: Truth and Human Rights in Guatemala* (New York: Palgrave MacMillan, 2003), 74.

46. Greg Grandin, *The Last Colonial Massacre: Latin America in the Cold War* (Chicago: University of Chicago Press, 2004), 24.

47. Sanford, *Buried Secrets*, 57.

48. Williams, *Export Agriculture*, 147–51.

49. Grandin, *Last Colonial Massacre*, 155.

50. Victoria Sanford, "Breaking the Reign of Silence: Ethnography of a Clandestine Cemetery," in *Human Rights in the Maya Region: Global Politics, Cultural Contentions, and Moral Engagements*, ed. Pedro Pitarch, Shannon Speed, and Xochitl Leyva Solano (Durham, NC: Duke University Press, 2008), 233–55, 243.

51. Mario Payeras, *Days of the Jungle: The Testimony of a Guatemalan Guerrillero, 1972–1976* (New York: Monthly Review Press, 1983), 21.

52. Payeras, *Days of the Jungle*, 35–36; Manz, *Paradise in Ashes*, 77.

53. Sanford, *Buried Secrets*, 82–83.

54. Payeras, *Days of the Jungle*, 71.

55. Payeras, *Days of the Jungle*, 76. See also Manz, *Paradise in Ashes*, 78–79.

56. Stoll, *Between Two Armies*, 73.

57. Payeras, *Days of the Jungle*, 79.
58. Payeras, *Days of the Jungle*, 82.
59. Stoll, *Between Two Armies*, 4–5.
60. Sanford, *Buried Secrets*, 99.
61. Sanford, *Buried Secrets*, 99.
62. Manz, *Paradise in Ashes*, 86.
63. Human Rights Office, Archdiocese of Guatemala, *Guatemala, Never Again!* (New York: Orbis Books, 199), 220–22.
64. Sanford, *Buried Secrets*, 126–27.
65. Richard Wilson, *Maya Resurgence in Guatemala: Q'Eqchi' Experiences* (Norman: University of Oklahoma Press, 1995), 218.
66. Archdiocese of Guatemala, *Guatemala, Never Again!*, 117.
67. Sanford, *Buried Secrets*, 147.
68. Sanford, *Buried Secrets*, 184.
69. Grandin, *Last Colonial Massacre*, 128.
70. Manz, *Paradise in Ashes*, 161.
71. Benjamin D. Paul and William J. Demarest, "The Operation of a Death Squad in San Pedro la Laguna," in Carmack, *Harvest of Violence*, 119–54, 153–54.
72. Manz, *Paradise in Ashes*, 166–67.
73. Jennifer L. Burrell, *Maya After War: Conflict, Power, and Politics in Guatemala* (Austin: University of Texas Press, 2013), 32.
74. Grandin, *Last Colonial Massacre*, 187.
75. Richard A. White, *The Morass: United States Intervention in Central America* (New York: Harper & Row, 1984), cited in Brockett, *Land, Poverty, and Power*, 118.
76. Manz, *Paradise in Ashes*, 20.
77. Scott Wright, "Oscar Romero and Juan Gerardi: Truth, Memory, and Hope," in *Truth and Memory: The Church and Human Rights in El Salvador and Guatemala*, ed. Michael A. Hayes and David Tombs (London: MPG Books, 2001), 11–43, 20–21.
78. Konefal, *For Every Indio Who Falls*, 151.
79. Konefal, *For Every Indio Who Falls*, 151.
80. Grandin, *Last Colonial Massacre*, 188.
81. George Black, "Israeli Connection: Not Just Guns for Guatemala," *NACLA Report on the Americas* 17, no. 3 (1983): 43–45.
82. Lou Cannon, "Reagan Praises Guatemalan Military Leader," *Washington Post*, December 5, 1982.
83. Sanford, *Buried Secrets*, 169–71.
84. Sanford, *Buried Secrets*, 15, 148.

CHAPTER 5: NICARAGUA
1. Jeffrey L. Gould, *To Lead as Equals: Rural Protest and Political Consciousness in Chinandega, Nicaragua, 1912–1979* (Chapel Hill: University of North Carolina Press, 1990), 16.
2. Ernesto Cardenal, "Solentiname, The End," *Index on Censorship* 8, no. 1 (1979): 11–13; 11.
3. See Williams, *The Catholic Church and Politics in Nicaragua and Costa Rica*, 49–51; Michael Dodson and Laura Nuzzi O'Shaughnessy, *Nicaragua's Other Revolution: Religious Faith and Political Struggle* (Chapel Hill: University of North Carolina Press, 1990), 124–30; Lynn Horton, *Peasants in Arms: War and Peace in the Mountains of Nicaragua, 1979–1994* (Athens: Ohio University Center for International Studies, 1998), 66–68.
4. Gould, *To Lead as Equals*, 274–75.

5. Robert J. Sierakowski, *Sandinistas: A Moral History* (Notre Dame, IN: University of Notre Dame Press, 2020), 140, 160.

6. Sierakowski, *Sandinistas*, 194.

7. Stephen Kinzer, *Blood of Brothers: Life and War in Nicaragua* (New York: G. P. Putnam's Sons, 1991), 150.

8. Joseph Collins, *What Difference Could a Revolution Make?* (Oakland, CA: Institute for Food and Development Policy, 1982), 4.

9. Collins, *What Difference Could a Revolution Make?*, 89.

10. José Luis Rocha, "Agrarian Reform in Nicaragua in the 1980s: Lights and Shadows of Its Legacy," in *A Nicaraguan Exceptionalism: Debating the Legacy of the Sandinista Revolution*, ed. Hilary Francis (London: University of London Press, 2020), 103–26, 106.

11. Collins, *What Difference Could a Revolution Make?*, 33.

12. Frances Moore Lappé and Joseph Collins, *Now We Can Speak: A Journey Through the New Nicaragua* (Oakland, CA: Institute for Food and Development Policy, 1982), 10.

13. Horton, *Peasants in Arms*; Rocha, "Agrarian Reform," 112–13.

14. See Laura Enríquez, *Harvesting Change: Labor and Agrarian Reform in Nicaragua, 1979–1990* (Chapel Hill: University of North Carolina Press, 1991).

15. Collins, *What Difference Could a Revolution Make?* 43.

16. Collins, *What Difference Could a Revolution Make?* 46.

17. Collins, *What Difference Could a Revolution Make?* 139.

18. Horton, *Peasants in Arms*, 160.

19. Kinzer, *Blood of Brothers*, 129.

20. Roxanne Dunbar-Ortiz, *Blood on the Border: A Memoir of the Contra War*, orig. 2005; Norman: University of Oklahoma Press, 2016), 99.

21. Charles R. Hale, *Resistance and Contradiction: Miskitu Indians and the Nicaraguan State, 1984–1987* (Palo Alto, CA: Stanford University Press, 1994), 15.

22. Charles R. Hale, "*Resistencia para que?* Territory, Autonomy and Neoliberal Entanglements in the 'Empty Spaces' of Central America," *Economy and Society* 40, no. 2 (May 2011): 184–210, 190.

23. Martin Diskin, "The Manipulation of Indigenous Struggles," in *Reagan Versus the Sandinistas: The Undeclared War on Nicaragua*, ed. Thomas W. Walker (Boulder, CO: Westview Press, 1987), 80–96, 89.

24. Envío Team, "The Atlantic Coast: War or Peace?" *Envío* 52 (October 1985), https://www.envio.org.ni/articulo/3412.

25. Hale, *Resistance and Contradiction*, 14.

26. Dunbar-Ortiz, *Blood on the Border*, 167.

27. Hale, "*Resistencia para que?*," 190.

28. Nancy Saporta Sternbach, Marysa Navarro-Aranguren, Patricia Chuchryk, and Sonia E. Alvarez, "Feminisms in Latin America: From Bogotá to San Bernardo," *Signs* 17, no. 2 (Winter 1992): 393–434, 403.

29. Sierakowski, *Sandinistas*, 10.

30. Sierakowski, *Sandinistas*, 128–29.

31. Sierakowski, *Sandinistas*, 2–3. See also Margaret Randall, *Sandino's Daughters Revisited: Feminism in Nicaragua* (New Brunswick, NJ: Rutgers University Press, 1994), 13.

32. See Marguerite Guzmán Bouvard, *Revolutionizing Motherhood: The Mothers of the Plaza de Mayo* (Lanham, MD: SR Books, 1994; Lorraine Bayard de Volo, *Mothers of Heroes and Martyrs: Gender Identity Politics in Nicaragua, 1979–1999* (Baltimore: Johns Hopkins University Press, 2001).

33. Kinzer, *Blood of Brothers*, 97.

34. Reed Brody, *Contra Terror in Nicaragua: Report of a Fact-Finding Mission, September 1984–January 1985* (Boston: South End Press, 1985), 19. A twenty-page appendix to the book gives a chronology of hundreds of such attacks.

35. Brody, *Contra Terror in Nicaragua*, 20–21.

36. Kinzer, *Blood of Brothers*, 203.

37. Horton, *Peasants in Arms*, 173.

38. Horton, *Peasants in Arms*, 176.

39. Kinzer, *Blood of Brothers*, 295–96.

40. Horton, *Peasants in Arms*, 193.

41. Horton, *Peasants in Arms*, 43.

42. Horton, *Peasants in Arms*, 49, 55, 143.

43. Horton, *Peasants in Arms*, 57.

44. Horton, *Peasants in Arms*, 71–72.

45. Horton, *Peasants in Arms*, 210.

46. Horton, *Peasants in Arms*, 126.

47. Horton, *Peasants in Arms*, 136–37.

48. Hale, "Miskitu: Revolution in the Revolution," *NACLA Report on the Americas* XXV, no. 3 (December 1991), https://nacla.org/article/miskitu-revolution-revolution.

49. Carlos Vilas, "War and Revolution in Nicaragua: The Impact of the U.S. Counter-Revolutionary War on the Sandinista Strategies of Revolutionary Transition," *Socialist Register* (1988): 182–219, 190.

50. Vilas, "War and Revolution," 197.

51. Mitchell Seligson and Vincent McElhinny, "Low-Intensity Warfare, High-Intensity Death: The Demographic Impact of the Wars in El Salvador and Nicaragua," *Canadian Journal of Latin American and Caribbean Studies* 21, no. 42 (1996): 211–41, 213.

52. Vilas, "War and Revolution," 211.

53. See Dianna Melrose, *Nicaragua: The Threat of a Good Example?* (Oxford, UK: Oxfam, 1989), vii.

54. Kinzer, *Blood of Brothers*, 352–53.

55. Roger N. Lancaster, *Life Is Hard: Machismo, Danger, and the Intimacy of Power in Nicaragua* (Berkeley: University of California Press, 1992), 286.

56. Rocha, "Agrarian Reform," 115; Sierakowski, *Sandinistas*, 232.

57. Anne Larson, "Nicaragua's Real Property Debate," *Revista Envío* 138 (January 1993), https://www.envio.org.ni/articulo/1666; Envío Team, "El rompecabezas de la propiedad," *Revista Envío* 133 (December 1992), https://www.envio.org.ni/articulo/757.

58. Horton, *Peasants in Arms*, 273.

59. Horton, *Peasants in Arms*, 286.

60. Dora María Téllez, quoted in Envío Team, "Behind the Birth of the Recontras," *Envio* 123 (October 1991), https://www.envio.org.ni/articulo/2841.

61. Rocha, "Agrarian Reform," 117; Marc Edelman and Andrés León, "Cycles of Land Grabbing in Central America: An Argument for History and a Case Study in the Bajo Aguán, Honduras," *Third World Quarterly* 34, no. 9 (October 2013): 1697–1722, 1706.

62. Vilas, "War and Revolution," Enríquez, *Harvesting Change*, 154.

CHAPTER 6: EL SALVADOR

1. Tommie Sue Montgomery, *Revolution in El Salvador: Origins and Evolution* (Boulder, CO: Westview Press, 1982), 80.

2. Montgomery, *Revolution in El Salvador*, 76.

3. Elisabeth Jean Wood, *Insurgent Collective Action and Civil War in El Salvador* (New York: Cambridge University Press, 2003), 14.

4. Jeffrey M. Paige, "Land Reform and Agrarian Revolution in El Salvador," *Latin American Research Review* 31, no. 2 (1996): 127–39, 133.

5. Paige, "Land Reform," 133.

6. Joaquín M. Chávez, "El Salvador—The Creation of the Internal Enemy: Pondering the Legacies of U.S. Anticommunism, Counterinsurgency, and Authoritarianism in El Salvador (1952–18), in *Hearts and Minds: A People's History of Counterinsurgency*, ed. Hannah Gurman (New York: New Press, 2013), 104–34, 116.

7. Chávez, "El Salvador," 105.

8. William H. Durham, *Scarcity and Survival in Central America: Ecological Origins of the Soccer War* (Palo Alto, CA: Stanford University Press, 1979), 2.

9. Todd, *Beyond Displacement*, 28.

10. Todd, *Beyond Displacements*, chapter 1; 180–81.

11. Armstrong and Shenk, *El Salvador*, 80.

12. Montgomery, *Revolution in El Salvador*, 105.

13. Montgomery, *Revolution in El Salvador*, 106; Francisco Joel Arriola, "Federación Cristiana de Campesinos Salvadoreños (FECCAS) y Unión de Trabajadores del Campo (UTC): La formación del movimiento campesino salvadoreño revisitada," *Diálogos: Revista Electrónica de Historia* [Costa Rica] 2019, https://www.scielo.sa.cr/scielo.php.

14. Arriola, "FECCAS."

15. Statement of Rev. William L. Wipfler, dir., Caribbean and Latin American Department, National Council of Churches, in House of Representatives, Committee on International Relations, "Human Rights in Guatemala, Nicaragua, and El Salvador: Implications for U.S. Policy," June 9, 1976 (Washington, DC: US Government Printing Office, 1976), 79.

16. Chávez, "El Salvador," 123.

17. Armstrong and Shenk, *El Salvador*, 67.

18. Armstrong and Shenk, *El Salvador*, 77; Erik Ching, *Stories of Civil War in El Salvador: A Battle over Memory* (Chapel Hill: University of North Carolina Press, 2016), 35.

19. Chávez, "El Salvador," 124–25.

20. Wood, *Insurgent Collective Action*, 12.

21. Mark Danner, *The Massacre at El Mozote* (New York: Vintage Books, 1994), 147.

22. Todd, *Beyond Displacement*, 57, 58.

23. Chávez, "El Salvador," 134.

24. Jeffrey L. Gould, "Ignacio Ellacuría and Salvadoran Revolution," *Journal of Latin America Studies* 47, no. 2): 285–315, 289.

25. Armstrong and Shenk, *El Salvador*, 94.

26. Armstrong and Shenk, *El Salvador*, 94.

27. Gould, *Solidarity under Siege*, 103.

28. Gould, *Solidarity under Siege*, 112, 125.

29. Danner, *Massacre at El Mozote*, 26–27.

30. Edward F. Lehoucq, "Reform with Repression: The Land Reform in El Salvador," ISHI Occasional Papers in Social Change, no. 6 (Philadelphia: Institute for the Study of Human Issues, 1982), https://libres.uncg.edu/ir/uncg/f/F_Lehoucq_Reform_1982.pdf.

31. Armstrong and Shenk, *El Salvador*, 146.

32. Paul Heath Hoeffel, "The Eclipse of the Oligarchs," *New York Times Magazine*, September 6, 1981.

33. Lehoucq, "Reform with Repression." For on-the-ground studies of the ways that reform and repression were linked, see P. Shiras, "The False Promise—and the Real

Violence—of Land Reform," *Food Monitor* (January-February 1981); L. R. Simon and J. C. Stephens, *El Salvador Land Reform. 1980–1981: Impact Audit* (Boston: OXFAM America, 1981).

34. Chris Hedges, "Salvador Land Reform Plowed Under By Rightists," *Christian Science Monitor*, October 18, 1983.

35. Todd, *Beyond Displacement*, 58–59.

36. Hedges, "Salvador Land Reform Plowed Under By Rightists."

37. Armstrong and Shenk, *El Salvador*, 149.

38. Richard Severo, "Roberto d'Aubuisson, 48, Far Rightist in Salvador," *New York Times*, February 21, 1992.

39. Gould, *Solidarity Under Siege*, 196.

40. Todd, *Beyond Displacement*, 53.

41. William M. LeoGrande, "After the Battle of San Salvador," *World Policy Journal* 7, no. 2 (Spring 1990): 331–56, 333.

42. Leigh Binford, "Grassroots Development in Conflict Zones of Northeastern El Salvador," *Latin American Perspectives* 24, no. 2 (March 1997): 56–79, 65.

43. Charles Clements, *Witness to War: An American Doctor in El Salvador* (New York: Bantam Books, 1984).

44. Ching, *Stories of Civil War*, 44; Binford, "Grassroots Development," 59.

45. Todd, *Beyond Displacement*, 50; Clements, *Witness to War*.

46. Ching, *Stories of Civil War*, 43.

47. Danner, *Massacre at El Mozote*, 17.

48. Danner, *Massacre at El Mozote*, 85–86.

49. Danner, *Massacre at El Mozote*, chapter 7.

50. White House officials quoted in Karen DeYoung, "El Salvador: Where Reagan Draws the Line," *Washington Post*, March 9, 1981.

51. Danner, *Massacre at El Mozote*, 130.

52. Danner, *Massacre at El Mozote*, 137.

53. See Todd, *Beyond Displacement*.

54. Seligson and McElhinny, "Low-Intensity Warfare, High-Intensity Death," 229.

55. Todd, *Beyond Displacement*, 3.

56. Todd, *Beyond Displacement*, 172.

57. Ralph Sprenkels, *After Insurgency: Revolution and Electoral Politics in El Salvador* (Notre Dame, IN: University of Notre Dame Press, 2018), 146.

58. Steve Cagan, "Salvadoran Refugees at the Camp at Colomoncagua, Honduras," *DRCLAS Revista* (Spring 2016), https://revista.drclas.harvard.edu/book/salvadoran -refugees-camp-colomoncagua-honduras-1980–1991. See also Vincent J. McElhinny, "Between Clientelism and Radical Democracy: The Case of Ciudad Segundo Montes," in Lauria-Santiago and Binford, eds., *Landscapes of Struggle*, 147–65; Steve Cagan and Beth Cagan, *This Promised Land El Salvador: The Refugee Community of Colomoncagua and Their Return to Morazán* (New Brunswick, NJ: Rutgers University Press, 1991).

59. Todd, *Beyond Displacement*, chap. 7, 217, 219.

60. Wood, *Insurgent Collective Action*, 28.

CHAPTER 7: HONDURAS: STAGING GROUND FOR WAR AND REAGANOMICS

1. Brockett, *Land, Power, and Poverty*, 43.

2. James Guadalupe Carney, *"To Be a Christian Is . . . To Be a Revolutionary"* (New York: Harper & Row, 1987), 190.

3. Durham, *Scarcity and Survival*, 154, 157–61.

4. Brockett, *Land, Power, and Poverty*, 133.

5. J. Mark Ruhl, "Agrarian Structure and Political Stability in Honduras," *Journal of Interamerican Studies and World Affairs* 26, no. 1 (February 1984): 33–68, 55.

6. Ruhl, "Agrarian Structure," 54.

7. Miguel Alonzo Macías, *La capital de la contrarreforma agraria: El Bajo Aguán de Honduras* (Tegucigalpa, Honduras: Editorial Guaymuras, 2001), 43.

8. Annie Bird, *Human Rights Violations Attributed to Military Forces in the Bajo Aguán Valley in Honduras* (Rights Action, February 20, 2013), http://rightsaction.org/sites/default/files/Rpt_130220_Aguan_Final.pdf, 7.

9. Brockett, *Land, Power, and Poverty*, 53–54.

10. Brockett, *Land, Power, and Poverty*, 134–35; Williams, *Export Agriculture*, 179–83.

11. Richard Boudreaux, "Honduras in Turmoil," *Los Angeles Times*, February 25, 1989.

12. Philip L. Shepherd, "The Tragic Course and Consequences of U.S. Policy in Honduras," *World Policy Journal* 2, no.1 (Fall 1984): 109–154, 121.

13. Russell Watson and David C. Martin, "A Secret War for Nicaragua," *Newsweek*, November 8, 1982, 42–55, 44–45.

14. Shepherd, "Tragic Course and Consequences," 122, 114, 115–16.

15. Dawn Paley, *Drug War Capitalism* (Oakland, CA: AK Press, 2014), 198.

16. Ginger Thompson and Gary Cohn, "Torturers' Confessions," *Baltimore Sun*, June 13, 1995.

17. "Hear No Evil, See No Evil," *Baltimore Sun*, June 19, 1995.

18. Gary Cohn and Ginger Thompson, "A Carefully Crafted Deception," *Baltimore Sun*, June 18, 1995.

19. Donald E. Schultz and Deborah Sundloff Schultz, *United States, Honduras, and the Crisis in Central America* (Boulder, CO: Westview Press, 1994), 199.

20. Shepherd, "Tragic Course and Consequences," 115.

21. David Bacon, "If San Pedro Sula Is the Murder Capital of the World, Who Made It That Way?," *American Prospect*, June 13, 2019, https://prospect.org/economy/san-pedro-sula-murder-capital-world-made-way.

22. Adrienne Pine, *Working Hard, Drinking Hard: On Violence and Survival in Honduras* (Berkeley: University of California Press, 2008), 138, 139.

23. Brecher et al., "A Secret War for Nicaragua."

24. Ariel Torres Funes, "A 'Green Prison' Where Impunity Reigns," PEN Canada, March 2016. https://pencanada.ca/news/el-tumbador.

25. US Senate, Committee on Foreign Relations, Subcommittee on Terrorism, Narcotics and International Operations, "Drugs, Law Enforcement and Foreign Policy" (Washington, DC: US Government Printing Office, December 1988), 75.

26. Committee on Foreign Relations, "Drugs, Law Enforcement, and Foreign Policy," 36.

27. Anne Manuel, "Death Squad Debris," *Washington Post*, November 28, 1993.

28. Pine, *Working Hard, Drinking Hard*, 55.

29. Pine, *Working Hard, Drinking Hard*, 57, 58.

30. Stuart Schrader, *Badges Without Borders: How Global Counterinsurgency Transformed American Policing* (Berkeley: University of California Press, 2019).

31. Pine, *Working Hard, Drinking Hard*, 84.

32. Tanya M. Kerrsen, *Grabbing Power: The New Struggles for Land, Food, and Power in Northern Honduras* (Oakland, CA: Food First Books, 2013), 7.

33. Bird, "Human Rights Abuses," 13.

34. Macías, *La capital de la contrarreforma agraria*, 39.

35. Bird, "Human Rights Abuses," 6.

36. Bacon, "San Pedro Sula."

37. Pine, *Working Hard, Drinking Hard*, 164.

38. Pine, *Working Hard, Drinking Hard*, 139.

39. Bacon, "San Pedro Sula."

40. Pine, *Working Hard, Drinking Hard*, 161.

41. Daniel R. Reichman, *The Broken Village: Coffee, Migration, and Globalization in Honduras* (Ithaca, NY: Cornell University/ILR Press, 2011), 95–96, 77.

42. Reichman, *Broken Village*, 172–73.

43. Paley, *Drug War Capitalism*, 202.

44. Hillary Clinton, *Hard Choices: A Memoir* (New York: Simon & Schuster, 2014), 206.

45. Dana Frank, *The Long Honduran Night* (Chicago: Haymarket Books, 2018), 18–19.

46. Frank, *Long Honduran Night*, 36–37.

47. Bacon, "San Pedro Sula."

48. Frank, *Long Honduran Night*, 70.

49. Heather Gies, "Garifuna Under Siege," *NACLA Report on the Americas* 50, no. 2 (June 2018).

50. Frank, *Long Honduran Night*, 80.

51. Paley, *Drug War Capitalism*, 215–16, 209.

52. Frank, *Long Honduran Night*, 192.

53. Paley, *Drug War Capitalism*, 15.

54. Parker Asmann, "Honduras Drop in Homicides One Part of Complex Security Situation," *InSight Crime*, June 27, 2019, https://www.insightcrime.org/news/analysis/honduras-homicide-dip-one-part-complex-security-situation.

55. Gustavo Palencia, "Honduran President Sworn in Amid Protests After Election Chaos," Reuters, January 27, 2018.

56. Edelman and León, "Cycles of Land Grabbing," 1712.

57. Bird, "Human Rights Violations," 17.

58. Frank, *Long Honduran Night*, 54–55.

59. Jared Olson, "Honduras's Deadly Water Wars," *The Nation*, March 24, 2020.

60. Frank, *Long Honduran Night*, 83.

61. Bird, "Human Rights Violations," 13.

62. Olson, "Deadly Water Wars."

63. Frank, *Long Honduran Night*, 86, Bird, "Human Rights Violations," 43–44.

64. Goldman Environmental Prize, "Berta Cáceres," https://www.goldmanprize.org/recipient/berta-caceres.

65. Olson, "Deadly Water Wars."

66. Frank, *Long Honduran Night*, 225.

CHAPTER 8: CENTRAL AMERICA SOLIDARITY IN THE UNITED STATES

1. Van Gosse, "'The North American Front': Central American Solidarity in the Reagan Era," in *Reshaping the U.S. Left*, ed. Mike Davis and Michael Sprinker (New York: Verso, 1988), 1–43, 32.

2. Christian Smith, *Resisting Reagan: The U.S. Central America Peace Movement* (Chicago: University of Chicago Press, 1996), 158.

3. The name uses a take-off on the name of the Guatemalan department of Huehuetenango, but it's an imaginary Central America–like location.

4. Paul Farmer, *Infections and Inequalities: The Modern Plagues* (Berkeley: University of California Press, 2001), 96, 148.

5. Tracy Kidder, *Mountains Beyond Mountains: The Quest of Dr. Paul Farmer, A Man Who Would Cure the World* (New York: Random House, 2004), 211.

6. Smith, *Resisting Reagan*, 141.

7. Lafeber, *Inevitable Revolutions*, 246.

8. See Renny Golden and Michael McConnell, *Sanctuary: The New Underground Railroad* (New York: Orbis Books, 1986).

9. Norma Stoltz Chinchilla, Nora Hamilton, and James Loucky, "The Sanctuary Movement and Central American Activism in Los Angeles," *Latin American Perspectives* 36, no. 6 (November 2009): 101–26, 108–110.

10. Quixote Center, "About Us," https://www.quixote.org/about.

11. Gosse, "North American Front," 32–33.

12. Smith, *Resisting Reagan*, 81.

13. Smith, *Resisting Reagan*, 83.

14. Smith, *Resisting Reagan*, 82–83.

15. Héctor Perla Jr., "Si Nicaragua Venció, El Salvador Vencerá: Central American Agency in the Creation of the U.S.-Central American Peace and Solidarity Movement," *Latin American Research Review* 43, no. 2 (2008): 136–58, 150.

16. Quoted in Héctor Perla Jr., "Heirs of Sandino: The Nicaraguan Revolution and the U.S.-Nicaragua Solidarity Movement," *Latin American Perspectives* 36, no. 6 (November 2009): 80–100, 92.

17. Gosse, "North American Front."

18. Gosse, "North American Front," 35.

19. Perla, "Si Nicaragua Venció," 152.

20. Perla, "Heirs of Sandino," 85.

21. Several sources cite the figure of one hundred thousand Americans traveling to Nicaragua by 1986, though this is hard to confirm. See Mark Falcoff, "Revolutionary Tourism in Nicaragua," *Public Opinion* (American Enterprise Institute, Summer 1986). Nicaraguan tourism minister Henry Lewites claimed that one hundred thousand foreigners visited Nicaragua in 1986, about 40 percent of them from the US. See Marjorie Miller, "Run by Ex-Gunrunner: Nicaragua's Tourism Up Despite War," *Los Angeles Times*, March 12, 1986.

22. Gosse, "North American Front," 32.

23. TecNica Volunteers, "TecNica History and Background," https://www.tecnicavolunteers.org/backgr/the-background-of-tecnica.

24. Richard Boudreaux, "Linder's Death Heightens Zeal: 300 U.S. Volunteers Vow Sandinista Commitment," *Los Angeles Times*, May 2, 1987.

25. Michael Harris and Victor Lopez-Tosado, "Science for Nicaragua," *Science for the People* 18, no. 3 (May/June 1986): 22–25.

26. Susanne Jonas and David Tobin, *Guatemala: And So Victory Is Born Even in the Bitterest Hours* (New York: North American Congress on Latin America, 1974); Arturo Arias, *Taking Their Word: Literature and the Signs of Central America* (Minneapolis: University of Minnesota Press, 2007), 108.

27. Washington Office on Latin America, "Our History," https://www.wola.org/history-of-wola.

28. Barbara Crossette, "Groups Trying to Sway U.S. Policy," *New York Times*, November 18, 1981; Council on Hemispheric Affairs, "COHA's History," http://www.coha.org/cohas-history.

29. David Lowe, "Idea to Reality: NED at 30," National Endowment for Democracy, https://www.ned.org/about/history.

30. Andrew Battista, "Unions and Cold War Foreign Policy in the 1980s: The National Labor Committee, the AFL-CIO, and Central America," *Diplomatic History* 26, no. 3 (Summer 2002): 419–51.

31. Beth Sims, *Workers of the World Undermined: American Labor's Role in U.S. Foreign Policy* (Boston: South End Press, 1992), 87–88.

32. See Sims, *Workers of the World Undermined* and Tom Barry and Deb Preusch, *AIFLD in Central America: Agents as Organizers* (Albuquerque, NM: Inter-Hemispheric Education Resource Center, 1986).

33. Battista, "Unions and Cold War Foreign Policy," 447.

34. Roque Dalton, *Miguel Mármol* (Willimantic, CT: Curbstone Press, 1987); Roque Dalton, *Poems*, trans. Richard Schaaf (Willimantic, CT: Curbstone Press, 1984); Roque Dalton, *Poetry and Militancy in Latin America* (Willimantic, CT: Curbstone Press, 1982); *Poemas Clandestinos/Clandestine Poems* (Willimantic, CT: Curbstone Press, 1990). Curbstone's later anthology *Poetry Like Bread* (ed. Martín Espada, 1994; new and expanded edition 2000) brought together "poets of the political imagination" including most of Central America's best-known revolutionary poets.

35. Susan Meiselas, *Nicaragua* (New York: Aperture, 1981).

36. Perla, "Heirs of Sandino," 82. Perla makes a related argument in "Si Nicaragua Venció," 138.

CHAPTER 9: PEACE TREATIES AND NEOLIBERALISM

1. Henry Veltmeyer and James Petras, "New Social Movements in Latin America: The Dynamics of Class and Identity," in *The Dynamics of Social Change in Latin America*, ed. Henry Veltmeyer and James Petras (London: MacMillan, 2000), 99–121.

2. Richard Stahler-Sholk, "Resisting Neoliberal Homogenization: The Zapatista Autonomy Movement," *Latin American Perspectives* 34, no. 2 (March 2007): 48–63, 51.

3. Rose J. Spalding, *Contesting Trade in Central America: Market Reform and Resistance* (Austin: University of Texas Press, 2014), 67.

4. Lisa Johnston, "Why It's a Good Time to Take Another Look at Sourcing in Central America (Yes, Again)," *Sourcing Journal*, August 15, 2019, https://sourcingjournal.com /topics/sourcing/central-america-sourcing-opportunities-164635.

5. Pine, *Working Hard, Drinking Hard*, 28.

6. Leisy J. Abrego, *Sacrificing Families: Navigating Law, Labor, and Love Across Borders* (Palo Alto, CA: Stanford University Press, 2014), 14.

7. International Center for Transitional Justice, "Transitional Justice Issues: Truth and Memory," 2020, https://www.ictj.org/our-work/transitional-justice-issues/truth-and -memory.

8. Charles R. Hale, "What Went Wrong? Rethinking the Sandinista Revolution, in Light of Its Second Coming," *Latin American Research Review* 52, no. 4 (2017): 720–27; Jeffrey L. Gould, "Nicaragua: A View from the Left," *NACLA Report on the Americas* (July 25, 2018).

9. Hilary Francis, "Introduction: Exceptionalism and Agency in Nicaragua's Revolutionary Heritage," in Francis, ed., *A Nicaraguan Exceptionalism?*, 1–20, 6.

10. Jon Lee Anderson, "Nicaragua on the Brink, Once Again," *New Yorker*, April 27, 2018, https://www.newyorker.com/news/news-desk/nicaragua-on-the-brink-once -again.

11. Francis, "Introduction," 11; Justin Wolfe, "Conclusion: Exceptionalism and Nicaragua's Many Revolutions," in Francis, ed., *A Nicaraguan Exceptionalism?*, 179–84, 183.

12. UN Security Council, Annex, *From Madness to Hope: The 12-Year War in El Salvador: Report of the Commission on the Truth for El Salvador*, S/25500, 1993, https://www.usip.org/sites/default/files/file/ElSalvador-Report.pdf.

13. Margaret Popkin, *Peace Without Justice: Obstacles to Building the Rule of Law in El Salvador* (University Park: Pennsylvania State University Press, 2000), 6.

14. Lisa Kowalchuk, "The Salvadoran Land Struggle in the 1990s: Cohesion, Commitment, and Corruption," in Lauria-Santiago and Binford, eds., *Landscapes of Struggle*, 187–205, 189.

15. Kowalchuk, "The Salvadoran Land Struggle," 189.

16. Ellen Moodie, *El Salvador in the Aftermath of Peace: Crime, Uncertainty, and the Transition to Democracy* (Philadelphia: University of Pennsylvania Press, 2010), 43–44.

17. Luis Noe-Bustamante, Antonio Flores, and Sono Shah, "Facts on Hispanics of Salvadorian Origin in the United States, 2017," https://www.pewresearch.org/hispanic/fact-sheet/u-s-hispanics-facts-on-salvadoran-origin-latinos.

18. Aldo Lauria-Santiago and Leigh Binford, "Culture and Ideology in Contemporary El Salvador," in Lauria-Santiago and Binford, eds., *Landscapes of Struggle*, 207–210, 207–8.

19. Moodie, *El Salvador in the Aftermath of Peace*, 43–44.

20. Lauria-Santiago and Binford, "Culture and Ideology," 208.

21. Moodie, *El Salvador in the Aftermath of Peace*, 43–44, 46.

22. Lauria-Santiago and Gould, *To Rise in Darkness*, 278.

23. Sprenkels, *After Insurgency*, 10.

24. Sprenkels, *After Insurgency*, 12.

25. Sprenkels, *After Insurgency*, 23.

26. Sprenkels, *After Insurgency*, 5.

27. Sprenkels, *After Insurgency*, 2.

28. Sprenkels, *After Insurgency*, 4.

29. Hilary Goodfriend, "El Salvador's Backslide," *NACLA Report on the Americas*, February 14, 2019, https://nacla.org/news/2019/02/14/el-salvador%E2%80%99s-backslide.

30. Vincent J. McElhinny, "Between Clientelism and Radical Democracy: The Case of Ciudad Segundo Montes," in Lauria-Santiago and Binford, eds., *Landscapes of Struggle*, 147–65, 164.

31. McElhinny, "Between Clientelism and Radical Democracy," 159.

32. Voices on the Border, "Ciudad Segundo Montes Celebrates 24 Years," November 25, 2013, https://voiceselsalvador.wordpress.com/2013/11/25/ciudad-segundo-montes-celebrates-24-years.

33. Sprenkels, *After Insurgency*, 181–82.

34. Sprenkels, *After Insurgency*, 165–66.

35. Sprenkels, *After Insurgency*, 169.

36. Irina Carlota Silber, "Not Revolutionary Enough? Community Rebuilding in Postwar Chalatenango," in Lauria-Santiago and Binford, eds., *Landscapes of Struggle*, 166–86, 167.

37. Grandin, *Last Colonial Massacre*, 194.

38. Patricia Foxen, *In Search of Providence: Transnational Mayan Identities* (Nashville, TN: Vanderbilt University Press, 2007), 206.

39. Sanford, *Buried Secrets*, 17.

40. For updates on the different cases, see "International Justice Monitor: Guatemala Trials," https://www.ijmonitor.org/category/guatemala-trials/.

41. See Sandra Cuffe, "Day of the Disappeared: 'The Pain Never Ends' in Guatemala," *Al Jazeera*, August 30, 2019, https://www.aljazeera.com/indepth/features/day -disappeared-pain-ends-guatemala-190830153353465.html; Rachel López, "From Impunity to Justice and Back Again in Guatemala," Open Global Rights, November 5, 2019, https://www.openglobalrights.org/from-impunity-to-justice-and-back-again-in -guatemala.

42. Burrell, *Maya After War*, 82.

43. Foxen, *In Search of Providence*, 207.

44. Foxen, *In Search of Providence*, 205.

45. Foxen, *In Search of Providence*, 213.

46. Foxen, *In Search of Providence*, 208.

47. Foxen, *In Search of Providence*, 216.

48. Foxen, *In Search of Providence*, 209. See also Stener Ekern, "Are Human Rights Destroying the Natural Balance of All Things? The Difficult Encounter between International Law and Community Law in Mayan Guatemala," in Pitarch, Speed, and Leyva Solano, eds., *Human Rights in the Maya Region*, 123–43.

49. Burrell, *Maya After War*, 12.

50. Richard Stahler-Sholk, "Resisting Neoliberal Homogenization: The Zapatista Autonomy Movement," *Latin American Perspectives* 34, no. 2 (March 2007): 48–63.

51. Nicholas Copeland, *The Democracy Development Machine: Neoliberalism, Radical Pessimism, and Authoritarian Populism in Mayan Guatemala* (Ithaca, NY: Cornell University Press, 2019), 7–8.

52. Copeland, *Democracy Development Machine*, 22.

53. Copeland, *Democracy Development Machine*, 9.

54. Burrell, *Maya After War*, 37.

55. Rachel Seider, "Legal Globalization and Human Rights: Constructing the Rule of Law in Post-Conflict Guatemala," in Pitarch, Speed, and Leyva Solano, eds., *Human Rights in the Maya Region*, 67–88, 82.

56. Burrell, *Maya After War*, 87.

57. Burrell, *Maya After War*, 86.

58. International Labour Organization, C169, "Indigenous and Tribal People's Convention, 1989 (C-169), https://www.ilo.org/dyn/normlex/ en/f?p=NORMLEXPUB:12100:0::NO::P12100_ILO_CODE:C169.

59. Hale, "*Resistencia para qué?*" 194.

60. Naomi Klein, *This Changes Everything: Capitalism vs. the Climate* (New York: Simon and Schuster, 2014).

61. See Robin Broad and John Cavanagh, "El Salvador Gold: Toward a Mining Ban," in Thomas Princen, Jack P. Manno, and Pamela L. Martin, eds., *Ending the Fossil Fuel Era* (Cambridge, MA: MIT Press, 2015), 167–92, 179–80 and 190–91n33, for sources on this provision.

62. Global Witness, *Enemies of the State?*, July 30, 2019, https://www.globalwitness .org/en/campaigns/environmental-activists/enemies-state/, 23.

63. Michael L. Dougherty, "The Global Gold Mining Industry, Junior Firms, and Civil Society Resistance in Guatemala," *Bulletin of Latin American Research* 30, no. 4 (2011): 403–18, 411–13.

64. See the documentary "Sipakapa no se vende" by Caracol Productions, https:// www.youtube.com/watch?v=F36SqLpqQmQ.

65. Institute for Policy Studies and Earthworks, "Guatemalan Government Discriminates against Xinca, Puts Escobal Mine Consultation at Risk," September 6, 2019.

https://earthworks.org/publications/report-guatemalan-government-discriminates
-against-xinka-puts-escobal-mine-consultation-at-risk.

66. Robin Broad and John Cavanagh, "Like Water for Gold in El Salvador," *The Nation*, July 11, 2011, https://www.thenation.com/article/archive/water-gold-el-salvador; Broad and Cavanagh, "El Salvador Gold: Toward a Mining Ban."

67. Emily Achtenberg, "Resistance to Mining in El Salvador," *ReVista: Harvard Review of Latin America* (Winter 2014), https://revista.drclas.harvard.edu/book/resistance
-mining-el-salvador.

68. Michael L. Dougherty, "El Salvador Makes History," *NACLA Report on the Americas* (April 12, 2017), https://nacla.org/news/2017/04/19/el-salvador-makes-history.

69. Claire Provost and Matt Kennard, "World Bank Tribunal Dismisses Mining Firm's $250 Million Claim Against El Salvador," *The Guardian*, October 14, 2016, https://www.theguardian.com/global-development/2016/oct/14/el-salvador-world-bank
-tribunal-dismisses-oceanagold-mining-firm-250m-claim; Esty Dinur, "How El Salvador Won on Mining," *The Progressive*, April 1, 2018, https://progressive.org/magazine/how
-el-salvador-won-on-mining; Sarah Anderson, Manuel Pérez-Rocha, and Michael L. Dougherty, "The Rise of the Corporate Investment Rights Regime and 'Extractive Exceptionalism': Evidence from El Salvador," in Kalowatie Deonandan and Michael L. Dougherty, eds., *Mining in Latin America: Critical Approaches to the New Extractivism* (New York: Routledge, 2016), 229–49.

70. Cultural Survival, "Observations on the State of Indigenous Human Rights in El Salvador," prepared for the Universal Periodic Review Working Group of the United Nations Human Rights Council, March 2019, 4, https://www.culturalsurvival.org/sites
/default/files/El-Salvador-UPR-final.pdf.

71. On royalties, see Dougherty, "Global Gold Mining," 413.

72. Richard Ashby Wilson, "Making Rights Meaningful for Mayas: Reflections on Culture, Rights, and Power," in Pitarch, Speed, and Leyva Solano, eds., *Human Rights in the Maya Region*, 305–21, 313.

73. World Population Review, "Murder Rate by Country, 2020," February 17, 2020, http://worldpopulationreview.com/countries/murder-rate-by-country.

74. Moodie, *El Salvador in the Aftermath of Peace*, 41.

75. Wilson, "Making Rights Meaningful for Mayas," 314; Deborah T. Levenson, *Adiós Niño: The Gangs of Guatemala City and the Politics of Death* (Durham, NC: Duke University Press, 2013).

76. Pine, *Working Hard, Drinking Hard*, 49.

77. United States, The White House, "Fact Sheet: What You Need to Know About the Violent Animals of MS-13," May 21, 2018, https://www.whitehouse.gov/articles
/need-know-violent-animals-ms-13/.

78. President Donald J. Trump, State of the Union Address, February 5, 2019, https://www.whitehouse.gov/briefings-statements/president-donald-j-trumps-state
-union-address-2.

79. Dara Lind, "MS-13, Explained," *Vox*, February 5, 2019, https://www.vox.com
/policy-and-politics/2018/2/26/16955936/ms-13-trump-immigrants-crime.

80. Bacon, "San Pedro Sula."

81. Lind, "MS-13."

82. José Miguel Cruz, "Central American Gangs Like MS-13 Were Born Out of Failed Anti-Crime Policies," *The Conversation*, May 8, 2017, https://theconversation.com
/central-american-gangs-like-ms-13-were-born-out-of-failed-anti-crime-policies-76554.

83. Levenson, *Adiós Niño*, 6.

84. Pine, *Working Hard, Drinking Hard*, 33.

85. Bacon, "San Pedro Sula."

86. Cruz, "Central American." For the role of aggressive policing and imprisonment in strengthening gangs in the United States, see Benjamin Lessing, "Inside Out: The Challenge of Prison-Based Criminal Organizations," Brookings Institution Local Orders Paper Series, September 2016, https://www.brookings.edu/wp-content/uploads/2016/09/fp_20160927_prison_based_organizations.pdf.

87. Levenson, *Adiós Niño*, 4.

88. Roberto Lovato, "Why Is Nicaragua's Homicide Rate So Far Below That of Its Central American Neighbors?," *The Nation*, February 2, 2018, https://www.thenation.com/article/archive/why-is-nicaraguas-homicide-rate-so-far-below-that-of-its-central-american-neighbors.

89. Jennifer Goett, "In Nicaragua, the Latest Zombie Megaproject," *NACLA Report on the Americas* (May 20, 2016), https://nacla.org/news/2016/05/20/nicaragua-latest-zombie-megaproject.

CHAPTER 10: MIGRATION

1. María Cristina García, *Seeking Refuge: Central American Migration to Mexico, the United States, and Canada* (Berkeley: University of California Press, 2006), 2, 34, 9.

2. García, *Seeking Refuge*, 9–10.

3. Pew Research Center: Hispanic Trends: Table "Foreign-Born by Region of Birth, 1960–2017," June 3, 2019, https://www.pewresearch.org/hispanic/2019/06/03/facts-on-u-s-immigrants-trend-data; D'Vera Cohn, Jeffrey Passel, and Ana González-Barrera, "Recent Trends in Northern Triangle Immigration," Pew Research Center, December 7, 2017, https://www.pewresearch.org/hispanic/2017/12/07/recent-trends-in-northern-triangle-immigration.

4. Luis Noe-Bustamante, Antonio Flores, and Sono Shah, "Facts on Hispanics of Nicaraguan Origin in the United States, 2017," Pew Research Center, September 16, 2019, https://www.pewresearch.org/hispanic/fact-sheet/u-s-hispanics-facts-on-nicaraguan-origin-latinos; "Facts on Hispanics of Guatemalan Origin in the United States, 2017," https://www.pewresearch.org/hispanic/fact-sheet/u-s-hispanics-facts-on-guatemalan-origin-latinos; "Facts on Hispanics of Honduran Origin in the United States, 2017," https://www.pewresearch.org/hispanic/fact-sheet/u-s-hispanics-facts-on-salvadoran-origin-latinos; and "Facts on Hispanics of Salvadorian Origin in the United States, 2017," https://www.pewresearch.org/hispanic/fact-sheet/u-s-hispanics-facts-on-salvadoran-origin-latinos.

5. Cohn, Passel, and González-Barrera, "Recent Trends."

6. Pew Research Center, "Foreign-Born by Region of Birth."

7. García, *Seeking Refuge*, 40.

8. Barack Obama, "Remarks by the President in an Address to the Nation on Immigration," November 20, 2014, https://obamawhitehouse.archives.gov/the-press-office/2014/11/20/remarks-president-address-nation-immigration.

9. Gregory T. Carter, "Race and Citizenship," in *The Oxford Handbook of American Immigration and Ethnicity*, ed. Ronald H. Bayor (New York: Oxford University Press, 2016), 166–82, 169.

10. See Michelle Alexander, *The New Jim Crow: Mass Incarceration in the Age of Colorblindness* (New York: New Press, 2010); Aviva Chomsky, *Undocumented: How Immigration Became Illegal* (Boston: Beacon Press, 2014).

11. Muzaffar Chishti, Doris Meissner, and Claire Bergeron, "At Its 25th Anniversary, IRCA's Legacy Lives On," Migration Policy Institute, November 16, 2011, https://www .migrationpolicy.org/article/its-25th-anniversary-ircas-legacy-lives.

12. García, *Seeking Refuge*, 91.

13. García, *Seeking Refuge*, 90.

14. Sarah J. Mahler and Dusan Ugrina, "Central America: Crossroad of the Americas," Migration Policy Institute, April 1, 2006, https://www.migrationpolicy.org/article /central-america-crossroads-americas.

15. García, *Seeking Refuge*, 91.

16. García, *Seeking Refuge*, 91.

17. Smith, *Resisting Reagan*, 300.

18. Cecilia Menjívar, *Fragmented Ties: Salvadoran Immigrant Networks in America* (Berkeley: University of California Press, 2000), 88–89.

19. Cecilia Menjívar, "Liminal Legality: Salvadoran and Guatemalan Immigrants' Lives in the United States," *American Journal of Sociology* 111, no. 4 (January 2006): 999–1037.

20. See US Citizenship and Immigration Services, "Nicaraguan Adjustment and Central American Relief Act (NACARA) 203," https://www.uscis.gov/humanitarian /refugees-asylum/asylum/nicaraguan-adjustment-and-central-american-relief-act -nacara-203-eligibility-apply-uscis.

21. Faye Hipsman and Doris Meissner, "In-Country Refugee Processing: A Piece of the Puzzle," Migration Policy Institute, August 2015, 2, https://www.migrationpolicy.org /research/country-processing-central-america-piece-puzzle.

22. TRAC Immigration, Syracuse University, "Asylum Decisions and Denials Jump in 2018," https://trac.syr.edu/immigration/reports/539.

23. US Border Patrol, "Border Patrol Agent Nationwide Staffing by Fiscal Year," https://www.cbp.gov/sites/default/files/assets/documents/2019-Mar/Staffing%20FY 1992-FY2018.pdf.

24. Ted Hesson, "The Border Patrol's Recruiting Crisis," *Politico*, February 10, 2019, https://www.politico.com/story/2019/02/10/border-patrol-recruitment-crisis-1157171.

25. David Bacon, "Undocumented Youth Are Here Through No Fault of Their Own. But It's Not Their Parents' Fault Either," *In These Times*, November 5, 2015.

26. US Citizenship and Immigration Service (USCIS), "Approximate Active DACA Recipients: Country of Birth," September 4, 2017, https://www.uscis.gov/sites/default /files/USCIS/Resources/Reports%20and%20Studies/Immigration%20Forms%20Data /All%20Form%20Types/DACA/daca_population_data.pdf.

27. Josh Dawsey, "Trump Attacks Protections for Immigrants from 'Shithole' Countries," *Washington Post*, January 11, 2018; Donald Trump, Twitter, November 12, 2019, https://twitter.com/realDonaldTrump/status/1194219655717642240; Dartunorro Clark, "Trump Holds White House Event Focused on 'American Victims of Illegal Immigration,'" NBC News, June 22, 2018, https://www.nbcnews.com/politics/white-house/trump -looks-shift-border-policy-debate-american-victims-illegal-immigration-n885881.

28. García, *Seeking Refuge*, 112.

29. García, *Seeking Refuge*, 38–39.

30. García, *Seeking Refuge*, 34–35, 36, 37.

31. García, *Seeking Refuge*, 37.

32. García, *Seeking Refuge*, 38–40.

33. Richard C. Jones, "Causes of Salvadoran Migration to the United States," *Geographical Review* 79, no. 2 (April 1989): 183–94.

34. García, *Seeking Refuge*, 110.

35. Eric Schmitt, "Salvadorans Illegally in U.S. Are Given Protected Status," *New York Times*, March 3, 2001.

36. García, *Seeking Refuge*, 35.

37. Watanabe, "Enduring Yet Ineffable Community, 200.

38. Burrell, *Maya After War*, 36, 88.

39. Manz, *Paradise in Ashes*, 236, 237.

40. Manz, *Paradise in Ashes*, 239, 238.

41. Carrie Seay-Fleming, "Beyond Violence: Drought and Migration in Central America's Northern Triangle," Wilson Center New Security Beat, April 12, 2018, https:// www.newsecuritybeat.org/2018/04/violence-drought-migration-central-americas -northern-triangle.

42. Hipsman and Meissner, "In-Country Refugee Processing," 2–3, 8.

43. Office of Refugee Resettlement, "Facts and Data," https://www.acf.hhs.gov/orr /about/ucs/facts-and-data.

44. John Gramlich and Luis Noe-Bustamante, "What's Happening at the U.S.-Mexico Border in 5 Charts," Pew Research Center, November 1, 2019, https://www .pewresearch.org/fact-tank/2019/11/01/whats-happening-at-the-u-s-mexico-border -in-5-charts.

45. US Border Patrol, "Total Illegal Alien Apprehensions by Fiscal Year," https:// www.cbp.gov/sites/default/files/assets/documents/2020-Jan/U.S.%20Border%20Patrol %20Total%20Monthly%20Family%20Unit%20Apprehensions%20by%20Sector%20 %28FY%202013%20-%20FY%202019%29_0.pdf; Gramlich and Noe-Bustamante, "U.S.-Mexico Border."

46. Rob O'Dell, Daniel González, and Jill Castellano, "'Mass Disaster' Grows at the U.S.-Mexico Border, But Washington Doesn't Seem to Care," *USA Today*, n.d. [December 27, 2017].

47. David Stoll, *El Norte or Bust! How Migration Fever and Microcredit Produced a Financial Crash in a Latin American Town* (Lanham, MD: Rowman & Littlefield, 2013), xi.

48. Stoll, *El Norte or Bust!*, 5.

49. Reichmann, *Broken Village*, 167.

50. Gies, "Garifuna Under Siege."

51. Gould, *Solidarity Under Siege*, 163–64.

52. Vince Bielski, Cindy Forster, and Dennis Bernstein, "The Death Squads Hit Home," *Progressive*, October 1987, 15–19; 16.

53. Smith, *Resisting Reagan*, 300; Bielski, Forster, and Bernstein, "The Death Squads Hit Home," 18.

54. Foxen, *In Search of Providence*, 257, 123.

55. Foxen, *In Search of Providence*, xxxiv.

56. Foxen, *In Search of Providence*, xxxiv; Juan Alecio Samayoa Cabrera v. John Ashcroft, https://d279m997dpfwgl.cloudfront.net/wp/2017/12/SamayoaFirstCircuit.pdf, Jo-Marie Burt and Paulo Estrada, "After 25 Years in the United States, Guatemalan Accused of Mass Atrocities to Face Charges," *International Justice Monitor*, December 12, 2019, https://www.ijmonitor.org/2019/12/after-25-years-in-united-states-guatemalan -accused-of-mass-atrocities-to-face-charges.

57. Burt and Estrada, "After 25 Years," US Customs and Immigration Enforcement; "ICE Removes Former Civil Patrol Leader Accused of Human Rights Abuses in Guatemala," December 2, 2019, https://www.ice.gov/news/releases/ice-removes-former-civil -patrol-leader-accused-human-rights-abuses-guatemala.

58. Foxen, *In Search of Providence*, xxxiv. See also Amanda Milkovitz, "Providence Man Accused of War Crimes Ordered Deported to Guatemala," *Providence Journal*, March 29, 2018; Amanda Milkovitz, "Accused Guatemalan War Criminal Living in RI Faces Deportation," *Providence Journal*, March 2, 2018; Simón Ríos, "For Guatemalan War Survivors, Arrest of Accused War Criminal Is A Cause for Hope," WBUR, December 13, 2017; Brianna Rennix, "A Tale of Two Atrocities," *Current Affairs*, March 4, 2018.

59. Héctor Tobar, *The Tattooed Soldier* (New York: Delphinium Books, 1998/Penguin, 2000).

60. Richard Luscombe, "Florida No Longer Safe Haven for War Criminals as U.S. Prosecutors Take Action," *Guardian*, March 23, 2015.

61. Center for Justice and Accountability, "Romagoza Arce v. García and Vides Casanova: The Perpetrators," https://cja.org/what-we-do/litigation/romagoza-arce-v-garcia -and-vides-casanova/perpetrators; Linda Cooper and James Hodge, "Former Salvadoran Defense Minister, Tied to Killings of Romero and Churchwomen, Deported Back to El Salvador," *National Catholic Reporter*, January 13, 2016.

62. Center for Justice and Accountability, "Command Responsibility for the Infamous Church Women Murders," https://cja.org/what-we-do/litigation/amicus-briefs /ford-v-garcia; Center for Justice and Accountability, "Human Rights Crimes under Salvadoran Defense Ministers," https://cja.org/what-we-do/litigation/romagoza-arce-v -garcia-and-vides-casanova; Center for Justice and Accountability, "U.S. Removal Proceedings, General Vides Casanova," https://cja.org/where-we-work/el-salvador/related -resources/u-s-removal-proceedings-general-vides-casanova; Luscombe, "Florida No Longer Safe Haven."

63. See Lisa Creamer, "Salvadoran Colonel Who Lived For Years in Everett Extradited to Spain in 1989 Jesuit Murders," WBUR, November 29, 2017; US Department of Justice, "U.S. Extradites Former Salvadoran Military Officer to Spain to Face Charges for Participation in 1989 Jesuit Massacre," November 29, 2017, https://www.justice.gov/opa /pr/us-extradites-former-salvadoran-military-officer-spain-face-charges-participation -1989-jesuit; Mark Arsenault, "War Crime Suspect Found in Everett," *Boston Globe*, August 17, 2011.

64. Much information about this case can be found in Sebastian Rotella, "Finding Oscar: Massacre, Memory, and Justice in Guatemala," ProPublica, May 25, 2012, https:// www.propublica.org/article/finding-oscar-massacre-memory-and-justice-in-guatemala; and in the 2016 Steven Spielberg documentary "Finding Oscar," findingoscar.com.

65. See Patricia Flynn and Mary Jo McConahay, "Discovering Dominga," https:// itvs.org/films/discovering-dominga; Guatemala Human Rights Commission, "Río Negro Massacres," https://www.ghrc-usa.org/our-work/important-cases/rio-negro; Laura Briggs, *Somebody's Children: The Politics of Transracial and Transnational Adoption* (Durham, NC: Duke University Press, 2012), 166–68.

66. George W. Liebmann, *The Last Diplomat: John D. Negroponte and the Changing Face of American Diplomacy* (London: I. B. Tauris & Co., 2012), 139.

67. Briggs, *Somebody's Children*.

68. Briggs, *Somebody's Children*, 178; Erin Elizabeth Siegal, *Finding Fernanda: Two Mothers, One Child, and a Cross-Border Search for Truth* (Boston: Beacon Press, 2011), 35.

69. Rachel Nolan, "Destined for Export: The Troubled Legacy of Guatemalan Adoptions," *Harpers Magazine*, April 2019, https://harpers.org/archive/2019/04/destined-for -export-guatemalan-adoptions; Siegal, *Finding Fernanda*, ix.

70. Nolan, "Destined for Export."

71. Pro-Búsqueda, "Campaña en Estados Unidos," http://www.probusqueda.org.sv
/que-hacemos/campana-en-estados-unidos.

72. Burrell, *Maya After War*, 52.

73. Burrell, *Maya After War*, 159.

74. Leisy J. Abrego, *Sacrificing Families: Navigating Law, Labor, and Love Across Borders* (Palo Alto, CA: Stanford University Press, 2014).

75. Abrego, *Sacrificing Families*, 22.

76. Menjívar, *Fragmented Ties*, 236–37.

77. Sarah J. Malher, *American Dreaming: Immigrant Life on the Margins* (Princeton, NJ: Princeton University Press, 1995), 215.

CONCLUSION: TRUMP'S BORDER WAR

1. See Nicole Einbinder, "How the Trump Administration Is Rewriting the Rules for Unaccompanied Minors," *Frontline*, February 13, 2018; Andrea Castillo, "Trump Is Stripping Immigrant Children of Protections, Critics Say," *Los Angeles Times*, September 2, 2019.

2. Caitlin Dickerson, "Hundreds of Immigrant Children Have Been Taken from Parents at U.S. Border," *New York Times*, April 20, 2018. Reuters later put together statistics showing that 1,800 children had been separated from their parents between October 2016 and February 2018. See Micah Rosenberg, "Exclusive: Nearly 1800 Families Separated at U.S.-Mexico Border in 17 Months Through February," Reuters, June 8, 2018.

3. Dara Lind, "The Trump Administration's Separation of Families at the Border, Explained," *Vox*, August 18, 2018.

4. Dara Lind, "Trump's DHS Is Using an Extremely Dubious Statistic to Justify Splitting Up Families at the Border," *Vox*, May 8, 2018.

5. Richard Gonzales, "ACLU: Administration Is Still Separating Migrant Families Despite Court Order to Stop," NPR, June 30, 2019.

6. Camilo Montoya-Galvez, "Lawmakers Condemn 'Horrific' Conditions Faced by Asylum-Seekers Returned to Mexico," CBS News, January 17, 2020.

7. Human Rights Watch, "U.S. 'Remain in Mexico' Program Harming Children," February 12, 2020, https://www.hrw.org/news/2020/02/12/us-remain-mexico-program
-harming-children.

8. Priscilla Alvarez, "Migrant Families Have Sent Roughly 135 Children Across the U.S.-Mexico Border Alone, U.S. Government Says," CNN, November 26, 2019.

9. Christopher Sherman, Martha Mendoza, and Garance Burke, "US Held Record Number of Migrant Kids in Custody This Year," *Frontline*, PBS, November 12, 2019.

10. Nicole Acevedo, "Why Are Migrant Children Dying in U.S. Custody?," NBC News, May 29, 2019.

11. See Dara Lind, "The Horrifying Conditions Facing Kids in Border Detention, Explained," *Vox*, June 25, 2019; Ginger Thompson, "A Border Patrol Agent Reveals What It's Really Like to Guard Migrant Children," ProPublica, July 16, 2019.

12. Whitney Eulich, "How Mexico Became Trump's Wall," *Christian Science Monitor*, March 6, 2020.

13. Whitney Eulich, "2,000 Miles, 72 Hours, a Tough Choice: Asylum in Guatemala, or Go Home?" *Christian Science Monitor*, March 13, 2020.

14. See Elizabeth Oglesby, "How Central American Migrants Helped Revive the U.S. Labor Movement," *The Conversation*, https://theconversation.com/how-central
-american-migrants-helped-revive-the-us-labor-movement-109398.

15. Catherine E. Soichet, "They Thought Living in Churches Would Protect Them. Now They Fear Nowhere Is Safe," CNN, December 22, 2018.

16. In a recent example, a *New York Times* reporter pointedly and repeatedly overruled Bernie Sanders's attempt to recall the US war against Nicaragua in the 1980s. See Sydney Ember, "Sanders Defends Views on Foreign Policy," *New York Times*, May 19, 2019.

INDEX

National University: attacked by Salvadoran military, 130, 137
Native Americans, US, 8, 21, 46, 54–55
NED (National Endowment for Democracy, United States), 181
négritude, 44
Negroponte, John, 66, 151, 153, 154, 155, 239
neoliberalism, 190, 208, 210, 216–17; in Central America, 189–92; counterinsurgency and, 72; in El Salvador, 197–98; in Guatemala, 205–7; in Honduras, 156, 161–62; migration and, 231, 232–34; peace treaties and, 188–217; United States and, 63, 146, 154; violence and, 166, 215
neo-Sandinismo, 195, 196
Neruda, Pablo, 44; "The United Fruit Company," 39
New Deal, 46
Newsweek, 66, 151, 154
New York Times, 80, 82, 140, 184, 243–44
New Zealand, 7, 207
NGOs (nongovernment organizations), 97–98, 158, 190, 199, 200, 211, 220, 240
NicaNet (National Network in Solidarity with the Nicaraguan People), 178
Nicaragua, 32, 35, 101, 103, 107, 120, 175, 209; Atlantic coast of, 110–13, 119; banana economy in, 38, 167; Britain and, 24–25; Carter's policies toward, 61–62; Catholicism and, 58, 116; gangs in, 215–16; Indigenous people in, 2, 4, 12, 35, 41–42, 66, 70, 110–12, 115, 228; peace process in, 120–21; refugees and migrants from, 219, 224, 227–28; solidarity travel to, 167, 172, 174, 179–80, 217, 267n21; US covert war in, 65–66, 119, 168, 174–75, 277n16; US influence in, 24–25, 30–34, 35, 60, 219, 267n21; US occupation of (1912–33), 4, 34–37, 41; Vanderbilt and, 32–33
Nicaraguan revolution, 61, 99–123, 195; economy after, 194–96; elections after, 121–22; gender and, 113–14; impact of, 189, 195–96; Liberation Theology and, 101–2; Sandinistas in

power after, 104–13; solidarity of US Americans with, 178
nickel mining (Guatemala), 80, 81
NISGUA (Network in Solidarity with Guatemala), 180
Nixon, Richard M., 59–60
NLC (National Labor Committee in Support of Democracy and Human Rights in El Salvador), 183
Non-Aligned Movement, 62
North, Oliver, 63, 68–69, 189
North America, British, 6, 8
Northern Triangle (Central America), 230, 231

Oakland (California), refugee organizing in, 177–78
OAS (Organization of American States), 62, 122, 160, 161, 162
Obama, Barack, 160, 220, 225, 226, 231, 247
Obando y Bravo, Miguel, 61–62, 102
Ocasio-Cortez, Alexandria, 245
OFRANEH (Black Fraternal Organization of Honduras), 162
oil companies and petroleum industry, 80, 81, 90; Guatemala and, 75, 76, 211
oil crisis of 1973, 54, 59, 78, 80
Operación Limpieza (Nicaragua), 103
Operation Big Pine II (US troops in Honduras), 151
Operation PBSUCCESS (CIA in Guatemala), 51
Orbis Books, 180
ORDEN (Salvadoran paramilitary force), 132–35
ORPA (Revolutionary Organization of the People in Arms, Guatemala), 86, 94
ORR (Office of Refugee Resettlement, United States), 242–45
Ortega, Daniel, 67, 119, 121–22, 194, 195, 216, 217
Ortíz, Dianna, torture of, 96–97
ortodoxos, in Sandinista party, 194

Pacific coast of El Salvador, 52, 124
PACs (Civil Defense Patrols, Guatemala), 94–95, 98
Paley, Dawn, 163

Palmerola, Honduras. *See* Soto Cano Air Base, Palmerola, Honduras,
palm oil industry, 156, 158, 162, 165
Panama, 70
Panama canal, 34, 35
Panama Canal Zone, School of the Americas in, 53
pan-Mayanism, 207–8
Panzós massacre (Guatemala), 87, 88–90
Paraguay, Somoza assassinated in, 62
paramilitary forces, 84, 89, 132, 192, 203, 212. *See also* death squads, paramilitary; ORDEN; PACs
Pastor, Robert, 184
Pastora, Edén, 115
patriarchy, 82, 113
Payeras, Mario, 90, 92–93
Paz y Paz, Claudia, 203–4
Peace Corps, 77
peace process: in El Salvador, 29, 71, 144–45, 189, 193, 196; in Guatemala, 71, 98, 189, 193, 202, 206–7; neoliberalism and, 188–217; in Nicaragua, 120–21
peasants, 25, 54; in El Salvador, 28, 127–28, 129, 131–32; in Guatemala, 89; in Honduras, 127–28, 147–48; land and, 4, 49, 56; in Nicaragua, 100, 116–18; organizing of, 82, 88, 90, 101, 126, 128, 129, 135, 147, 148; as refugees, 127–28, 136; uprisings of, 4, 27–28. *See also* campesinos; land reform
Pelosi, Nancy, 166
peons and debt peonage, 26, 35, 82, 89
people of color, colonialism and, 7
People's University (El Salvador), 28
Perla, Héctor, 178, 185
Peru, 7, 146
Petén (Guatemala), 81–82, 211
Peurifoy, John, 51, 52
Pew Research Center, 219
PGT (Guatemala's communist party), 48, 49, 75, 86
Pierce, Franklin, 32
"piñata laws" (Nicaragua), 122
Pine, Adrienne, 154, 155, 156, 192
"pink tide" (Latin America), 159, 216
plantation agriculture and plantations, 7, 8, 23, 24, 49; in British Caribbean, 6,

7. *See also under names of export agriculture crops*
Plaza of the Revolution (Managua), 104
Pledge of Resistance, 168, 172, 173–75
Polochic River (Guatemala), 89
Popol Vuh, quoted by Menchu, 4–5
poverty, 7, 168, 171; in Guatemala, 206–7; in Honduras, 146–47, 161, 164; in Nicaragua, 100
Pratt, Richard H., 42
prisons, prisoners, 181, 215; in El Salvador, 131; gangs and, 215; in Guatemala, 52, 74, 230, 235; in Honduras, 233; in Nicaragua, 105; political, 49, 102, 103; US, 214, 237, 242
privatization, 153, 159, 162, 183, 190, 239
Pro-Búsqueda (El Salvador), 239
"progress": "disappearing Indian" and, 42; imposed by United States, 40, 41
proletarios, as Sandinista faction, 103
Prolonged Popular War, as Sandinista faction, 103
protests and marches, 4, 63, 87, 195. *See also* resistance
Providence, R.I., 234–36, 240
Puerto Cortés free trade zone (Honduras), 147, 153

Q'eqchi' (Indigenous population in northeastern Petén region of Guatemala), 81; massacre of, 89
Quakers, Sanctuary Movement and, 173
Quest for Peace, 174
Quiché. *See* El Quiché; Ixil region of northern Quiché
Quilalí (Nicaragua), 117
Quixote Center (United States), Quest for Peace and, 174
quotas on US immigration, 221

race, racism, 21, 29, 87, 220, 240; anti-Indigenous, 42, 43, 94; of elites, 41–44; Europeans and, 6, 7; nationalist ideology and, 30, 44
"race to the bottom" of world economies, 158, 192
radicalization of peasants, 78, 86, 129, 131–32
Radio Venceremos, 140

294 INDEX